Liberalism and the Welfare State

Liberalism and the Welfare State

ECONOMISTS AND ARGUMENTS FOR THE WELFARE STATE

Edited by

ROGER E. BACKHOUSE
BRADLEY W. BATEMAN
TAMOTSU NISHIZAWA
DIETER PLEHWE

OXFORD
UNIVERSITY PRESS

OXFORD
UNIVERSITY PRESS

Oxford University Press is a department of the University of Oxford. It furthers the University's objective of excellence in research, scholarship, and education by publishing worldwide. Oxford is a registered trade mark of Oxford University Press in the UK and certain other countries.

Published in the United States of America by Oxford University Press
198 Madison Avenue, New York, NY 10016, United States of America.

CIP data is on file at the Library of Congress
ISBN 978–0–19–067668–1

9 8 7 6 5 4 3 2 1

Printed by Sheridan Books, Inc., United States of America

CONTENTS

Liberalism and the Welfare State

I Introduction

I.1. Economic Arguments and the Cases for and against the Welfare State

The welfare state has not fared well in capitalist countries since the financial crisis of 2008, coming increasingly under attack. (A timeline showing some of the main events related to the welfare state in the three countries studied here is provided in an Appendix to this chapter. It is selective but serves to give an idea of the timing of changes.) While capitalism and democracy expanded in tandem for several decades, social citizenship and equality have now been relegated to the bottom on the list of agenda items in most democracies. Following the financial crisis of 2008 and the use of government funding to bail out much of the financial sector, the need for austerity has been used as a justification for reducing the level of welfare provision. When combined with the doctrine that tax burdens on business must be reduced to stimulate growth, this has served to further increase inequality[1] and to undermine many of the ideas on which postwar European welfare states rested, generous welfare states being important for taming both inequality and poverty (Brady 2009). Inequality has also increased in developing countries. Although many developing countries have succeeded in fighting poverty in terms of reducing the absolute number of poor according to standard definitions, this has not served to reduce inequality. Global poverty may have fallen, but this is mainly an effect of the rapid development of the Chinese economy (Ross 2013), which continues to be governed by a one-party Communist regime with its own peculiar needs of legitimacy, including the fight against poverty. Generalized notions of global competition, fiscal restraint, and the need to reduce public debt have been construed to legitimize austerity regimes in Europe (and the United States), undermine established welfare regimes in poor peripheral countries, and modify or at least preempt the expansion of welfare regimes in rich countries (Pierson 2001b; Taylor-Gooby 2005; Orenstein 2008; Blyth 2013; Schäfer and Streeck 2013).

However, the financial crisis only marked a new stage of the arguments against the welfare state, which had been under increasing pressure for several decades, with governments in many countries modifying pension, unemployment insurance, and public health systems. These changes have been viewed in contrasting ways. Some observers claim that these changes have not fundamentally altered the system, since citizens are still protected against old-age poverty, the increasing risks in volatile labor markets, and the lifetime vagaries of health and safety. Some countries even expanded certain types of welfare provision, notably health insurance coverage in the United States under the Obama administration and the system of old-age care insurance in Germany. Thus, despite the cutting back of welfare provision, many advocates of free-market economics and government restraint continue to bewail the continuing burden of the state, pointing in particular to the rising costs of supporting aging populations. In complete contrast, other observers have discerned a dramatic transformation of the welfare regimes established after World War II. Protestors bemoan the reduction of payments, the changing modalities, and the decline of the welfare state. Unsurprisingly, titles like "the end of the welfare state" have been chosen to sell books, and even to write newspaper obituaries such as Aditya Chakrabortty's "The Welfare State, 1942–2013."[2]

Insofar as there is a crisis of the welfare state, it is clearly connected to change in attitudes: a change in the ideational basis for the welfare state. It can no longer be taken for granted that welfare states are designed to provide a *comprehensive* protection against the vagaries of capitalist development, or militate *against* inequality. The new formula of "flexicurity" has been promoted in the EU, for example, in order to combine the goals of increasing labor market flexibility and social protection (Commission 2007).[3] The need for a new balance has been conceived in part because of the difficulties involved in sustaining a universal welfare state regime in Nordic countries. The original "flexicurity"[4] reforms in Denmark in 1994 and 1996 were reinforced by reforms of the Swedish welfare state from 1998 onward (based on the work of the Lindbeck Commission, Lindbeck et al. 1994; for criticism see Atkinson 1995). The partial privatization of the Swedish welfare state under the leadership of Social Democratic government in turn has been widely praised as a model to be followed in other strong welfare countries like Austria, for example.[5] "Flexicurity" was eventually popularized by Andre Sapir, a Belgian economist who wrote an influential Bruegel report on the topic of welfare reforms at the request of the European Commission in 2003. Sapir basically claims that a combination of liberal and social democratic welfare regimes can achieve a better balance of flexibility and social protection, a claim that has been strongly repudiated (Keune and Serrano 2014).

While arguments that there is a convergence of different models of the welfare state are strongly disputed, there is little doubt that there has been a widespread move toward more limited liberal welfare regimes, featuring the commercialization of welfare state services, individualistic approaches (self-responsibility, insurance principle), and reductions in entitlement (Seeleib-Kaiser 2013). Because of the quite diverse strategies and processes needed in the different countries to achieve similar ends, Seeleib-Kaiser (2001) speaks of divergent convergence, concurring with Cerny (1997), who argues that divergence and convergence are two sides of the same coin of intensified globalization. The welfare state's weight as a system of secondary redistribution has been decreasing overall as a result, regardless of remaining stark differences between the various countries. For the time being, economists who argue against redistribution in order not to undermine market efficiency and economic growth seem to have the upper hand when it comes to discussing the reforms of the welfare state.

If there has been a change in the way the welfare state is conceived, this raises a question about the ideas that previously underpinned the extension of the welfare state and the accompanying decline in inequality, and why those ideas were no longer effective in supporting the policies they had supported for several decades. This volume is concerned with one element in this package of ideas, namely the role of economists and economic ideas.

The rise of the welfare state was undoubtedly the outcome of diverse sets of ideas about social welfare and the distribution of the fruits of economic progress. Arguments for welfare provision have been grounded in political and ethical philosophy and in analysis of individual and social psychology as well as economic reasoning. For example, political, ethical, and psychological arguments have been used to argue that it is necessary to counter the effects of very unequal wealth distribution and social inequality. However, in debates over the welfare state, economists have never been far away. There are, no doubt, many reasons for this, not the least of which is that the arguments against the welfare state are overwhelmingly made on economic grounds. The main case against welfare provision rests on the argument that an unregulated market, free of government intervention, is a more effective way of lifting people out of poverty; and that inequality provides the incentives needed to create prosperity. The decline in growth rates in recent decades has thus been attributed to the growth of the welfare state (Fic and Ghate 2004). This argument is problematic since growth rates have declined across the Organisation for Economic Co-operation and Development (OECD) world, and some countries with generous welfare states have done better than countries with small welfare states. But the argument seems to have traction in public debates because of a simple equation of high and growing welfare expenses with economic burden, no matter which insights can be gained in comparative analysis.

Criticisms of the welfare state have been associated with the movement usually termed neoliberalism.[6] Although neoliberals accepted minimal welfare provisions against the worst risks—this is clear in Friedrich Hayek's *The Road to Serfdom* (1944), one of the classic texts of neoliberalism—neoliberal scholars systematically rejected policies aimed at increasing equality and expanding welfare provisions on economic as well as moral grounds. Against them, economists who have supported such provisions have generally presumed a moral case in favor, using economic reasoning to undermine the argument that such reforms are harmful. The main purely economic argument for welfare provision that can stand independently of any moral case is the argument that a grossly unequal distribution of income stifles economic growth through restraining demand, thereby harming the rich as well as the poor. Thus Gunnar Myrdal, a Swedish economist and Social Democrat, pointed to the correlation of race, gender, and poverty and the resulting inefficiencies in meeting stated objectives in society. However, though such arguments have been around for centuries, they have generally been a minority position among economists. The more radical position—represented by Pickett and Wilkinson (2009) and notably Cingano (2014) at the OECD—that *everyone* is worse off in a more unequal society, which provides an even stronger argument for welfare provision, is of recent origin and is not widely accepted by economists, who generally presume that an individual's welfare depends only on his or her own consumption.[7]

Right across the spectrum of capitalist democracies it has been common to construct a moral case for welfare provision. One limitation of such arguments is that they fail to challenge the economic arguments that the welfare state is counterproductive. For example, it has been argued that welfare has increased a culture of dependency (compare Medvetz 2012 on the effective reframing of welfare research in the United States). This argument claims to be based on economic rationality, and goes beyond deliberations on deserving versus undeserving recipients. It is therefore no accident that the recent reversal of the fortunes of the welfare state has occurred at a time when economics has been more prominent than ever in public discourse, giving economists greater voice than in previous generations (Rodgers 2011).

Moreover, the individualistic, primarily microeconomic theorizing that has come to dominate academic economics has, whether correctly or incorrectly, come to be widely identified with "neoliberalism," the ideology that is associated with undermining the intellectual basis for the welfare state. The most systematic attacks on the welfare state have been coming from groups that have loudly proclaimed their adherence to liberal principles, some of them describing themselves as neoliberal—as having developed a new form of liberalism, distinct from the nineteenth-century liberalism of John Stuart Mill—the most notable being the network of think tanks and pressure groups centered on the Mont Pelerin Society (Walpen 2004;

Plickert 2008; Mirowski and Plehwe 2009; Burgin 2012). Attacks on welfare provision in general (e.g., austerity) and reforms of individual parts of the welfare system (e.g., pensions) have been linked by a variety of authors to neoliberal scholarship and political and institutional entrepreneurship (Blyth 2013; Orenstein 2008; Appel and Orenstein 2013), but without observing the common Mont Pelerin denominators of "expansionary austerity" (rooted in Luigi Einaudi's Italian version of neoliberalism), Alvin Rabushka's "flat tax," or José Pinera's original proposals of private pensions in Pinochet's Chile. Einaudi, Rabushka, and Pinera are all economists who belong or belonged to the Mont Pelerin "thought collectives" (to use Karl Mannheim's terminology), which presented the demand for social protection that is "not inimical to the market" as one of its key principles in the founding declaration (compare Plehwe 2009).

Contrary to the concern of neoliberals in the 1930s, 1940s, and 1950s with social integration to stabilize capitalism, neoliberalism has frequently been misrepresented as a linear heir to classical liberalism (Razeen Sally 1998, member of the Mont Pelerin Society). Liberalism as a whole is presented as antithetical to the idea of the welfare state.[8] However, the historical record is far more complex. The political science literature has distinguished between social democratic, conservative, and liberal welfare regimes in countries like Sweden, Germany, and the United Kingdom, respectively (Esping-Andersen 1990). National regimes differ with regard to the fundamental norms and principles guiding social policy and the types and character of resulting institutions. Those based on universality principles use welfare provisions to increase equality, while conservative regimes legitimate both comprehensive protection and the maintenance of status hierarchies. Regimes based on liberal principles create systems that are primarily need based and therefore support individualist notions of risk and legitimate protection. Yet other regimes have been labeled rudimentary because they are less comprehensive, and therefore less complete, regardless of objectives and underlying understandings. Such a distinction of national systems helps to explain certain differences between countries. In order to separate cases clearly and cleanly, however, differences are sometimes amplified, and real cases are interpreted to closely match ideal cases, rather than observers asking if and to what extent real cases are ambivalent, and how and why they sometimes develop in ways unexpected by the literature informed by institutional path-dependency theory (Ferragina and Seeleib-Kaiser 2011).

In the British case of a liberal regime, for example, the post–World War II evolution from means-tested social insurance to a partly universalist system of secondary redistribution (notably the National Health System) presents a challenge to the classification of the United Kingdom as a liberal welfare regime. Although recent reforms arguably moved the British welfare state closer to the liberal individualist ideal type (Esping-Andersen 1990, 15), a closer examination of the ideational forces behind welfare state thinking is useful to understand historical programming and institutional transformations. For example, liberal individualism prevailed in Britain until the 1950s but was later compromised by socialist and conservative collectivist traditions until the rise of Thatcherism. Thatcher and her successors tried unsuccessfully to cut the two parts cleanly apart even though there was a clear move in the direction of liberal individualism.

Similar questions can be raised about whether the Swedish-Scandinavian regime still unequivocally qualifies as universalist and about whether the conservative model has moved away from limited universalism by way of expanding status differentiation (dualization). The liberal regime has arguably become more individualistic despite becoming more comprehensive. The most important changes across regimes are best described as retrenchment, or recommodification, and converge on a turn toward individual responsibilities and commercialization like the Hartz reforms of the German unemployment protection or the privatization of Swedish healthcare. While it is certainly useful to distinguish between retrenchment, cost-cutting, and recalibration in order to observe differences between countries in the common effort of coping with permanent austerity (Pierson 2001a), it is not clear whether cost-cutting and recalibration can always be fully isolated from retrenchment, and it is certainly problematic to suggest that neoliberal influences are only relevant in the cases of wholesale retrenchment. Pierson's attempt to distinguish reform efforts in conservative and social democratic regimes from the reforms in liberal regimes has become less convincing in light of the reforms of the past decade in Germany and Sweden, for example. Previous conceptions of universal and generous welfare regimes dedicated to reducing inequality now are widely regarded as unfeasible, utopian, and counterproductive in a rapidly changing world of globalized capitalism. No matter which type of welfare regime existed in the past, social policy is held to be in need of answering new and different sets of questions broadly directed by market liberal perspectives (Streeck 2014; Seeleib-Kaiser 2011).

At the core of the answer to these questions in many cases is the rise of individualistic conceptions of markets and efficiency, which counter notions of social citizenship (McCluskey 2003; Taylor-Gooby 2008). In the United States, the field of law and economics has limited the idea that the law serves as a universal set of principles standing in contradiction to economic reasoning, and has increased the influence of economic reasoning in legal deliberations. The resulting legal pragmatism has generalized notions of "moral hazard" to encompass virtually all kinds of social protection (Baker 1996). The law-and-economics movement has thereby been able to supply ammunition against the expansion of social citizenship and has been effectively used to push back universalist notions of welfare and equality. Welfare regimes are caught in an untenable position: welfare benefits are the only effective protection against the vagaries of the capitalist market economy, but the provision of a welfare state is widely held to hinder the dynamics of market economies. This catch-22 thus creates a reason for decreasing welfare benefits so that capitalism can generate the prosperity on which welfare depends. The problem here is the perceived dichotomy of equity and efficiency. Welfare objectives are relegated to questions of redistribution, which are per definition not concerned with the size of the pie, whereas market efficiency is concerned with growth and the increase of wealth in general. Such a perspective implies that the protection of those adversely affected by markets is always achieved at the expense of achieving additional gains. Such a perspective has been challenged on the grounds that the relationship between the two goals is more complicated and that welfare provision may promote economic progress (McCluskey 2003).

This volume explores the role of economists in laying the intellectual foundations for arguments for and against the welfare state. Economists and economic ideas matter more than ever with regard to welfare (state) debates, and yet they and their history remain poorly understood in economics. Discussions of welfare have rarely ventured into discussions of the history of economics beyond noting changes, such as the rise of neoliberalism, while failing to distinguish between strands of economic thinking to which historians of economics attach much importance. On the other side, historians of economics, though conscious of competing arguments about welfare, have rarely focused attention on the relationship between these ideas and the welfare state. Our claim is that there is much to be learned by bringing together the history of economic thought and arguments over the welfare state. The problem is far from trivial not only because of national differences but also because the role of economists in society changed significantly during the twentieth century. By the end of the nineteenth century, the time when the first significant moves toward a welfare state were being taken, economics was, in most countries, only just beginning to become institutionalized as a specialized academic discipline. The rise of the welfare state thus coincided with the period when the number of economists increased dramatically, economists' position, in relation to government and the public, was changing significantly, and there were shifts in the relative importance of different types of economic thinking (see, for example, Coats 1981, 1986, 1997, 2000). Such research has established that there were considerable differences between countries.

I.2. Complicating Welfare State Discourse: Three Not-So-Neat Cases

This volume illustrates the complexity of economists thinking about the relationship between liberalism and the welfare state in the twentieth century through case studies of three countries: Britain, Germany, and Japan. It makes sense to focus on these countries because, in the discussion of varieties of liberal and nonliberal capitalism and in the discussion of liberal and conservative welfare regimes, they are traditionally considered "neat cases." In the literature on comparative capitalism, the United Kingdom is considered a liberal market economy (like the United States), quite distinct from the coordinated market economies of Germany and Japan. In the comparative welfare literature, the United Kingdom and Japan are frequently considered liberal welfare states, although some consider Japan a special—liberal Confucian—case. Germany is represented as a clear-cut conservative welfare regime. Liberalism (United Kingdom) and conservatism (Germany) are the dominant worldviews backing up the distinct regimes. However, closer analysis reveals peculiarities and complexity that contradict the apparent simplicity of the three cases. For example, the odd combination of coordinated capitalism and limited welfare state in Japan can be explained if we pay attention to the peculiar combination of business- and state-related welfare. Neither Germany nor the United Kingdom is as clear-cut a case as they are usually presented in light of the historical controversies, for the historical evolution from less to more, and from more to less, comprehensive welfare regimes and the increased emphasis on individual responsibility and asset-based welfare defy explanation in terms of strictly national path dependencies. The historical evolution becomes easier to explain if we understand better the earlier struggles between different wings of economic thought on welfare in each of the countries. The three countries we have chosen exhibit sufficient contrasts for a comparative study to be worthwhile, even though we leave aside the so-called extreme cases: the liberal capitalism found in the United States and the social democratic welfare state capitalism represented by Sweden. There has been significant change in both of these countries, making them less "extreme"—Obamacare in the United States and privatization and commercialization of welfare provision in Sweden—but though analysis of these welfare regimes would support our argument about the complexity of the relationship between liberalism and welfare, we opted for a closer analysis of three countries. We do, however, go beyond the strictly national focus that is traditional in the comparative welfare literature in acknowledging the transnational dimensions of liberalism and neoliberalism, both in the country studies and the two chapters on international dimensions of neoliberalism.

I.3. Competing Economic Ideas and the Changing Perspectives on the Welfare State

The starting point for this volume is Britain. Backhouse, Bateman, and Nishizawa examine the period up to 1945, when a comprehensive welfare state was established. Despite being instituted by a socialist government, the British welfare state rested as much on the ideas of liberals as on socialist thinking. The initial moves toward a welfare state had taken place under a Liberal government, inspired by the so-called New Liberalism, which sought to move the Liberal Party in a more collectivist direction, but without compromising what were believed to be the important features of liberalism. These thinkers spanned different academic disciplines, and some had no academic affiliations. Liberalism was never far away.

George Peden's chapter, "Liberal Economists and the British Welfare State: From Beveridge to the New Right," takes the account of the British case a stage further, exploring the history of welfare state thinking after World War II. He begins by explaining the ideas that lay behind the welfare state established by Attlee, locating it in New Liberalism, which was one of the fundamentals of Beveridge's and Keynes's understanding of a universal system of social insurance. This was initially supported, however, even by more conservative elements of the British liberal community like Lionel Robbins. Though they moved toward collectivism, Peden argues that New Liberals maintained a strong belief in self-help and thrift. This limited departure from classical liberalism is consistent with there being less distance between Hayek, Beveridge, and Keynes on questions of social insurance than popular stereotypes would suggest. Comprehensive social insurance offered protection against significant risks that were beyond individual control (poverty related to old age and children) but, at least in the early years of the British welfare state, did not aim at redistribution; even the postwar Labour governments maintained an austere version of universal insurance. The picture changed in the course of the 1950s and 1960s. Successive Conservative and Labour governments modified and improved welfare schemes, increased benefits, and thereby changed the character of the system. Incentives for self-help were lost, and social insurance became more of a redistribution scheme. The public health (National Health Service) and the education system likewise moved the British welfare state away from liberal individualism. This was the background for the wider range of neoliberal critiques of the British welfare state that started to be made in the 1960s and grew stronger in the course of the 1970s. The New Right in Britain was clearly inspired by a wide range of domestic and foreign neoliberal economists like Alan Peacock and James Buchanan, and by think tanks like the Institute of Economic Affairs. Conservative social insurance reforms under Thatcher as well as approaches to commercialize public health and higher education were both consistent in terms of direction toward individualism and limited by many constraints. Peden's chapter clarifies the range and the directing force of liberal and other ideas—of both domestic and foreign provenance—behind British welfare as well as the discourse-shaping power of political and institutional configurations.

Hagemann then turns to the German case, very different from the British in that policymaking was, until the 1970s, dominated by "ordoliberalism" and the related, yet more pragmatic, idea of a "social-market economy," very different from the blend of socialist, Keynesian, and liberal ideas that lay behind British policymaking. The intellectual foundation for the policies of Ludwig Erhard, the dominant figures in German politics in the 1950s and 1960s, were Walter Eucken, associated with the Freiburg school tradition of ordoliberalism, and Alfred Müller-Armack, who coined the term "social-market economy." In a stark departure from laissez-faire notions of the market, ordoliberalism rested on the idea that the state is needed to organize competition. This was not socialism because prime importance was attached to property rights; neither was it consistent with Keynesianism, for there was an emphasis on monetary stability and a reliable legal order rather than influencing economic process.

Ordoliberal and social-market ideas focused on reconciling what would otherwise be conflicts over economic resources (Müller-Armack's irenic formula and evolutionary principle). But the influence of organized labor and the conflict constellation in Germany led to measures not seen in Britain, though they were briefly debated during the 1960s, such as worker representation on company boards, aimed at reducing conflict between capital and labor (*Sozialpartnerschaft*). Hagemann argues that, though it may have taken longer to influence policymaking than in other countries, Keynesianism became important in German academic economics in the 1950s, notably because of Erich Schneider in Kiel. It had less influence on policy because its natural political supporters, in the Social Democratic Party, remained ambiguous and to a certain extent Marxist in orientation until 1959, when the SPD accepted the idea of the social-market economy, albeit with a greater emphasis on employment policy than was found in the Christian Democratic Union and Christian Social Union (CDU/CSU). The legislative basis for Keynesian policies was established in 1967, with the Stability and Growth Act associated with Karl Schiller, later the economics and finance minister, who considered his perspective as a search for a compromise between ordoliberalism and Keynesianism.

Turning to Japan, Nishizawa and Ikeda examine the historical and intellectual background of the shift towards neoliberal policymaking in contemporary Japan. The chapter tackles a variety of liberal traditions and ideas in Japan that were linked to the German historical school and British New Liberalism. But contrary to European developments, these ideas played a limited role in Japan before World War II. Liberal traditions in support of welfare capitalism were revived and further developed politically in postwar years. While Japanese Marxism was by and large confined to academic institutions and oppositional parts of the trade union movement after the war, reforms conducted under the auspices of the Liberal Party–Liberal Democratic Party governments from the late 1940s onward appropriated ideas developed by liberal economists like Nakayama Ichiro and Tsuru Shigeto. American occupation played a considerable role in limiting the opportunities of socialist ideas to gain practical relevance in the late 1940s and early 1950s, though working-class militancy certainly reinforced the perceived need for social reforms in Japan.

The Japanese variety of "new liberalism" took the shape of liberal idealism and limited social liberalism within a state-directed version of developmental capitalism. While neoliberal ideas remained under the surface until the 1980s, Japan's weak welfare state was arguably more in line with ideas of limited welfare than the more comprehensive systems that developed elsewhere (compare Teranishi's chapter in this volume). The weight of social liberal ideas was linked to corporate welfare, backed by employment-oriented policies. Limited public sector welfare spending thus coincided with state private sector coordination that enabled welfare security primarily based on the employment system (lifelong employment, etc.). Although explicit neoliberal worldviews played much less a role in Japan than in Germany directly after World War II, for example, pockets of neoliberal thought existed in Japan throughout the postwar period, displaying close links to both European and American circuits. The strong neoliberal bent of Japanese welfare capitalism from the 1980s onward in any case relied on domestic as well as foreign sources. The history and diffusion of neoliberal ideas about the welfare state in Japan can be traced through people like Yamamoto Katsuichi, a unique neoliberal economist, and Nishiyama Chiaki, who studied with Hayek in the United States in the 1950s, and served as president of the Mont Pelerin Society.

I.4. The Turn to Retrenchment of the Welfare State

The book then turns to the period when there was a turn from developing the welfare state to retrenchment. Starting again with the United Kingdom, the first chapter in this part covers the role of economists in this process, discussing three economists and their relationship with leading British business associations. Neil Rollings finds fault with popular and academic characterizations of the British history of neoliberalism in general, arguing that greater attention needs to be paid to economists such as Arthur Shenfield, Barry Cracewell-Milnes, and John Jewkes. His examination of the work and their careers calls for a closer look at the relationship of corporate and academic circles in the United Kingdom.

Matt Beech continues the discussion of the history and prospect of the British welfare state by laying out two hypotheses about the British developments. For many observers, New Labour was simply the heir of Thatcherism. Others point to the reversal of the decline of British welfare expenditures since Blair took office. Matt Beech's chapter discusses the relative merits of these two perspectives. It acknowledges continuities from the Thatcher years, but he rejects an oversimplified path dependency argument by way of pointing to changing objectives.

Daniel Kinderman examines the reasons behind the shift in Germany's welfare state following unification. An employer initiative to inform a new social-market economy was founded to renew the original ideas, which were opposed to trade unions and social democracy. The push for a more individualistic model and a decrease in social spending was promoted during a time of increasing public constraints. High transfers from West to East Germany and continuously high levels of unemployment created an urgent need for reform, which was paradoxically executed by the Social Democratic and Green Party coalition and not by the center-right coalitions closer to the employers' campaign. The weight of economic ideas and the extent to which they were positively received in Social Democratic circles helps explain the move from a more universalist to a more limited liberal welfare regime. Contrary to those who think the social-market economy was a Social Democratic idea, Kinderman's chapter reminds us of the neoliberal share in the origins of Germany's social model, and thus to a continuity in economic thought at odds with the stereotypes of the welfare state and comparative capitalism literatures.

The discussion then moves to Japan in Teranishi's chapter, which examines the nature and logic of the Koizumi reforms. Between 2001 and 2006, the Japanese government pursued a policy line dedicated to deregulation and structural reform. For Japan, the Koizumi reforms had a historical significance similar to the Thatcher and Reagan years in the United Kingdom and the United States, respectively. The chapter first compares the Koizumi reform policy with the fiscal policy of Inoue Jun-Nosuke in 1930–31, and argues that public support for both policies can be attributed to the congruence with the global standard of the time, that is, the gold standard in Inoue's case and neoliberalism in Koizumi's. The chapter investigates a core aspect of Japanese policymaking, namely the relationship between the popular notion of Japan as a developmental state and the concept of neoliberalism. Teranishi critically examines the "Japan as a development-oriented state hypothesis" by Chalmars Jonson and Noguchi Yukio. According to Teranishi, the system during the high-growth era was not established for a general developmental purpose, suggesting the development of welfare capitalism akin to European models. A company-based cooperative system involving capital and labor became dominant and succeeded in improving income distribution; but the Western type of social democratic system was abandoned at the same time. The system during the high-growth era protected weak industries as well as small and medium-sized firms and stabilized employment. The labor market reform orchestrated by Koizumi in turn destroyed the traditional employment system in weak industries and generated the massive expansion of temporary and atypical (nonstandard full-time) employment contracts. Teranishi argues that the core of Koizumi reform was justified by a neoliberal reasoning that, though consistent with the Anglo-American tradition, was situated in an economic policy tradition that had roots in Japanese history.

Fabio Masini then turns to an important dimension of neoliberalism that is generally neglected in analyses conducted at the national level. Neoliberal economists sought to promote their policies through supranational institutions that would establish two collective goods—capital mobility and free trade—and would also constrain the measures national governments could take in support of the welfare state. These discussions reveal two distinct versions of federalism. Masini argues that Hayek began to support supranational institutions to limit the power of nation-states. He had in mind not just the excesses of Nazi, fascist, and communist states but also the defenses of monetary nationalism by liberal economists such as Roy Harrod and Maynard Keynes. Yet he did not want international cooperation of the type he believed had contributed to the crisis of the 1930s, as when central banks cooperated over measures to prevent the price level falling. His goal was to use supranational institutions to prevent public, and political, interventions over monetary policy: it was not to create a new forum in which democratic control over policy could be exercised. Masini argues that Hayek's support for political federalism was instrumental to his worldview of a spontaneous social order. Masini then contrasts this view with those of Lionel Robbins and Luigi Einaudi, who sought supranational institutions as a means of resolving conflicts that traditional diplomacy was unable to solve. For them, federalism should not imply a reduction in government, as it did for Hayek. Robbins's constitutional federalism, a means for resolving disputes, was more consistent with the welfare state emerging after World War II than was Hayek's instrumental federalism. Masini argues that an originally rich debate on federalism among neoliberals has suffered from an increasingly narrow and instrumental perspective.

The volume is rounded off with a review of neoliberal economic ideas related to the financial crisis and the future of the welfare state by Dieter Plehwe. The global financial crisis of 2007–8 challenged the notion that free markets could operate effectively with very limited controls, provoking some public choice theorists to argue that regulation was likely to fail because of the economic interests of regulated industries and regulators. The crisis instead has certainly underlined the concern about market failure, no matter the extent to which regulators were complicit. However, how did those who were in support of privatization, deregulation, and financial liberalization react to the crisis, and what are the implications of their reflections for the future of the welfare state? Plehwe approaches this question through looking at the discussion at the special meeting of the Mont Pelerin Society in New York in 2009, and some of the strategies pursued by think tanks in the aftermath of this meeting. The chapter shows that leading scholars in this group claim convergence between Hayek and Keynes on how to react to a great crisis. While conceding the need to fight a depression and deflation, most scholars considered the contemporary financial and economic crisis to be less severe than the Great

Depression, and demanded an end to Keynesian stimulus programs. Attention should instead be redirected to the high level of public debt, to the return to sound monetary politics, and to the preservation of free trade. The central message of the president of the Mont Pelerin Society back in 2009 was defend the economic globalization status quo ante crisis.

In addition to the survival of core beliefs such as the superiority of the market, a central feature of the New York deliberations was the revival of ordoliberalism, discussed in Hagemann's and Kinderman's chapters. For a long time, ordoliberal thinking had been relegated to the back shelves as neoliberals primarily used Hayekian, Chicago, or Virginia perspectives to promote deregulation and liberalization. After the crisis, ordoliberal ideas became more attractive because they offered an alternative to more left-leaning approaches to market regulation. The chapter goes on to consider some activities orchestrated in the aftermath of the crisis by the Atlas Economic Research Foundation that were dedicated to free trade and sound money and the wide range of activities pursued by think tanks that belong to the European Stockholm network. While some think tanks approached the crisis from a radical antistate perspective, others were more balanced and emphasized a need for limited reregulation. However, despite this seeming diversity, different wings of neoliberal thought shared a support for austerity regimes that would inevitably lead to further retrenchment, cost-cutting, and other reforms of the welfare state inspired by what could be considered a now common logic of—more or less social—market citizenship.

In a concluding chapter we tie these ideas together, drawing general conclusions about the relationship between economists' ideas, liberalism, and the welfare state.

Appendix: Timeline of Main Events in British, German, and Japanese Welfare States

	BRITAIN	GERMANY	JAPAN
16th century		Compulsory elementary education in German states	
1717		Compulsory elementary education in Prussia	
1840s	1842: Progressive income tax	1845: Local health insurance (Prussia)	
1870s	1870: Compulsory elementary education	1876: Unification of health insurance (Prussia)	

	BRITAIN	GERMANY	JAPAN
1880s		Laws establishing health, accident, and retirement/disability insurance, based on equal contributions from employers and workers, separation of public and private health insurance (Bismarck era)	
1890s			Elementary school act (compulsory elementary education)
1900–1914	Introduction of old-age pensions, labor exchanges, and unemployment insurance; rise in income tax (Liberal government)		1911: Factory act (less than 12 hours for women under 15 years old)
1918–39		1919: Invalidity law 1927: Unemployment insurance (Weimar Republic)	1922: Health insurance act (for manual workers) 1938: National health insurance act (not compulsory insurance) 1939: Staff (white collar) health insurance act
1940–45	Conservative-led coalition government of Winston Churchill 1942: Beveridge report (social insurance and allied services) 1944: Butler education act (compulsory education to age 15)	1941: Expansion of mandatory health insurance for retirees (Nazi era)	1944: Employees' pension insurance act 1945: Trade union act 1946: Public assistance act (poverty relief, at this stage at government discretion)

	BRITAIN	GERMANY	JAPAN
1945–51	1944: Establishment of comprehensive welfare state based on insurance principle (Attlee) 1945: Family Allowances Act 1946: National Health Service Act 1948: National Insurance Act 1951: National Health Service Act (introduction of charges for spectacles and dentures)	German constitution stipulates the imperative of a social government under the law (Article 28), equality principle (nondiscrimination, Article 3), and basic and human rights (Article 79) that cannot be rescinded	1946: Japanese constitution stipulates, "All Japanese people have the right to minimum of healthy and cultural life" (Article 25). 1947: Unemployment insurance act 1948: Children's welfare act 1949: Physically handicapped people's welfare act 1950: New public assistance act: universal entitlements for eligible poor to different kinds of assistance, ranging from housing and medical care to education
1950s	1952: Family Allowances and National Insurance Act (increased weekly allowance for noneldest children) 1956: Family Allowance and National Insurance Act—increased weekly allowance for non-eldest children 1959: National Insurance Act ñ establishes earnings-related pensions	1957: Dynamic public retirement system (linked to average wage development) (Adenauer Era)	1954: New employees' pension insurance act 1958: National health insurance act (effective 1961) 1959: National universal pension act (effective 1961)

	BRITAIN	GERMANY	JAPAN
1960s	1965: Family Allowances Act 1965: National Insurance (Industrial Injuries) Act 1966: Social Security Act established Supplementary Benefits (means-testing of noncontributory benefits)	Expansion of health insurance coverage and improvements of accident insurance Income support for children with low-income family background in secondary schools and higher education Social Democrat–Liberal government era	1960: Ikeda government, Income-doubling policy
1970s	1970: Local Authority Social Services Act establishes local responsibility for the delivery of many social services 1970: Chronically Sick and Disabled Persons Act 1970: National Insurance Act establishes attendance allowance for disabled people 1972: School-leaving age raised to 16 1973: Social Security Act (graduated pensions replaced by earnings-related contributions)	From 1977: Laws to control cost development in health insurance, inclusion of workers in cofinancing of health insurance	1973: "The first year under the welfare system." Medical expenses (of one's own expenses) for old age (more than 70 and the approved between 65 and 70) became free. Japanese system of employment and the corporate welfare system 1974: Employment insurance act (after oil shock)

	BRITAIN	GERMANY	JAPAN
1990s	1991: Disability Working Allowance Act 1994: Social Security Act establishes Incapacity Benefit 1995 Jobseekers Act (introduction of Jobseekers Allowance)	Unification: expansion of West German welfare regimes to former GDR Two-tier wage regime with lower pay in new German *Länder* 1995: Establishment of old-age care insurance, opening of expanded care supply services to private firms (commercialization of care and subsequently health sector)	1989: 10-year strategy for aged people's health and welfare ("Goldplan"). 1991: Childcare leave act (increasing two-income family) 1993: Part-time workers act 1994: "Angel plan": measures to deal with 1.57 shock (low birth rate). 1994: Employees' pension payment starting year raised (gradually from 60 to 65) Aged people employment promotion act amended (to raise the retiring age to above 60) 1997: Long-term care insurance act (for those older than 65). 1999: Dispatched workers' act amendment (liberalization of the workers dispatch business, increasing irregular employment)

	BRITAIN	GERMANY	JAPAN
2000s	1998: National Minimum Wage Act 1999: Introduction of the Minimum Income Guarantee or pensioners 1999: Welfare Reform and Pensions Act increases conditionality in the form of interviews for certain out-of-work benefits; widowers receive equal entitlements to widows; establishes Stakeholder Pensions 1999: Comprehensive Spending Review sets out reinvestment program across the public services from 2001 to 2002. 2002: Tax Credits Act introduces Child Tax Credit and Working Tax Credit (means-tested benefits for low-income households) 2002: State Pension Credit Act replaces the Minimum Income Guarantee 2004: Introduction of Education Maintenance Allowance (Blair government)	reforms of pension system: reduction to less than 50 percent of last net wages, state subsidies for private insurance, increase of retirement age to 67 2003–2005: Hartz reforms of unemployment insurance, job center, consolidation of secondary support of unemployed (after 12 months) and social security, reduction of skill level protection, stronger requirements to take lower-paid work, stronger training support, change of labor exchange office to job center following British/Dutch examples	2000: Pension act amendment (raising the pension payment starting year). Health act for aged people amendment (aged patients' expenses). 2001: Koizumi (austerity, marketization) reforms 2002: Health insurance act amendment: gradual increase of one's own medical expenses 2003: Dispatched workers' act amendment (further liberalization). Organic law for dealing with the falling birth rate. 2004: Pension system reform (standard insurance premium fixed and macroeconomic slide of pension payment). Aged people employment promotion act amendment (up to 65).

References

Appel, Hilary, and Mitchell A. Orenstein. 2013. "Ideas versus Resources: Explaining the Flat Tax and Pension Privatization Revolutions in Eastern Europe and the Former Soviet Union." *Comparative Political Studies* 46 (2): 123–52.

Armingeon, Klaus, and Michelle Beyeler. 2004. *The OECD and European Welfare States*. Cheltenham: Edward Elgar

Atkinson, Anthony B. 1995. "Welfare State Necessarily an Obstacle to Economic Growth? The Scope for a European Growth Initiative." *European Economic Review* 39: 723–30.

Atkinson Anthony B., and Salvatore Morelli. 2011. "Economic Crises and Inequality." Human Development Research Paper UNDP 2011/06.

Blyth, Mark. 2013. *Austerity: History of a Dangerous Idea*. New York: Oxford University Press.

Brady, David. 2009. *Rich Democracies, Poor People: How Politics Explain Poverty*. New York: Oxford University Press.

Burgin, Angus. 2012. *The Great Persuasion*. Cambridge, MA: Harvard University Press.

Cerny, Philip G. 1997. "Paradoxes of the Competition State: The Dynamics of Political Globalization." *Government and Opposition* 32 (2): 251–74.

Cingano, F. 2014. "Trends in Income Inequality and Its Impact on Economic Growth." OECD Social, Employment and Migration Working Papers No. 163. http://dx.doi.org/10.1787/5jxrjncwxv6j-en.

Coats, A. W., ed. 1981. *Economists in Government: An International Comparative Study*. Durham, NC: Duke University Press.

Coats, A. W., ed. 1986. *The Role of Economists in International Organizations: An Exploratory Study*. London: Praeger.

Coats, A. W., ed. 1997. *The Internationalization of Economics after 1945*. Durham, NC: Duke University Press.

Coats, A. W., ed. 2000. *The Development of Economics in Western Europe*. London: Routledge.

Esping-Andersen, Gösta. 1990. *Three Worlds of Welfare Capitalism*. Cambridge: Polity Press.

Ferragina, Emanuele, and Martin Seeleib-Kaiser. 2011. "Welfare Regime Debate: Past, Present, Futures?" *Policy and Politics* 39 (4): 583–611. doi.org/10.1332/030557311X603592.

Fic, Tatiana, and Chetan Ghate. 2004. "The Welfare State, Thresholds, and Economic Growth." DIW Discussion Paper 424, German Institute for Economic Research, Berlin.

Fölster, Stefan, and Nima Sanandaji. 2014. *Renaissance for Reforms*. London: Institute of Economic Affairs; Stockholm: Timbro.

Hayek, Friedrich A. von. 1944. *The Road to Serfdom*. London: Routledge.

Keune, Maarten, and Amparo Serrano, eds. 2014. *Deconstructing Flexicurity and Developing Alternative Approaches*. New York: Routledge.

Lindbeck, Assar, et al. 1994. *Turning Sweden Around*. Cambridge, MA: MIT Press.

McCluskey, Martha. 2003. "Efficiency and Social Citizenship: Challenging the Neoliberal Attack on the Welfare State." *Indiana Law Journal* 78:783–876.

Medvetz, Tom. 2012. *Think Tanks in America*. Chicago: University of Chicago Press.

Mirowski, Philip, and Dieter Plehwe, eds. 2009. *The Road from Mont Pèlerin: The Making of the Neoliberal Thought Collective*. Cambridge, MA: Harvard University Press.

Myrdal, Gunnar. 1944. *An American Dilemma*. New York: Harper Brothers.

Orenstein, Mitchell A. 2008. *Privatization Pensions. The Transnational Campaign for Social Security Reform*. Princeton, NJ: Princeton University Press.

Pickett, Kate, and Richard G. Wilkinson. 2009. *The Spirit Level: Why More Equal Societies Almost Always Do Better*. London: Allen Lane.

Pierson, Paul. 2001a. "Coping with Permanent Austerity: Welfare State Restructuring in Affluent Democracies." In P. Pierson, ed., *The New Politics of the Welfare State*, 410–56. Oxford: Oxford University Press.

Pierson, Paul. 2001b. *The New Politics of the Welfare State*. Oxford: Oxford University Press.

Plehwe, Dieter. 2009. Introduction to Philip Mirowski and Dieter Plehwe, eds., *The Road from Mont Pèlerin*. Cambridge, MA: Harvard University Press.

Plickert, Philip. 2008. *Wandlungen des Neoliberalismus*. Stuttgart: Lucius & Lucius.

Rodgers, Daniel. 2011. *Age of Fracture*. Cambridge, MA: Belknap Press of Harvard University Press.

Ross, John. 2013. "China Accounts for 100% of the Reduction in the Number of the World's People Living in Poverty." November 24. http://ablog.typepad.com/keytrendsinglobalisation/2013/11/china-world-poverty.html.

Sally, Razeen. 1998. *Classical Liberalism and International Economic Order*. London: Routledge.

Schäfer, Armin, and Wolfgang Streeck, eds. 2013. *Politics in the Age of Austerity*. Cambridge: Polity Press.

Seeleib-Kaiser, Martin. 2001. *Globalisierung und Sozialpolitik: Ein Vergleich der Diskurse und Wohlfahrtssysteme in Deutschland, Japan und den USA*. Frankfurt am Main: Campus.

Seeleib-Kaiser, Martin, ed. 2011. *Welfare State Transformations: Comparative Perspectives*. New York: Palgrave.

Seeleib-Kaiser, Martin. 2013. "Welfare Systems in Europe and the United States: Conservative Germany Converging toward the Liberal US Model?" *International Journal of Social Quality* 3 (2): 60–77.

Streeck, Wolfgang. 2014. *Buying Time*. London: Verso.

Svalvors, Stefan, and Peter Taylor-Gooby, eds. 1999. *The End of Welfare*. New York: Routledge.

Taylor-Gooby, Peter, ed. 2005. *Ideas and Welfare State Reform in Western Europe*. Basingstoke: Palgrave Macmillan.

Taylor-Gooby, Peter. 2008. *Reframing Social Citizenship*. New York: Oxford University Press.

Wacquant, Loïc. 2010. "Crafting the Neoliberal State: Workfare, Prisonfare, and Social Insecurity." *Sociological Forum* 25 (2): 197–220.

Walpen, Bernhard. 2004. *Die offenen Feind und ihre Gesellschaft*. Hamburg: Vsa Verlag.

I | Varieties of Liberalism and the Early Welfare State

UNITED KINGDOM, GERMANY, AND JAPAN

1 | Liberalism and the Welfare State in Britain, 1890–1945

ROGER E. BACKHOUSE, BRADLEY W. BATEMAN, AND TAMOTSU NISHIZAWA

1.1. The Liberal Origins of the British Welfare State

In the general election of July 5, 1945, Clement Attlee's Labour Party achieved a landslide victory over the Conservatives led by the highly popular wartime prime minister, Winston Churchill. There was an overwhelming desire for change and for a society that was fairer and more just than the one people remembered from before the war. The Labour Party was socialist, committed to achieving its social goals through public ownership of key industries, and proposed nationalizations, including railways, coal, gas, electricity, steel, and the Bank of England. The intellectual basis for its welfare reforms obviously rested on the writings of socialists associated with the Labour Party, such as R. H. Tawney, G. D. H. Cole, and Harold Laski. However, the document that laid down the principles on which the welfare state was established, *Social Insurance and Allied Services* (1942), had been written by a committed Liberal, William Beveridge. Moreover, the welfare state came to rest on the idea that government could and should manage the level of aggregate demand to ensure full employment, an idea that rapidly became synonymous with the name of an even more prominent Liberal, John Maynard Keynes. Not only did the maintenance of full employment meet a major social goal, but it was a virtual precondition for ensuring that a comprehensive system of national insurance was affordable.

The intertwining of liberalism and the welfare state had a long history, going back at least to the New Liberalism that had developed from the 1880s, with the aim of pulling the Liberal Party away from Gladstonian liberalism toward a more collectivist outlook in which state intervention was used to promote welfare through mitigating the worst effects of the market. The policies advocated by the New Liberals were implemented in the Liberal governments of Henry Campbell-Bannerman and Herbert Henry Asquith in the decade before World War I, notably due to the efforts of David Lloyd George and the young Winston Churchill, with whom the rational bureaucrats such as Llewellyn Smith and the younger William Beveridge worked out the liberal reform. The foundations of the welfare state were laid through measures that included the institution of old-age pensions, unemployment insurance, and progressive income taxation. In the interwar period, as the Labour Party gradually displaced the Liberal Party as the main opposition to the Conservatives, this complex interplay of liberalism and reform continued. Traditional liberal notions of noninterference, "sound finance," and free trade vied with the idea that the state should do more to encourage the welfare of its citizens. Within the Labour Party, the strands of socialist thinking represented by Tawney, Cole, Laski, George Bernard Shaw, and Beatrice and Sidney Webb were never far from liberalism. The Liberal journalist and theorist of imperialism John A. Hobson had moved to the Labour Party, and there was continual exchange of ideas between these thinkers and liberals. Debates within the Liberal Party were just as intense, if not more so, given its declining position in the polls, notably in the Liberal summer schools in the late 1920s. There were also divisions of opinion inside the Conservative Party, which encompassed "one nation" conservatives, holding to a Burkean faith in traditional forms of social organization, as well as those more skeptical about the welfare state. As Freeden (2003, 8) has argued, the welfare state was supported by an "ideational composite of welfare thinking" and is not appropriately conceived as either the result of a collectivist assault on individualism or as the outcome of rivalry between liberal (or conservative) and socialist viewpoints.

The arguments used to support the idea of a welfare state cut across this variety of political positions. Again Freeden (2003, 12): "All major ideologies drew on three main categories in drawing up welfare measures . . . the socialization of virtue, the normalization of risk and the legitimization of need," categories that permeated the Beveridge report. It had long been accepted that it was desirable that people should save to cover times when they could no longer support themselves, notably in old age, and also that there was a case for mutual aid. The welfare state could be seen as an extension of such activities. The welfare state could also be seen as providing social insurance, compensating for chance events that undermined the idea of equality of opportunity or as enabling basic human needs to be satisfied through ensuring that no one fell below a minimum level of income. Though some conservatives questioned the use of such arguments to justify welfare provision by the state, none of these arguments was confined to socialists. Arguments about human needs, for example, could be applied to nonmaterial needs such as the need to participate in society and translated into arguments about citizenship that resonated with conservatives and liberals. The Cambridge Liberal economist Alfred Marshall recalled his passage from psychology to economics: "'its [psychology's] fascinating inquiries into the possibilities of the higher and more rapid development of human faculties" brought him into touch with the question, "How far do the conditions of life of the British (and other) working classes generally suffice for the fullness of life?" (quoted in Keynes 1971–89, 10:171).

However, notwithstanding that arguments over the welfare state cannot usefully be analyzed in terms of competition between collectivist and individualist ideologies, it is nevertheless useful to see debates over the welfare state against the background of debates over liberalism. To argue this is not to argue that there was a single ideology called liberalism, or that it implied particular positions on the welfare state. The reason for juxtaposing the two is that in Britain during this period the meaning of liberalism was contested in ways that were linked to positions on the welfare state. The argument being made is related specifically to Britain, for the way the term "liberalism" was used in other countries was not the same: it is that, even if liberalism did not lose its nineteenth-century valences as thoroughly as happened in the United States in the 1930s, its meaning was transformed for reasons specific to Britain.

1.2. New Liberalism to the Beveridge Report

The reason for the centrality of liberalism to debates over the welfare state is the role of the Liberal Party and, within it, the New Liberalism, the high point of which was undoubtedly the reforms introduced in the decade before World War I. There were ongoing debates about the meaning of liberalism, debates in which ideas about individual freedom and the role of the state were, as far back as John Stuart Mill's classic, *On Liberty* (1859), entwined with ideas of utilitarianism. Utilitarianism may have been subject to intense criticism, and it had certainly become unfashionable in many quarters at the end of the nineteenth century, but it never went away. The ideas of the leading New Liberal theorists, Leonard Hobhouse, professor of sociology at LSE, and Hobson, the journalist, theorist of imperialism, and self-confessed economic heretic, rejected traditional liberal doctrines such as laissez-faire, yet attached importance to freedom from coercion. Though supporting collective empowerment of disadvantaged groups, their arguments against imperialism were rooted in the ideas of liberal thinkers such as Richard Cobden. While the influences on the politicians, notably Lloyd George and Churchill, who pushed these reforms through are uncertain, both the general direction of the Liberal reforms and the intellectual basis on which they rested had wide support. The political situation, in which Labour representatives supported a Liberal government, were in tune with a political philosophy that, though it remained Liberal, committed above all to free trade, saw an increased role for collective action to mitigate the social problems that arose in a market economy.

At Cambridge, Alfred Marshall, who sought to establish economics as a scientific discipline, had built an analytical apparatus that could be used to support reform, even if he was himself hesitant in pushing it too far. In this, he was following a long tradition among British economists who, through much of the nineteenth century, had followed the line taken by John Stuart Mill in considering there to be a prima facie case for nonintervention, but that reasons could be adduced for intervention in an increased number of cases (Robbins 1978; Hutchison 1978; Medema 2011). Like his one-time mentor, Henry Sidgwick, and his successor, A. C. Pigou, all of them Liberals, Marshall continued this trend to develop a theoretical framework on which the case for the welfare state could be based. His economics dominated the English-speaking world, and a fortiori British economics, in the early twentieth century, and Pigou's *The Economics of Welfare*, which went through four editions (1920–32), a development of his prewar *Wealth and Welfare* (1912), developed his ideas to provide a case for extensive social provision, coming close to the case for a welfare state. For example, *The Economics of Welfare* culminated with a chapter titled "A National Minimum Standard of Real Income." In arguing for what he described as "an objective minimum of conditions," he explained that these conditions must be general and not confined to just one aspect of life. Thus "The minimum includes some defined quantity and quality of house accommodation, of medical care, of education, of food, of leisure, of the apparatus of sanitary convenience and safety where work is carried on, and so on" (Pigou 1932, book 4, chap. 13, sec. 2). Thus on one occasion, he related the national minimum to housing conditions (Rowntree and Pigou 1914).

With World War I and its aftermath the situation changed dramatically. Though Lloyd George remained prime minister, the Liberal Party had split, one wing remaining in government in coalition with the Conservatives and the other headed by Asquith. The party was reunited in 1923 when the Conservatives adopted a policy of protection, but by then the Labour Party had overtaken it and, with Liberal support, formed a brief minority administration. In 1924, the Liberal Party was reduced to only 40 MPs, squeezed between the other two parties. Free trade may have served to reunite the Lloyd George and Asquith wings of the party, but it was hardly a sufficient basis on which to establish a credible electoral program. There was a clear need to rethink Liberalism: faced with a Labour Party that was seeking power in its own right, and which aimed for an explicitly socialist program, represented by Clause IV of its constitution, adopted in 1918:

> To secure for the workers by hand or by brain the full fruits of their industry and the most equitable distribution thereof that may be possible upon the basis of the common ownership of the means of production, distribution and exchange, and the best obtainable system of popular administration and control of each industry or service.

The traditional limits of liberalism were clearly being tested. This was the background to the debates held at the Liberal Summer Schools from 1922 onward, events that attracted large audiences, involving many leading figures in the party, but focused on the ideas of experts who were not necessarily supporters of the party. The economists involved included Keynes on international debt and reparations, Josiah Stamp on public finance, Walter Layton on state involvement in industry, and Hubert Henderson on the problem of unemployment. Hobhouse spoke on wages and other experts on problems in specific industries (Cecil et al. 1922). The aim was to develop a more practical liberalism, informed by the experience in government and in various public inquiries, and economics was clearly in the forefront of their discussions. The aim was to make a market economy work better. Though there was opposition to protection (J. M. Robertson, chairman of the National Liberal Federation) and to a capital levy to reduce the burden of the government debt accumulating during the war (Stamp), speakers were not shy of advocating government intervention, whether in the form of unemployment relief (Henderson), the use of trade boards to determine minimum wages, and even wages above this level (Hobhouse), nationalization of coal stocks so that the mining industry could be reorganized (McNair), measures to give urban leaseholders an incentive to improve their property (Comyns Carr), and measures to encourage farmers to raise productivity (Acland). The pragmatic view in evidence is nicely illustrated by Layton's remark that though Liberals attached great importance to individual freedom, "For Liberals there is no inherent sanctity in the conceptions of private property, or of private enterprise. They will survive, and we can support them only so long as they appear to work better in the public interest than any possible alternatives" (Layton, in Cecil et al. 1922). The perspective that the Manchester Liberals were adopting resonated with the analysis Pigou was offering in successive editions of *The Economics of Welfare.*

Lionel Robbins, a prominent liberal (though not Liberal) economist at the London School of Economics, is often presented as having attacked Pigouvian welfare economics. However, though he was more skeptical about government intervention than the New Liberals, opposing interventions such as minimum wages, he was not averse to government intervention per se. For example, he supported subsidies and controls to solve the housing problem. Though he might see fewer opportunities for government to improve the working of the economic system, and though he believed that some economists such as the Liberal Hobson and the socialist Tawney were illegitimately blurring the distinctions between economic science and their own value judgements, he remained, with qualifications, a utilitarian in his political judgments.[1]

Whereas in 1922 it was possible to argue that the main measures needed to reform the system were already in place, as the decade wore on the limitations of the system became more evident. Capitalism was called into question by the existence of a socialist system in the Soviet Union. There were thus economists calling for socialist solutions to the problems Britain was confronting. These ranged from the Marxist socialism of Laski and H. D. Dickinson through the Fabianism of the Webbs and the syndicalism and Christian socialism of Tawney and others. Yet there was no clear divide between this spectrum of views and those of New Liberals such as Hobson and Hobhouse who had incorporated collectivist elements into their liberalism. Socialism was defended both by referring to the success of Soviet planning, as in the Webbs' *Soviet Communism: A New Civilization?* (1936) and by using theoretical arguments such as those found in the so-called socialist calculation debate in which Dickinson and Abba Lerner joined "market socialists" based in the United States to counter the critiques leveled by the Austrian economist Ludwig von Mises.

The issue that changed the terms of the debate over the role of the state was unemployment. Clearly, the Great Depression called capitalism into question in a way that had not happened before; this was even more true in Britain, where unemployment had already emerged as a new problem in the early 1920s. Every year that it remained around 10 percent raised further doubts about whether traditional remedies were working. In the 1920s it became clear that the problem of unemployment had to be reconceptualized: the idea gained ground among both economists and policymakers that it was a structural problem, caused by problems in major industries, and this displaced earlier views of unemployment as attributable to problems of individual workers. It might be necessary to turn to more drastic measures, such as protection, abandoning the gold standard, or more vigorous government involvement in industrial restructuring—there was a stream of royal commissions and other inquiries into what could be done about particular industries such as coal and cotton textiles—but such measures, with the exception of abandoning free trade, did not raise problems of principle for liberals. Countercyclical public works policy, long mooted as a means of alleviating the cycle, became more prominent as a possible remedy for unemployment, especially after the return to gold took exchange rate and interest rate adjustments off the agenda.

The situation changed after 1929: unemployment became, along with the budget deficit, the overriding concern of economic policy. It was tackled as a problem of the business cycle. There had been major studies of the business cycle before World War I, but such work developed apace in the 1920s, when "business barometers" such as the one produced at LSE and other statistical work began to provide a much clearer picture of fluctuations in economic activity. The increased prominence of thinking in terms of the cycle is illustrated by Pigou's work. In 1914, his discussion of the cycle had been but one part of a larger project on welfare economics: welfare, he claimed, depended on the size of the national dividend, its distribution, and its stability. In the 1920s, his discussion of the cycle, and hence unemployment, was left out of *The Economics of Welfare*, and became the subject of a new book,

Industrial Fluctuations (1927). When the nature of the problem had changed still further, he brought out *The Theory of Employment* (1933).

As the world fell into depression, clear divisions arose as to the diagnosis of the problem and the appropriate policies to pursue. Liberals took contrasting positions on what should be done. Robbins and Friedrich Hayek, recently arrived from Austria, took a stand against expansionary monetary or fiscal policy. The most prominent opposition to these arguments came, not from socialists, but from other liberals, such as Keynes and Henderson, supporting the efforts of Lloyd George to stem flow of the electoral tide against the Liberal Party. Keynes might acknowledge "the end of laissez-faire," but he remained self-consciously a Liberal, in both senses of the word. *The General Theory* (1936) marked a fundamental change in his economic theory but did not involve any change in his political philosophy. As he had argued in "The End of Laissez-Faire" (1926, in 1971–89, vol. 9), he had always been committed to the idea that the state should take responsibility for those things that would otherwise not be done at all, which included, in 1926 and in 1936, ensuring appropriate levels of saving and investment. He saw such action by the state as entirely consistent with liberalism.

The conversion of the Treasury to demand management, in 1941, was driven by the exigencies of war. The aim was not to increase employment but to enable the Treasury to reconcile competing demands on resources without excessive inflation. It was the wartime government, albeit responding to public opinion, that took the crucial step of implementing the recommendations contained in *Social Insurance and Allied Services* (1942), the report written by Beveridge, a longtime Liberal, that built on principles many Liberals had embraced since the much more limited introduction of pensions and unemployment insurance in the first two decades of the century.

1.3. Philosophical Foundations for the Analysis of Welfare

All his life, Keynes was a committed liberal, both philosophically and politically. As an undergraduate be became heavily involved in Liberal politics, and he remained committed to the Liberal Party, arguing that though his heart lay on the left, he could never join the Labour Party, a class party representing a class that was not his own.[2] The philosophical beliefs that supported his position were explained in an essay, "My Early Beliefs," written in September 1938 (Keynes 1949).[3] The essay is useful because it treats in some detail the effect on Keynes and his contemporaries at Cambridge of the philosopher G. E. Moore. Moore's book *Principia Ethica* (1903) was published at the end of Keynes's first year at Cambridge. "Its effect on *us*, and the talk that preceded and followed it, dominated, and perhaps still dominate, everything else" (Keynes 1971–89, 10:435). Keynes was particularly influenced by the book because he had become a member of the secret society known as the Apostles during his first year, and Moore had also been a member as a Cambridge undergraduate and still often attended the group's Saturday night meetings. The group was already discussing Moore's ideas before *Principia Ethica* was published, hence Keynes's remark about "the talk that preceded" it. Likewise, they discussed Moore's work at length after the book was published, and made it a central element of membership in the group to have a "correct" understanding of what Moore had said in the book. Following the publication of Moore's book, Keynes read a series of papers to the group on themes related to it, including his first work ever on probability.[4]

Moore's ethics rested on the claim that good was something that was apprehended directly. Certain activities or things are seen to be good, but meaning of the term "good" cannot be broken down into elements of which it is composed. Some things were just good: they were not good because they were pleasurable or for any other reason. In other words, he rejected utilitarianism. One of the most intriguing things about Keynes's 1938 autobiographical essay is his recounting of how Moore's disdain for utilitarianism played a crucial role in the lives of the young Apostles. "We were amongst the first of our generation, perhaps alone amongst our generation, to escape from the Benthamite tradition" (Keynes 1971–89, 10:96).[5] *Principia Ethica* contained a strong argument against John Stuart Mill's utilitarianism (which it took as paradigmatic) and dismissed Mill's ethics out of hand (Moore 1903, 68–81, 104–5). Moore did not deny that people experienced pleasure (or utility); rather he denied that the pleasure that people felt was always "good" or desirable. In other words, he denied that utility was a sufficient basis for a theory of ethics; he denied that people would always act so as to maximize their utility, or that they would want to do so.

Pigou, like Keynes, was also a member of the Apostles and rejected utilitarianism. In the final edition of his *Economics of Welfare* (1932), Pigou wrote not of the good, but of welfare. He claimed that "the elements of welfare are states of consciousness and, perhaps, their relations" and that "welfare can be brought under the category of greater and less" (1932, 10). Though he referred to these as "satisfactions," he did not mean this to be utilitarianism. States of consciousness and satisfactions were plural and were not equated with the pleasure that formed the subject of utilitarianism. He then narrowed his focus still further, asserting that he was concerned only with what he called "economic welfare," namely welfare that could be brought into relation with the measuring rod of money. This was emphatically not the whole of welfare, and might not even be correlated with total welfare. Even if total welfare could be defined (and it is not clear that he considered its different elements commensurable—he even wrote that a good human being, living a virtuous life, might be an element in welfare, irrespective of what he produced), economic welfare might not be a good index or barometer of welfare.

This may have reinforced technical considerations in causing Pigou to abandon the Marshallian method of analyzing consumers' surplus in favor of marginal analysis, comparing the social costs and benefits of different activities, and analyzing market failure in terms of the divergence between social and private costs. However, though he saw the ethical foundation of his method as being nonutilitarian, his methods were consistent with utilitarianism. Moreover, having explained that economic welfare might bear no relation to total welfare (if indeed the latter could be defined), he backtracked (see Backhouse 2010, 127–28). First, he argued that he was not concerned with the sum of economic welfare, merely with how different activities increased or decreased economic welfare. The relevant question was whether actions that raised (or lowered) economic welfare would be offset by changes in noneconomic welfare. Then he submitted that "in the absence of special knowledge, there is room for a judgment of probability: unless there is evidence to the contrary, we can regard the change in economic welfare "as *probably* equivalent in direction, though not in magnitude, to the effect on total welfare" (Pigou 1932, 20). This concession was tantamount to admitting that economic welfare *could*, at least for the changes he was concerned to analyze, be considered a proxy for total welfare.

Following Moore's strictures, Keynes parted more decisively from utilitarianism in that he assumed neither that people always acted so as to maximize their utility nor that they should. Because of these two strictures, Keynes never employed utilitarian criteria as the ultimate guide in evaluating economic policy. Though he did occasionally speak of economic agents who used utility in their decision-making, this was never the sole or even the most important motivation. So, for instance, in the *General Theory* (1936, 8) there are six motivations to consumption, only one of which might reasonably be conflated with utility: "Enjoyment, Shortsightedness, Generosity, Miscalculation, Ostentation, and Extravagance." Likewise, the two other main behavioral functions in the *General Theory*, the marginal efficiency of investment and the liquidity preference function, are not underpinned by utility maximization. In fact, both of these functions may famously be animated by animal spirits and are impossible to fully understand as a part of Keynes's larger system without grasping that agents represented in them are driven by fundamental issues of uncertainty that can lead them to herd behavior. In addition to developing a theory that did not rely on utility maximization, Keynes also developed a nonutilitarian means of evaluating the performance of the economy. His desideratum was not maximizing individual or social utility functions; it was maximizing and stabilizing the level of employment. This criterion for evaluating macroeconomic performance was, for Keynes, decidedly not utilitarian.

Paradoxically, given popular conceptions of their work, the two most prominent utilitarians among Liberals involved in discussions of the welfare state were Hobson and Lionel Robbins. In contrast to Pigou, Hobson called explicitly for a "new utilitarianism," one that, instead of the earlier, individualistic utilitarianism, viewed problems from the perspective of society as a whole.[6] He wrote,

> Our setting must be in the full sense of the work, "utilitarian." The premature abandonment of the utilitarian setting by many thinkers, through pique arising from the narrow and degrading interpretation given to the term, has not been justified. . . . The particular vices of some special form of utilitarianism, the insistence that desirability was entirely to be measured by the quantity and never by quality, the stress on physical enjoyment, and the short range of measurement, which were somewhat incorrectly attributed to Bentham's system, are not inherent in utilitarianism, and need not deter us from using its convenient language. (Hobson 1901, 4–5)

However, though nailing his colors firmly to the utilitarian mast, Hobson's utilitarianism resembled, in significant respects, Pigou's and Keynes's Mooreian antiutilitarian positions. Neither would have dissented from Hobson's claim, made in respect of Adam Smith, that welfare (true wealth) should encompass not simply goods but also knowledge, freedom, health, and character.

Where Hobson parted company with Pigou was in rejecting the idea that money could be used to measure welfare, thereby making the analysis of welfare scientific. Attacking the notion of a scientific welfare economics, Hobson drew upon John Ruskin to mount a critique of contemporary society, developing what he called a human standard of welfare. Making very specific judgments about the values of different activities—such as the greater value attached to artistic work than other forms of human endeavor—he challenged the idea that increases in production and consumption necessarily contributed to welfare. The production of some goods, even though consumers might want to consume them, was harmful.

This approach to utilitarianism was anathema to Lionel Robbins, who considered the way Hobson brought values into economics to be not simply wrong but dangerous. His *Essay on the Nature and Significance of Economic Science* (Robbins 1932), commonly believed to be an attack on Pigou, was nothing of the sort (Backhouse 2009). His target was those, such as Hobson, who blurred the boundaries between science and ethics. The book argued merely that ethical judgments were not a part of economic science. He did question some of Pigou's arguments, but they were on the same side in wanting the economist to be scientific, restricting what was claimed in the name of economic science to what could be said without smuggling in unwarranted ethical judgements. A few years later he wrote that in his youth he was attracted by what he called "provisional utilitarianism"—the idea that summing utilities on the assumption that every person counted equally and using this as a first approximation in evaluating policy—was "less likely to lead one astray than any of the absolute systems" (Robbins 1938, 635). This led him to appreciate Pigou's "delicate balancing of gain and loss through intricate repercussions of policy," but as time went on he wanted to make a clearer separation between politics and economics (Robbins 1938, 635). However, he continued, despite having doubts about Pigou's approach, he "never thought of abandoning [his] provisional utilitarianism as a working political philosophy" (Robbins 1938, 636).

The 1930s saw a move away from utilitarianism in economic theory in that the utilitarian criterion for social welfare—maximizing the sum of individual utilities—was decisively rejected. Utilities, as Robbins argued, were not interpersonally comparable, rendering such calculations problematic. What came, in the 1950s, to be termed "Pareto efficiency" or "Pareto optimality" was seen as an alternative to utilitarianism. However, such theorizing remained utilitarian in the sense that it rested on the assumption of maximizing agents, something Keynes had not been prepared to assume.

All the economists discussed in this section were liberals, and many of them supporters of the Liberal Party. All of them reflected on the philosophical foundations of their economic analysis, and yet they reached divergent views on utilitarianism and its serviceability as a basis for arguments about the welfare state. Keynes rejected utilitarianism entirely; Pigou rejected the philosophy but preserved much of the form of utilitarianism; Robbins rejected utilitarianism as a formal welfare criterion but confessed to being utilitarian in his political philosophy; and Hobson called for a new utilitarianism.

1.4. Conclusion

Modern opposition to the welfare state rests largely on an ideological aversion to collectivism, as being inherently inefficient and inimical to freedom. Given this, it is natural to attribute the creation of the welfare state to a collectivist frame of mind. This was emphatically not the case in Britain. Some supporters of the welfare state—including members of Attlee's Labour government—did use collectivist, socialist arguments to justify the reforms being introduced, but support for the welfare state from Liberals was just as strong. Many of the most important thinkers, behind the reforms introduced under both Asquith and Atlee, were liberals—Hobson, Beveridge, Keynes—for whom liberty was fundamental value. While they might recognize the necessity for an element of collectivism, they were in no way committed to collectivism, let alone socialism. Of course, not all liberals were supporters of the welfare state. Hayek and Robbins, though less extreme in their opposition to state welfare provision than many of their followers, were much more cautious in the range of measures that they thought compatible with a market economy. (See the chapter in this volume by George Peden for a discussion of Hayek's views on the welfare state.)

Those economists who did support the welfare state did not argue in terms of a utilitarian concept of efficiency, the basis on which modern economists might argue in favor of state intervention. Not even the economists argued in this way. Hobson was utilitarian but introduced Ruskinian value judgments at the heart of his analysis in a way that marks his approach as being very different from that of modern economists. Pigou and Keynes explicitly rejected utilitarianism for reasons that we have explained. Beveridge simply took for granted the importance of certain freedoms and did not try to reduce them to a single measure of well-being that could be maximized.

Given this, why have the nonutilitarian, liberal foundations on which British economists argued the case for the welfare state not been recognized? Part of the answer is that these foundations are unfamiliar to modern economists and crossed conventional ideological divisions: Keynes and Pigou rejected utilitarianism, but so too did Robbins and Hayek. Another part of the answer is that Keynes, whose name came to be associated above all others with welfarist policies, encouraged his followers to develop his ideas and to incorporate them in conceptual frameworks that were not necessarily his own. He said more than once that he was not concerned with the ultimate theoretical form that Keynesian macroeconomics took as long as it conveyed his central insights about the nature of unemployment in a capitalist economy.[7] Thus although his own work was nonutilitarian, this basis was lost in the proliferation of "Keynesian" theories based on different conceptual frameworks. If the ethical foundations for Keynes's theory were lost, what chance did the views of Pigou, lambasted as the representative "classical" economist, clearly on the losing side of the Keynesian revolution, have? Recognizing that Pigou's ethical framework was nonutilitarian was even harder because he presented many of his arguments in the language of utilitarianism.

The development of the British welfare state was intimately connected to developments in British liberalism, in turn linked to the fortunes of the Liberal Party. The first steps toward the welfare state were taken by the New Liberals, who dominated policymaking in the decade before World War I. Though it is debatable how much politicians drew on formal economic arguments, whether orthodox (Marshall and Pigou) or heretical (Hobson), liberal economists offered a range of arguments that could be used to support these developments. In the interwar period, the Liberal Party ceased to be a major political force, and the political pressure for improved social welfare provision came from the Labour Party, though it was not in a position to implement reform till 1945. However, the displacement of the Liberal Party by the Labour Party did not signify the displacement of liberalism as an intellectual force. Despite the Labour Party's socialist platform, the postwar British welfare state rested primarily on the ideas of two liberal economists, Keynes and Beveridge.

References

Backhouse, R. E. 2009. "Robbins and Welfare Economics: A Reappraisal." *Journal of the History of Economic Thought* 31 (4): 474–84.

Backhouse, R. E. 2010. "J. A. Hobson as a Welfare Economist." In R. E. Backhouse and T. Nishizawa, eds., *No Wealth but Life: Welfare Economics and the Welfare State in Britain, 1880–1945*, 114–35. Cambridge: Cambridge University Press.

Backhouse, R. E., and B. W. Bateman. 2010. "Whose Keynes?" In R. Dimand, R. Mundell, and A. Vercelli, eds., *Keynes's General Theory: A Reconsideration after Seventy Years*, 8–27. London: Palgrave Macmillan.

Backhouse R. E., and B. W. Bateman. 2012. "Keynes and the Welfare State." *History of Economic Thought and Policy* 1 (1): 7–19.

Backhouse R. E., and T. Nishizawa, eds. 2010. *No Wealth but Life: Welfare Economics and the Welfare State in Britain, 1880–1945*. Cambridge: Cambridge University Press.

Bateman, B. W. 1988. "G. E. Moore and J. M. Keynes: A Missing Chapter in the History of the Expected Utility Model." *American Economic Review* 78 (5): 1098–106.

Beveridge, W. 1942. *Social Insurance and Allied Services*. London: Her Majesty's Stationery Office.

Cecil, R., et al. 1922. *Essays in Liberalism, Being the Lectures and Papers Which Were Delivered at the Liberal Summer School at Oxford, 1922*. London: W. Collins and Son. Online at https://archive.org/details/essaysinliberali00libe.

Freeden, M. 2003. "The Coming of the Welfare State." In T. Ball and R. Bellamy, eds., *The Cambridge History of Twentieth Century Political Thought*, 5–44. Cambridge: Cambridge University Press.

Hayek, F. A. 1944. *The Road to Serfdom*. London: Routledge.

Hobson, J. A. 1901. *The Social Problem*. London: Nisbet.

Hutchison, T. W. 1978. *On Revolutions and Progress in Economic Knowledge*. Cambridge: Cambridge University Press.

Keynes J. M. 1936. *The General Theory of Employment, Interest, and Money*. London: Macmillan.

Keynes J. M. 1949. *Two Memoirs*. London: Rupert Hart-Davis.

Keynes J. M. 1971–89. *The Collected Writings of John Maynard Keynes*. Edited by D. Moggridge and E. Johnson. 30 vols. London: Macmillan.

Medema, S. G. 2011. *The Hesitant Hand: Taming Self-Interest in the History of Economic Ideas*. Princeton, NJ: Princeton University Press.

Mill, J. S. 1859. *On Liberty*. London: Macmillan.

Moore, G. E. 1903. *Principia Ethica*. Cambridge: University Press.

Pigou, A. C. 1912. *Wealth and Welfare*. London: Macmillan.

Pigou, A. C. 1920–1932. *The Economics of Welfare*. London: Macmillan.

Pigou, A. C. 1927. *Industrial Fluctuations*. London: Macmillan.

Pigou, A. C. 1933. *The Theory of Employment*. London: Macmillan.

Pigou, A. C., and S. Rowntree. 1914. *Lectures on Housing: The Warburton Lectures for 1914*. Manchester: Manchester University Press.

Robbins, L. C. 1932. *An Essay on the Nature and Significance of Economic Science*. London: Macmillan.

Robbins, L. C. 1938. "Interpersonal Comparisons of Utility: A Comment." *Economic Journal* 48 (192): 635–41.

Robbins, L. C. 1978. *The Theory of Economic Policy in English Classical Political Economy*. London: Macmillan.

Webb, B., and S. Webb. 1936. *Soviet Communism: A New Civilization?* 2 vols. New York: Charles Scribner's Sons.

2 Liberal Economists and the British Welfare State

FROM BEVERIDGE TO THE NEW RIGHT

GEORGE PEDEN

2.1. Introduction

Sir William Beveridge, whose report, *Social Insurance and Allied Services* (1942), did much to shape the welfare state, was a Liberal, as was John Maynard Keynes, whose *General Theory of Employment, Interest and Money* (1936) provided the basis for the postwar commitment to full employment. Yet the welfare state became the object of fundamental criticism by liberal economists, at first in Liberal Party publications, but increasingly from the 1960s through the Institute of Economic Affairs (IEA), a think tank that became associated with the New Right in British politics. How can one account for changing liberal attitudes to the welfare state?

The terms "liberal," "neoliberal," and "New Right" all have a range of meanings. I use "liberal," with a small *l*, as a generic term incorporating all varieties of liberalism. By "Liberal," with a capital *L*, I mean someone associated with the Liberal Party. Liberalism is traditionally associated in Britain with individual freedom, free markets, and a limited state. In the postwar period the party drifted between, on the one hand, advocating the use of the state to tackle the economic and social costs of free-market capitalism, and, on the other, expressing concern that reliance on the state would undermine the independence and individual responsibility required for true liberty. The party membership included not only Beveridge but also Arthur Seldon, who in 1955 became the first editorial adviser (and later director) of the IEA. It was only after the party took a leftward turn in the 1960s that neoliberalism became associated with Conservatism and the New Right (Sloman 2015, 190–95, 220–23, 238–39). Neoliberalism had various strands, including Austrian economics, German ordoliberalism, and the Virginia and Chicago schools, and changed over time. The Mont Pelerin Society, founded in 1947, on the initiative of Friedrich Hayek, provided an international network for spreading neoliberal ideas (Cockett 1994, 57, 100–121; Mirowski and Plehwe 2009). As Ben Jackson (2010) points out, neoliberalism had not evolved by 1947 into the precise ideological form it took in the 1970s, and Hayek and other members of the society initially tried to incorporate parts of the welfare state agenda into their thinking. Angus Burgin traces the hardening of neoliberal attitudes toward state intervention from the 1960s to the influence of Milton Friedman, who imparted a more confident emphasis on the benefits of impersonal market forces as the best way to secure personal liberty and welfare than members of the Mont Pelerin Society had previously shown (Burgin 2012, 125, 153–55, 178, 185, 222). It was also from the 1960s that respected academic economists wrote IEA papers and pamphlets urging greater use of markets and prices in welfare services (Tribe 2009).

"New Right" is another term that is hard to pin down: in Britain it incorporates different tendencies within the Conservative Party associated with Margaret Thatcher, both neoliberalism stressing the virtues of market forces, and neoconservativism emphasizing hierarchy, authority, and nation (Levitas 1986). Florence Sutcliffe-Braithwaite (2012) distinguishes neoliberalism from Thatcherism, which incorporated distinctive ideas on poverty and self-help, derived from Victorian values, as well as a Hayekian hostility to the state. This chapter is concerned with the neoliberal aspect of the New Right. The focus is on changes in liberal thought in Britain, but these were not independent of developments elsewhere. In particular, the IEA benefited from intellectual support from leading neoliberal economists from outside Britain, including Hayek, Friedman, and James Buchanan (Jackson 2012).

The term "welfare state" also has a range of meanings. The Labour Party committed itself to the Beveridge report, and the Attlee government's welfare legislation differed from earlier selective social services and the poor laws by being intended to ensure that all citizens were entitled to a basic income and had equal access to the best standards of health services, housing, and education (Briggs 1961, 228). In 1949 the Labour-supporting sociologist T. H. Marshall put forward the concept of social citizenship based on universal rights that were independent of the market value or social status of the claimant, with transfers between more and less fortunate individuals in the population (Marshall and Bottomore 1992, 28, 32–33). The Liberal Party was no less committed than Labour to the Beveridge report, but Liberals also believed that the market enabled individuals to be independent of the state. Members of the party, including its future leader, Joseph Grimmond, set up the Unservile State Group in 1953 to establish a sound basis for future policies. In a cooperative volume, *The Unservile State: Essays in Liberty and Welfare* (1957), one of the economists in the group, Alan Peacock, took as axiomatic that no one's opportunities to develop should be frustrated by material circumstances, and that therefore there was a good case for transfer payments such as family allowances, sickness benefits, and pensions, and financial support for access to health services, housing, and education. However, he argued that the latter need not be provided by state monopolies; instead independent providers should be encouraged to provide competition for the public sector. He believed that, as an article of faith, Liberals must assume the large majority of individuals, once freed from poverty, were able to take their own spending decisions when guided by a free market (Peacock 1957a). He later said the true object of the welfare state, for a Liberal, was to teach people to do without it (Peacock 1962, 11). Peacock became an early adherent of what would become known as public choice theory. An invitation to give a lecture at the University of Virginia in 1958 brought him into contact with Buchanan, and he was aware of Buchanan and Gordon Tullock's work on political and market choices by 1961 (Peden 2015, 501–2). Buchanan and Tullock's book, *The Calculus of Consent* (1962), demonstrated how free provision of welfare services would lead rational consumers individually and collectively to demand more than they would be willing as taxpayers to pay for. Liberal principles regarding the independence and individual responsibility of citizens, and public choice theory, were in conflict with an expansion of state welfare services beyond what had been established in the 1940s.

This chapter explores the relationship between liberal economists and the welfare state in three ways. First I look at the liberals whom Hayek associated with collectivism in the 1940s, Beveridge and Keynes, and ask how different their conceptions of the welfare state were from his. Then I look at liberal critiques of different aspects of the welfare state: income support, the National Health Service (NHS), education, housing, and employment policy. Third, I offer brief observations on the impact of the New Right on the welfare state in the 1980s.

2.2. Beveridge, Keynes, and Hayek

The Beveridge report recommended universal social insurance against interruptions of earnings resulting from ill health, unemployment, or old age, and means-tested national assistance for people who failed to fulfil the contribution conditions of insurance. Beveridge said the abolition of poverty would also require a national health service, family allowances, and measures to prevent a return to high unemployment (Beveridge 1942, 154–65). Treasury officials were worried about the implications of the enlarged social insurance scheme for the postwar budget. Prior to publication of the report, Keynes, then an adviser to the Chancellor of the Exchequer, and Lionel Robbins, then director of the Cabinet Office's Economic Section, had a series of meetings with Beveridge and persuaded him to reduce the immediate cost of his original proposals by phasing in old-age pensions and by being less generous with cash payments to parents, known as family allowances.[1] But otherwise, Keynes was supportive, describing the report as "a fine document" (Keynes 1980, 252; Harris 1997, 400–404).

The congruence of Keynes's and Beveridge's views on social insurance is not surprising. Both men had developed their political ideas during the period of New Liberalism before 1914. New Liberalism, which developed in the later nineteenth century, had a different philosophical basis from classical liberalism, with a more organic and less individualistic view of society. New Liberals believed the state should be used to cure social evils that were beyond the control of the individual. However, they retained a belief in the value of the free market and the virtue of self-help. For example, the system of national insurance against interruption of earnings on account of sickness or unemployment, which was introduced in 1911 for most wage earners, but not the salaried middle class, provided benefits below the wages of the poorest workers. Insured workers were thus encouraged to return to work as soon as possible. Subsistence payments could be obtained by applying to the Poor Law guardians, or, after 1929, local authority public assistance committees, or, after 1934, the Unemployment Assistance Board; such payments being means-tested and subject to evidence that the applicant was genuinely seeking work. National insurance was a system of compulsory, subsidized thrift, with wage earners, employers, and taxpayers all contributing to national health and unemployment insurance funds. Only wage earners were insured; thus a sick worker would receive a cash benefit and free medical treatment designed to enable him or her to return to work, but he or she would have to pay medical bills for dependents, unless they were covered by private insurance. New Liberals believed as much as classical liberals or neoliberals that self-help and thrift were necessary characteristics of freedom (Peden 1991, 15–16, 19–22, 26–32).

Beveridge and Keynes shared these ideas. Beveridge, while extending social insurance to all, recommended that contributions, benefits, and pensions should be flat-rate to minimize their redistributive effect, and, in order to encourage self-help, that benefits and pensions should be no more than "subsistence." Beveridge's proposals were based on a number of prewar social surveys in English cities that showed most poverty was caused by loss of earnings through old age, unemployment, or sickness, and could be cured by social insurance. However, he also recognized that up to a quarter of poverty was due to earnings being inadequate to maintain children. He therefore recommended that parents should receive subsistence allowances for their second and subsequent children. At a time when there was concern over a fall in the birth rate, family allowances were widely regarded as desirable, and an element of self-help was retained by making parents fully responsible for the cost of the first child (Beveridge 1942, 7–8, 120–22, 155–56).

Hayek had very little to say about social services in his wartime book, *The Road to Serfdom*. He thought there was no reason why the state should not guarantee a minimum standard of living to all its citizens, or help to organize a comprehensive system of social insurance against hazards, such as sickness, against which few individuals could make adequate private provision. His only condition was that the measures taken did not make the labor market less competitive. Otherwise he saw no incompatibility between social insurance and the preservation of individual freedom (Hayek 1944, 89–90). Hayek recognized that Beveridge did not intend social insurance to be an instrument of income redistribution (Hayek 1960, 303). There was nothing in the system of social insurance proposed by Beveridge and supported by Keynes that was contrary to Hayek's principles.

Hayek was much more concerned with the vogue for economic planning, and he was opposed to measures that would interfere with the labor market by guaranteeing particular groups of workers their current relative position compared with others. He saw that people might easily be persuaded to protect or subsidize particular producers, for example in agriculture. The principal economic purpose of *The Road to Serfdom* was to defend the price system as the best system of allocating resources against socialists and others who claimed that rational utilization of resources required central direction (Hayek 1944, 26–31, 36, 79, 89, 165). The latter group arguably included Beveridge. His thinking on collectivism in the 1940s was complex and far from consistent: he was much more skeptical than Keynes about how far economic liberalism, as opposed to noneconomic personal freedoms, could survive the changes brought about by war. In 1942 he believed that full employment would require state control of industry, but was converted in 1943–44 to Keynesian aggregate demand management by a group of socialist economists, including Nicholas Kaldor and Joan Robinson, whom he recruited to help him write his private report, *Full Employment in a Free Society*. He still believed in state regulation of private business investment and in price controls for essential goods and services. However, his continuing commitment to New Liberal ideals of self-help and the need to balance bureaucracy with voluntarism found expression in his last report, *Voluntary Action* (1948) (Beveridge 1944, 157, 202–3; Harris 1997, 426–43, 459–60, 467; Komine 2010; Marcuzzo 2010).

Beveridge had no impact on the content of the wartime coalition's white paper, *Employment Policy* (1944), which reflected thinking in Whitehall about what would be required to prevent a return to high unemployment. The white paper contained proposals for stabilizing investment, partly by using monetary policy and tax credits to influence the timing of private investment, and partly by offsetting variations in private investment with variations in public capital expenditure. Likewise there were proposals for maintaining consumer expenditure, partly by tax credits and partly by varying social insurance contributions, with higher contributions in periods of high employment and lower contributions when demand fell (Minister of Reconstruction 1944, 20–24). The economist who did most of the drafting of these sections was James Meade, who believed that economic stability and equitable distribution of income could only be achieved by extensive use of the market determination of prices and output (Meade 1948, v). Meade worked under Robbins in the Economic Section. Robbins had played a major part in developing a distinctive liberal school of economics at the London School of Economics (LSE) before the war, and in 1947 he drafted the Mont Pelerin Society's statement of its aims (Howson 2011, 664). Another liberal economist involved in the drafting of the white paper in the Ministry of Reconstruction was John Jewkes, who in 1962–64 would be president of the society. It is not surprising, therefore, that there was nothing in the white paper contrary to a continuation of the free market: indeed it referred to businessmen being guided in investment decisions by whether prices were likely to go up or down. The white paper explained that the policy of managing aggregate demand would work only if wages and prices were reasonably stable, but went on to say that there must always be room for adjustment of wages on account of changes in industry (Minister of Reconstruction 1944, 18). There was no mention of state controls on prices or wages. Keynes supported Robbins in opposing restrictions on industry, saying it should be the purpose of employment policy to provide a framework that would preserve the liberty and initiative of the individual in economic life (Keynes 1980, 369).

Keynes's own views on profits and planning in economic policy are brought out in his comments to Hayek about the *Road to Serfdom*, which he described as "a grand book." Keynes thought Hayek might have been even more robust in his defense of the profit motive and private enterprise against socialist teaching. On the other hand, Keynes believed a middle way was possible between laissez-faire and a planned economy, and was therefore less fearful than Hayek of planning by the state. He believed moderate planning would be safe provided it took place in a community where most people shared Hayek's moral position. Indeed, Keynes seems to have regarded planning designed to stabilize aggregate demand as an antidote to socialism (Keynes 1980, 385–88). Hayek, however, feared that state intervention would develop over time in ways that would restrict individual freedom: on the title page of *The Road to Serfdom* he quoted David Hume's remark, "It is seldom that liberty of any kind is lost all at once."

To conclude this section: Beveridge, Keynes, Robbins, and Hayek shared a good deal of common ground. They agreed the state had a role to play in organizing social insurance, and that social insurance should not discourage workers from entering the labor market. Where there was scope for disagreement was in how the principles of the Beveridge report and the white paper on employment policy were to be implemented.

2.3. Liberal Critics of Postwar Developments

Under Conservative governments in 1951–64 Britain lagged behind other Western European countries in terms of the growth of the proportion of GDP devoted to transfer incomes of all kinds: pensions and social insurance and means-tested benefits (Harris 1991, 36–58). Nevertheless Hayek became disenchanted with the way in which the welfare state was developing. In *The Constitution of Liberty* (1960) he developed a comprehensive critique of what he saw as the prospective political and economic consequences: increasing public expenditure, enterprise-paralyzing taxation, and the growth of bureaucracy with far-reaching powers and loss of individual rights. He believed that all monopolies, including centralized state provision of social insurance, become inefficient over time; increasing complexity made social insurance a matter for experts who tend to favor more generous provision; and politicians sought votes by using social insurance and pensions to redistribute income. He saw the free National Health Service as an open-ended commitment with financial implications of similar magnitude to social insurance. Demand for social housing was increased, he argued, by rent controls that discouraged investment in the private rental market. While he regarded the 1944 white paper's goal of high and stable employment as reasonable, he blamed Keynesian demand management for causing higher inflation than previously experienced in peacetime. Inflation made it harder for people to save for old age, thereby increasing their dependence on the state (Hayek 1960, 280–81, 287–300, 305, 324–28, 343–46). Robbins and Peacock thought Hayek's fears about the long-term consequences of the welfare state were greatly exaggerated (Robbins 1961; Peacock 2010, 139–40). In particular, Robbins was critical of Hayek's use of the blanket term "welfare state" instead of discussing social insurance or state-aided education on their merits. What follows looks at different aspects of the welfare state.

The Beveridge report was less influential on the system of income support than is often assumed. The economist who provided the most telling arguments against its full implementation was Hubert Henderson, who, like Beveridge and Keynes, was a Liberal. Like Keynes, Henderson was an economic adviser in the Treasury during the war, and he brought his critical powers to bear on Beveridge's proposals even before they were published. Beveridge hoped universal social insurance would restrict means testing to a small number of people who failed to pay contributions and who would therefore continue to rely on national assistance. Henderson, however, pointed out that universal social insurance would be an unnecessarily expensive way of abolishing poverty, since people with substantial savings and unearned income would qualify for benefits (Henderson 1955, 191–208). Treasury officials were impressed by his arguments, and tried unsuccessfully to have the Beveridge scheme restricted to the existing, largely working-class, insured labor force.

In the event, the Labour government made insufficient allowance for inflation in fixing pensions and benefits. When the National Insurance Act of 1946 came into force in 1948, 495,000 pensioners and 143,000 other people of pensionable age received means-tested national assistance supplements (which had replaced public assistance). In 1950 the Labour government responded to continuing inflation by increasing rates for national assistance but not national insurance pensions or benefits (Thane 2000, 369, 371). Notwithstanding Beveridge's intentions, it became normal for people without savings or other sources of income to undergo means testing to supplement national insurance benefits. Henderson's influence on Treasury thinking outlasted his death in 1952. In 1964 an official referred to Henderson's "famous Treasury paper" on the Beveridge report when commenting on the wastefulness of universal social insurance (Clarke 1964). An IEA study group, including Peacock, came to broadly similar conclusions to Henderson in 1967, but seems to have been unaware of his paper (Alexander et al. 1967).

Peacock meanwhile had questioned the need for an elaborate system of national insurance accounting separate from the budget accounts. He pointed out that national insurance differed from private insurance: first, national insurance contributions were not adjusted to individual risks; second, risk was minimized by government policy, for example through the NHS; third, ability to adjust benefits to maintain their real value depended on fiscal and monetary policy, not the existence of reserve funds. National insurance had some of the trappings of private insurance, with accumulated reserves and actuarial forecasting, but was open to political pressures to increase benefits faster than contributions (Peacock 1949, 1952). He was involved in the Liberal Party's plans for negative income tax, first put forward by Lady Juliet Rhys Williams as an alternative to the Beveridge report (Rhys Williams 1943; Sloman 2016). The Liberal Party's Yellow Book, *Reform of Income Tax and Social Security Arrangements* (1950), argued that income tax personal allowances and national insurance benefits should be replaced by new social security payments to which everyone, whether taxpayer or not, would be entitled without means test. National insurance contributions would be abolished, and direct taxation of incomes below a certain level would be fixed at a flat rate sufficient both to pay for the new benefits and to raise revenue previously raised by income tax. The Liberals' proposals were given short shrift by the Board of Inland Revenue when they were considered by the Royal Commission on the Taxation of Profits and Income in 1951, but they represent a liberal alternative to Beveridge's conception of social insurance in which fairness would be combined with personal responsibility.

The Beveridge report had recommended that national insurance benefits should be paid to the unemployed only if they were available for work and willing to undergo training after drawing benefits for a limited period (Beveridge 1942, 128). In practice, the unemployed could live off means-tested benefits indefinitely. In 1959 the Conservative government decided that national assistance benefits should be increased in line with the standard of living of the community as a whole, rather than in line with prices, as hitherto (Atkinson 1991, 129–31). Social security increasingly moved from providing a basic minimum to becoming a means of redistributing income. The consequence, in neoliberal analysis, was to increase the incentive for people to qualify for benefits by remaining or becoming unemployed or poor or homeless (Harris 1988).

The NHS likewise expanded far beyond Beveridge's original conception of a service that would reduce claims on the national insurance fund by preventing and curing disease (Beveridge 1942, 158–63, 199, 201). For example, hospital maternity departments increasingly came to be seen as the normal place for childbirth. An aging population increased demand for places in geriatric wards. The NHS administrative system in the 1950s was not well designed to reallocate resources—even a sympathetic historian describes it as having dysfunctional characteristics (Webster 1998, 62). Jewkes and his wife Sylvia claimed (*a*) the NHS was inherently inefficient, on account of the scale of bureaucracy required; (*b*) resources were allocated according to political expediency, so that preventative medicine, medical research, and the training of doctors were neglected rather than impose charges for doctor's services or hospital boarding costs; and (*c*) a free NHS acted as a disincentive for people to help themselves through private insurance and medical services. From the Jewkeses' perspective, the NHS was inferior to the prewar medical services, which were paid for by national or private insurance, and hospitals were free to people who could show need. They conceded that the prewar system was imperfect—and indeed many hospitals had been in financial difficulty in 1939—but argued that, with rising national income, Britain would have come to enjoy wider and better distributed health services under the old system (Jewkes and Jewkes 1961, 1963). By the 1960s it was possible to point to serious errors in centralized decision-making based on forecasts of manpower, costs, or demand. For example, the IEA claimed that the NHS was short of doctors because of an underestimate of demand by the Willink Committee in 1957 and the Ministry of Health's failure to respond to warnings that there was a large net loss of doctors by migration (Seale 1965). Buchanan, who spent time in London in 1965, frequently visiting the IEA, wrote a pamphlet calling for reform of the NHS to bring demand decisions and supply decisions into the same framework, either through the market or through setting limits on what individuals could demand (Buchanan 1965).

Primary and secondary education faced challenges after the war: a "baby boom" increased the number of pupils, and local authority housing programs moved families from urban centers to peripheral housing estates. Local education authorities had variable success in building new schools and staffing them with qualified teachers. In addition, there was debate about the respective merits of the prevailing selective system, whereby the type of a child's schooling was determined by examinations and intelligence test at age 11 or 12, and the comprehensive system. Consequently not every parent was convinced the best standard of education was being provided for her child. In his *Unservile State* essay in 1957, Peacock argued for greater competition between private and state schools as a means of raising standards. He was attracted by a scheme put forward in the United States by Friedman for giving parents vouchers to cover the cost of educating each child (Peacock 1957a, 118). In a pamphlet written for the IEA in 1964, Peacock and Jack Wiseman put forward a proposal for nontransferable vouchers that would be used by parents to pay fees to private or state schools of their choice. The intention was to widen access to the best standards of education, and, as the vouchers would be subject to tax as ordinary income, poor parents would have received more assistance than the better off (Peacock and Wiseman 1964, 35–36). The proposal was rejected by the Liberal Party conference—a decision that led Peacock to withdraw from regular contact with party leaders (Peacock 2010, 177–81)—but vouchers had continued support from the IEA (Maynard 1975).

Initially universities faced fewer challenges than schools did. The increase in student numbers after the war was modest, and, at a time when much professional training, including for accountants, bankers, nurses, and many schoolteachers, was provided outside the university system, university entrants represented only 4 percent of their age group in 1962. The chairman of a government committee that reviewed higher education in 1961–63 was none other than Robbins, whom Turner (2008, 6) identifies as being "among the most powerful exponents of neo-liberalism," but who in the context of university expansion saw no immediate need to resort to the price mechanism. Robbins retained the existing system whereby universities were largely financed by the taxpayer through grants administered by the independent University Grants Committee (UGC). He was impressed by arguments for a system of student loans, but his committee decided against them on the grounds that it was a bad thing for young people to emerge from education loaded with debt, and students continued to have fees paid by local authorities and to receive means-tested maintenance grants funded by the taxpayer. Robbins recognized that public funding exposed the universities to the danger of political pressures, but believed the UGC system could strike a balance between academic freedom and coordinated allocation of resources (Howson 2011, 889; Robbins 1963). Peacock and Wiseman (1964) were more skeptical, rightly anticipating that governments would be unwilling to provide from taxation the full cost of university expansion and that hitherto independent universities would increasingly be treated as part of the public sector. Robbins himself came to regret that he had not recommended a system of student loans (Robbins 1980, 35–36).

The shortage of housing created by World War II led to a huge expansion of building by local authorities. By the 1960s, however, many working-class people were buying houses, and Peacock, still an adviser to the Liberal Party, suggested that local authorities should be encouraged to allow sitting tenants to buy their homes (Peacock 1962). In 1968 the IEA published the results of a review of local authority housing that claimed that local authority bureaucracies were often inefficient and unresponsive to tenants' preferences. The IEA recommended the sale of houses to tenants or private landlords at market prices (Gray 1968), and in 1970s the Conservatives adopted a policy of giving sitting tenants the right to purchase at two-thirds of the market value of their homes.

2.4. Employment Policy and Inflation

Hayek and British liberal economists differed markedly on employment policy. As a product of the Austrian school of economics, Hayek believed unemployment was caused by failure of relative prices and wages to adjust to the demand for labor and its supply in each sector of the economy. It was, he said, always possible to reduce unemployment temporarily by monetary expansion, but employment thus created could only be maintained by continuing and accelerating inflation (Hayek 1978). In contrast, Robbins and Peacock believed Keynes had shown how inflation could be prevented through fiscal policy, although Robbins placed more emphasis than Keynes had done on supporting fiscal policy with monetary policy (Robbins 1954, 60–80; Peacock 1957b). During the long postwar boom chancellors aimed at budget surpluses on current expenditure to keep inflation down, although the size of the budget surplus was reduced at times when unemployment threatened to rise. Budget deficits on current expenditure only became a regular feature of public finance after 1973, when Anthony Barber reflated the economy to prevent unemployment rising above 1 million. The budget figures excluded borrowing by local authorities and public corporations, and the concept of the public sector borrowing requirement (PSBR) was introduced in Britain only in 1976. Retrospective figures for the PSBR, however, show that it had been almost always within the range of 2 to 4 percent of GDP before 1974. It is not surprising therefore that the IEA's attack on Keynesian budgetary profligacy came only in 1978, and was based on mistaken ideas about what had traditionally constituted a balanced budget (Buchanan, Wagner, and Burton 1978; Clarke 1998).

Even with fiscal restraint, public expenditure's share of GDP increased from 37 percent in 1955 to 42.9 percent in 1973. Social services more than accounted for the increase, their share rising 7.3 percentage points from 13.9 percent of GDP in 1955 to 21.2 in 1973 (Middleton 1996, 98). The resignation of a Chancellor of the Exchequer, Peter Thorneycroft, in 1958 in protest against the Cabinet's refusal to place a ceiling on public expenditure appeared in retrospect to be a proto-monetarist protest against Keynesianism. However, Thorneycroft and his junior ministers, Enoch Powell and Nigel Birch, were advised by Robbins and another liberal economist, Dennis Robertson, neither of whom could be described as a monetarist, as that term came to be understood in the 1970s and 1980s. Robbins and Robertson advised Thorneycroft that, if inflation was to be avoided, the government must rely less upon short-term debt in the form of Treasury bills to finance its expenditure, and the Bank of England rather reluctantly accepted Robbins's suggestion that commercial banks should deposit funds with the Bank, which it would lend to the Treasury. The idea of monetary targets lay in the future (Green 2000; Howson 2011, 798–802; Peden 2000, 486–93).

From 1948 to 1966 unemployment was more often than not below 2 percent, while retail prices almost doubled. Robbins doubted if the commitment to full employment could be maintained if wages and prices continued to rise and recommended that demand should be managed to ensure high employment at wage rates not increasing more rapidly than productivity (Robbins 1954, 18–40). Frank Paish, who was the Liberal Party's official economic adviser in the 1950s, caused controversy in academic and trade union circles by recommending that unemployment should be allowed to rise slightly, to create a margin of spare capacity and to alter workers' expectations. In the early 1950s he suggested an average of 3 to 4 percent, a figure he reduced in 1955 to 3 percent, and in 1958 to about 2 percent. He was not wedded to a particular figure because he recognized that the level consistent with stable prices would vary with circumstances, particularly changes in productivity (Paish 1966, 93–104; 1971, 23–51). Paish believed that the prices and incomes policies that governments pursued from the mid-1950s would be ineffective as long as there was excess demand for labor: even if unions cooperated, he noted, employers would be tempted to offer higher wages to induce workers to switch jobs. However, in 1969, when unemployment averaged 2.5 percent, implying, in his view, a sufficient margin of spare capacity to eliminate excess demand for labor, wages rose faster than before. Paish reluctantly came to the conclusion that temporary government control of wages and prices might be necessary to offset the monopoly power of the trade unions (Paish 1971, 68–84). Robbins, however, believed an attempt to control wages could do more harm than good, by affecting the general working of markets, and could only be justified in a grave emergency. Trade unions, he thought, should be left to learn from the consequences of their actions. However, in November 1972, faced with the Heath government's failure to control monetary growth, and with inflation rising rapidly, he reluctantly supported the introduction of a statutory freeze on prices and wages, since he believed that a deflationary financial policy alone would produce unacceptably high unemployment (Robbins 1971, 231; Howson 2011, 1031). In the event, the attempt to control wages provoked a coal miners' strike and brought down the Heath government in 1974. The political crisis and the subsequent experience of stagflation prepared the way for the rise of the New Right. The IEA played a crucial role by spreading neoliberal critiques of Keynesian macroeconomic policy (Friedman 1970; Hayek 1975; Walters 1978).

What is striking is how slow the New Right was to criticize microeconomic aspects of employment policy. Under the Distribution of Industry Act of 1945 the government had powers to encourage firms to move to areas of high unemployment, both by financial assistance or by withholding permission to build factories in areas of high employment. These powers were not much used until the decline of older industries, such as coal mining, shipbuilding, and textiles, from the late 1950s. Inevitably commercial decisions became entangled with social and political issues. In the late 1960s the Labour government was preserving shipbuilding jobs by granting financial assistance to firms in return for reorganization of the structure of the industry. The Conservative government came to power in 1970 declaring it would not subsidize what it called "lame ducks," but ended up not only giving financial assistance to shipbuilding but also nationalizing the major aero-engine firm, Rolls-Royce, when it was on the brink of bankruptcy. This kind of employment policy was precisely the kind of privilege for particular groups of workers that Hayek had denounced in *The Road to Serfdom*, but it took the Centre for Policy Studies (CPS), which Thatcher and Sir Keith Joseph had founded in 1974, until 1979 to condemn it (Burton 1979).

2.5. Impact of the New Right

The impact of neoliberalism on the welfare state during the period of the Thatcher government, 1979–90, was limited partly by the presence in the Cabinet of traditional "one-nation" Conservatives, and partly by continuity in official thinking. The IEA's ideas had been regarded in Whitehall prior to 1979 as being outside the mainstream of conventional wisdom, and, although IEA publications became prescribed reading thereafter, civil servants still offered advice along lines that they regarded as practical politics (Croham 1981). What follows are brief observations on how welfare policy changed.

By the 1980s it was widely accepted—on the left as well as on the right—that the social security system had become too complex, with high administrative costs and poor take-up of many means-tested benefits. The Conservative secretary of state for health and social security, Norman Fowler, called for the most comprehensive review since the Beveridge report, and the outcome was the Social Security Act of 1986. Benefits were rationalized, with the result that real incomes of the childless unemployed declined, sharpening the incentive to seek work, especially as income tax had been reduced. On the other hand, there were net real gains for low-income families, reflecting the government's concern to target benefits more accurately according to need (Dilnot and Webb

1989; Johnson and Stark 1989). While these changes were in line with New Right ideas—Peacock was a member of the review—they also had the support of, and indeed were drafted by, Whitehall officials.

The NHS was a target for New Right reformers, who saw it as subject to bureaucratic sclerosis, dominated by the interests of the medical professions, and poor value for money. Efforts were made to introduce business principles and methods into hospital management: in 1983 laundry and cleaning were put out to competitive tender; and in 1990 general practitioners were given the right to hold budgets with which to buy hospital care for their patients. Prescription and dental charges were raised steeply and more people took out private health insurance. Even so, at the end of the decade 90 percent of the population relied exclusively on the NHS for their healthcare, and the allocation of resources continued to be predominantly by queues rather than by price. The NHS was simply too popular with the electorate for the New Right to push reform as far as it would have liked (Allsop 1989; Green 1988).

It proved to be even harder to introduce New Right ideas into education. As secretary of state for education, Joseph was interested in the IEA's ideas for school vouchers. However, having attended private schools, he and his junior ministers were unfamiliar with the state system and were persuaded by officials that local authority schools would not be able to manage vouchers, and the idea was abandoned in 1983 (Timmins 1995, 419–20). To the IEA this decision was an example of public choice theory in action: the concentrated, articulate producer interests of the teachers' unions and bureaucrats were stronger than the dispersed, consumer interests of parents (Seldon 1986).

In contrast, New Right ideas had a major impact on local authority housing. The Housing Act of 1980 encouraged local authority tenants to become owner-occupiers. As a result, eventually 40 percent of the social housing stock was sold on very favorable terms. Moreover, local authority building was curbed, while private building increased. As a result of these changes the proportion of owner-occupiers among householders increased from just over half in 1979 to two-thirds 10 years later. A "property-owning democracy" had long been a Conservative ideal, but the way in which it was conceived in the 1980s reflected neoliberal influences (Francis 2012).

To sum up, the impact of New Right ideas on the welfare state in the 1980s was mixed, but significant. A new agenda for social reform had been set. The idea that there are free-market alternatives to provision of health and education services by public monopolies continued to inform welfare reform after Labour returned to office in 1997.

2.6. Conclusion

Liberal economists' attitudes to the welfare state were partly based on longstanding principles regarding the relationship between the citizen and the state, and partly a response to the tendency of the welfare state to develop in ways that enlarged the role of government. Hayek could agree with Beveridge on an austere form of social insurance, and yet strongly disapprove of how social insurance subsequently developed. Liberal economists looked for ways in which to minimize citizens' dependence on the state. Henderson and Peacock preferred social security to be based on means-tested need rather than on universal entitlement. Peacock was an early advocate of what would become known as social-market citizenship by adopting Friedman's idea of education vouchers and by advocating the sale of local authority houses. Yet liberal economists still expected the state to nurture and protect citizens. In 1963 Robbins looked to the state rather than to individuals to pay for the expansion of higher education. As regards full employment, Robbins and Paish expected the state to protect citizens from the effects of an unregulated market through judicious application of Keynes's macroeconomics, and when push came to shove in the 1970s they preferred state control of wages to mass unemployment. Liberal economists were on a spectrum, from New Liberalism to neoliberalism, with Beveridge and Keynes at one end and Hayek, Buchanan, and Friedman at the other. The success of the New Right, such as it was, was partly a reaction to an expansion of the welfare state and partly a consequence of the economic policy failures of the Heath government.

Acknowledgments

This chapter is based on research that began with a paper, "Economists and the British Welfare State: From New Liberalism to the New Right," presented in March 2010 at an international workshop at Hitosubashi University, Tokyo. A related article, "Neoliberal Economists and the British Welfare State," based on a paper presented in May 2016 at a conference of the European Society for the History of Economic Thought at University Paris 1–Panthéon-Sorbonne, can be found in the *Journal of the History of Economic Though* 39 (4) (2017). I am grateful to the editors of this volume and also Susan Howson, Ben Jackson, Stephen Meardon, and participants at the workshop and conference for comments and suggestions at various stages of the research.

References

Alexander, A. J., et al. 1967. *Towards a Welfare Society*. London: IEA.

Allsop, J. 1989. "Health." In M. McCarthy, ed., *The New Politics of Welfare: An Agenda for the 1990s?*, 53–81. London: Macmillan.

Atkinson, A. B. 1991. "A National Minimum? A History of Ambiguity in the Determination of Benefit Scales in Britain." In T. and D. Wilson, eds., *The State and Social Welfare: The Objectives of Policy*, 121–62. London: Longman.

Beveridge, W. 1942. *Social Insurance and Allied Services*. Cmd. 6404, House of Commons Parliamentary Papers.

Beveridge, W. 1944. *Full Employment in a Free Society*. London: George Allen & Unwin.

Beveridge, W. 1948. *Voluntary Action: A Report on Methods of Social Advance*. London: George Allen & Unwin.

Briggs, A. 1961. "The Welfare State in Historical Perspective." *Archives Européennes de Sociologie* 2:221–58.

Buchanan, J. M. 1965. *The Inconsistencies of the National Health Service*. London: IEA.

Buchanan, J. M., and G. Tullock. 1962. *The Calculus of Consent*. Ann Arbor: University of Michigan Press.

Buchanan, J. M., R. E. Wagner, and J. Burton. 1978. *The Consequences of Mr Keynes*. London: IEA.

Burgin, A. 2012. *The Great Persuasion: Reinventing Free Markets since the Depression*. Cambridge, MA: Harvard University Press.

Burton, J. 1979. *The Job Support Machine: A Critique of the Subsidy Morass*. London: Centre for Policy Studies.

Clarke, P. 1998. "Keynes, Buchanan and the Balanced Budget Doctrine." In *The Keynesian Revolution and Its Economic Consequences*, 190–212. Cheltenham: Edward Elgar.

Clarke, R. 1964. "Pensions." July 8. Sir Richard Clarke papers, CLRK 1/3/3/1, Churchill Archives Centre, Cambridge.

Cockett, R. 1994. *Thinking the Unthinkable: Think-Tanks and the Economic Counter-revolution, 1931–1983*. London: HarperCollins.

Croham, Lord. 1981. "The IEA as Seen from the Civil Service." In *The Emerging Consensus. . .?*, 205–26. London: IEA.

Dilnot, A., and S. Webb. 1989. "The 1988 Social Security Reforms." In A. Dilnot and I. Walker, eds., *The Economics of Social Security*, 239–67. Oxford: Oxford University Press.

Francis, M. 2012. "'A Crusade to Enfranchise the Many': Thatcherism and the Property-Owning Democracy." *Twentieth Century History* 23 (2): 275–97.

Friedman, M. 1970. *The Counter-revolution in Monetary Theory*. London: IEA.

Gray, H. 1968. *The Cost of Council Housing*. London: IEA.

Green, D. 1988. *Everyone a Private Patient: An Analysis of the Structural Flaws in the NHS and How They Could Be Remedied*. London: IEA.

Green, E. H. H. 2000. "The Treasury Resignations of 1958: A Reconsideration." *Twentieth Century British History* 11 (4): 409–30.

Harris, J. 1991. "Enterprise and the Welfare State: A Comparative Perspective." In T. Gourvish and A. O'Day, eds., *Britain since 1945*, 39–59. London: Macmillan.

Harris, J. 1997. *William Beveridge: A Biography*. Oxford: Clarendon Press.

Harris, R. 1988. *Beyond the Welfare State: An Economic, Political and Moral Critique of Indiscriminate State Welfare and a Review of Alternatives to Dependency*. London: IEA.

Hayek, F. A. 1944. *The Road to Serfdom*. London: George Routledge & Sons.

Hayek, F. A. 1960. *The Constitution of Liberty*. London: Routledge and Kegan Paul.

Hayek, F. A. 1975. *Full Employment at Any Price?* London: IEA.

Hayek, F. A. 1978. *A Tiger by the Tail: A 40-Years' Running Commentary on Keynesianism*. London: IEA.

Henderson, H. 1955. *The Inter-war Years and Other Papers*. Edited by Henry Clay. Oxford: Clarendon Press.

Howson, S. 2011. *Lionel Robbins*. Cambridge: Cambridge University Press.

Jackson, B. 2010. "At the Origins of Neo-liberalism: The Free Economy and the Strong State." *Historical Journal* 53 (1): 129–151.

Jackson, B. 2012. "The Think-Tank Archipelago: Thatcherism and Neo-liberalism." In B. Jackson and R. Saunders, eds., *Making Thatcher's Britain*, 43–61, 286–91. Cambridge: Cambridge University Press.

Jewkes, J., and S. Jewkes. 1961. *The Genesis of the British National Health Service*. Oxford: Blackwell.

Jewkes, J., and S. Jewkes. 1963. *Value for Money in Medicine*. Oxford: Blackwell.

Johnson, P., and G. Stark. 1989. *Taxation and Social Security, 1979–1989: The Impact on Household Incomes*. London: Institute for Fiscal Studies.

Keynes, J. M. 1980. *Collected Writings*. Vol. 27. London: Macmillan; Cambridge: Cambridge University Press.

Komine, A. 2010. "Beveridge on a Welfare Society: An Integration of His Trilogy." In R. Backhouse and T. Nishizawa, eds., *No Wealth but Life: Welfare Economics and the Welfare State in Britain, 1880–1945*, 207–19. Cambridge: Cambridge University Press.

Levitas, R., ed. 1986. *The Ideology of the New Right*. Cambridge: Polity Press.

Liberal Party. 1950. *Reform of Income Tax and Social Security Arrangements*. London: Liberal Publication Department.

Marcuzzo, M. C. 2010. "Whose Welfare State? Beveridge versus Keynes." In R. Backhouse and T. Nishizawa, eds., *No Wealth but Life: Welfare Economics and the Welfare State in Britain, 1880–1945*, 189–206. Cambridge: Cambridge University Press.

Marshall, T. H., and T. Bottomore. 1992. *Citizenship and Social Class*. London: Pluto Press.

Maynard, A. 1975. *Experiment with Education*. London: IEA.

Meade, J. E. 1948. *Planning and the Price Mechanism: The Liberal-Socialist Solution*. London: George Allen & Unwin.

Middleton, R. 1996. "The Size and Scope of the Public Sector." In S. J. D. Green and R. C. Whiting, eds., *The Boundaries of the State in Modern Britain*, 89–145. Cambridge: Cambridge University Press.

Minister of Reconstruction. 1944. *Employment Policy*. Cmd. 6527, House of Commons Parliamentary Papers.

Mirowski, P., and D. Plehwe, eds. 2009. *The Road from Mont Pèlerin: The Making of the Neoliberal Thought Collective*. Cambridge, MA: Harvard University Press.

Paish, F. W. 1966. *Studies in an Inflationary Economy: The United Kingdom, 1948–1961*. London: Macmillan.

Paish, F. W. 1971. *Rise and Fall of Incomes Policy*. London: IEA.

Peacock, A. T. 1949. "The National Insurance Funds." *Economica*, n.s. 16 (63): 228–42.

Peacock, A. T. 1952. *The Economics of National Insurance*. Edinburgh: William Hodge and Co.

Peacock, A. T. 1957a. "Welfare in the Liberal state." In G. Watson, ed., *The Unservile State: Essays in Liberty and Welfare*, 113–30. London: George Allan & Unwin.

Peacock, A. T. 1957b. "From Political Economy to Economic Science." *University of Edinburgh Journal* 18 (Summer): 249–57.

Peacock, A. T. 1962. *The Welfare Society*. Unservile State Papers, No. 2.

Peacock, A. T. 2010. *Anxious to Do Good: Learning to Be an Economist the Hard Way*. Exeter: Imprint Academic.

Peacock, A. T., and J. Wiseman. 1964. *Education for Democrats*. London: IEA.

Peden, G. C. 1991. *British Economic and Social Policy: Lloyd George to Margaret Thatcher*. Hemel Hempstead: Philip Allan.

Peden, G. C. 2000. *The Treasury and British Public Policy, 1906–1959*. Oxford: Oxford University Press.

Peden, G. C. 2015. "Alan Turner Peacock, 1922–2014." *Biographical Memoirs of Fellows of the British Academy* 14:495–516.

Rhys Williams, J. 1943. *Something to Look Forward To: A Suggestion for a New Social Contract*. London: Macdonald.

Robbins, L. 1954. *The Economist in the Twentieth Century and Other Lectures in Political Economy*. London: Macmillan.

Robbins, L. 1961. "Hayek on Liberty." *Economica*, n.s. 28 (109): 66–81.

Robbins, L. 1963. *Higher Education: Report of the Committee appointed by the Prime Minister under the chairmanship of Lord Robbins*. Cmnd. 2154, House of Commons Parliamentary Papers.

Robbins, L. 1971. *Autobiography of an Economist*. London: Macmillan.

Robbins, L. 1980. *Higher Education Revisited*. London: Macmillan.

Seale, J. 1965. "Medical Migration: A Study in the Inadequacy of Official Statistics." In D. Burn, J. Seale, and A. Ratcliffe, eds., *Lessons from Central Forecasting*, 25–39. London: IEA.

Seldon, A. 1986. *The Riddle of the Voucher: An Inquiry into the Obstacles to Introducing Choice and Competition in State Schools*. London: IEA.

Sloman, P. 2015. *The Liberal Party and the Economy, 1929–1964*. Oxford: Oxford University Press.

Sloman, P. 2016. "Beveridge's Rival: Juliet Rhys-Williams and the Campaign for Basic Income, 1942–1955." *Contemporary British History* 30 (2): 203–23.

Sutcliffe-Braithwaite, F. 2012. "Neo-liberalism and Morality in the Making of Thatcherite Social Policy." *Historical Journal* 55 (2): 497–520.

Thane, P. 2000. *Old Age in English History: Past Experience, Present Issues*. Oxford: Oxford University Press.

Timmins, N. 1995. *The Five Giants: A Biography of the Welfare State*. London: HarperCollins.

Tribe, K. 2009. "Liberalism and Neoliberalism in Britain, 1930–1980." In P. Mirowski and D. Plehwe, *The Road from Mont Pèlerin: The Making of the Neoliberal Thought Collective*, 68–97. Cambridge, MA: Harvard University Press.

Turner, R. 2008. *Neo-liberal Ideology: History, Concept and Policies*. Edinburgh: Edinburgh University Press.

Walters, A. 1978. *Economists and the British Economy*. London: IEA.

Webster, C. 1998. *The National Health Service: A Political History*. Oxford: Oxford University Press.

3 | Ordoliberalism, the Social-Market Economy, and Keynesianism in Germany, 1945–1974

HARALD HAGEMANN

3.1. Introduction

Welfare for Everybody (*Wohlstand für Alle*) was the title of a book Ludwig Erhard (1897–1977) presented to the public on the eve of the 1957 elections to the Bundestag. At that time the first minister of economics in the new Federal Republic of Germany from 1949 to 1963 was at his peak. Against the background of the West German economy, which experienced an unexpectedly high average rate of growth of the real national product of 8.2 percent per year in the 1950s, Erhard's reputation had risen, and his consultants had no major difficulties in stylizing Erhard as the "father" of the German "economic miracle" (*Wirtschaftswunder*) in the media. He also embodied the "miracle" visually, as in the famous photo when Erhard, well nourished and with his characteristic big cigar, presented his *Welfare for Everybody*, in which he advocated the concept of a social-market economy combining economic freedom with social cohesion. In contrast to subsequent debates on a Phillips curve trade-off, Erhard interestingly opted for an economy in which price stability and full employment should coexist.

Erhard contributed decisively to the success of the Christian Democrats in the 1957 elections to the Bundestag, the party getting 51 percent of the votes. This was the only time after World War II that a political party in Germany received an absolute majority of the votes. The staunchly liberal Erhard had strongly opposed proposals for the nationalization of basic industries (particularly iron, coal, and steel) and economic planning, which shortly after the war were not only widely advocated by socialists but even in the Ahlen program of February 1947, which had the flavor of a Christian-based socialism, by the Christian Democratic Union (CDU) in North Rhine-Westphalia, the important state including the Ruhr area.

With his clean political record, Erhard's career developed quickly after the war. After receiving a doctoral degree from Goethe University in Frankfurt in 1929, with the charismatic Franz Oppenheimer—well known for his "liberal socialism" and looking for a "third way"—as his thesis supervisor, Erhard worked for the Institute for Economic Research of the German industry for finished goods in Nuremberg. There he was dismissed from his position as director in 1942 because he refused to become a member of the Nazi Party. In October 1945 he became Minister of Economics in the first Bavarian government. In September 1947 Erhard was appointed chairman of the Sonderstelle Geld und Kredit (Special Bureau for Money and Credit), a secret group of experts preparing currency reform,[1] and in March 1948 he succeeded Johannes Semler (who was forced to resign by the Western Allies after he mentioned in a public speech that the corn included in US food aid would be considered "chicken feed" in Germany) as the director of the economic administration of the Wirtschaftsrat, the committee of economic experts elected from the members of the regional parliaments in the American-British bizone. After the Grundgesetz, the new constitution of the Federal Republic of Germany, was enacted on May 23, 1949, Erhard was elected member of the first Bundestag and became minister of economics on September 20, 1949, in the first Adenauer cabinet.

After World War II economic policy in the new Federal Republic of Germany was decisively shaped by the ordoliberal ideas of Walter Eucken and the Freiburg school and principles of the "social-market economy" (Watrin 1979). The social-market economy, sometimes called "Rhine capitalism" (with Bonn as the capital of the FRG in the first four decades), was the German version of a third way—between laissez-faire economic liberalism, which was discredited by the Great Depression, and a centrally planned economy—that economists and politicians in many countries were looking for, as, for example, in Sweden, which became the prototype of a Western welfare state in the first decades after World War II.

Whereas the Americans had a decisive influence on the West German currency reform of June 20, 1948, and thus on a key factor of the subsequent growth process, their influence on the predominant conception of economic policy after 1945 was quite minor. The fundamental ideas of the social-market economy and ordoliberalism, above all those of Walter Eucken and the Freiburg school, originated in the years 1938–45 in opposition to National Socialism and on the basis of strong Christian beliefs (Rieter and Schmolz 1993). The roots of ordoliberalism go back to the period after 1929, when economic and political liberalism was in its deepest crisis. The German conceptions of *Ordnungspolitik* and *Soziale Marktwirtschaft* are mainly a response to the three challenges of the Great Depression, with its devastating economic and political consequences, experiences with National Socialism, and experiences with central planning in Soviet-type socialism as also present in East Germany after 1945.

In the following I discuss the main ideas and principles of ordoliberalism and the Freiburg school in section 3.2. Section 3.3 deals with the related conception of the social-market economy as mainly shaped by Alfred Müller-Armack, and the main economic laws enacted on that basis. Whereas economic policy in Germany until the recession of 1966–67 was dominated by ordoliberal ideas, the resignation of Ludwig Erhard (who had succeeded Konrad Adenauer in 1963) as the chancellor in December 1966 and the subsequent formation of the first "Grand Coalition" of Christian and Social Democrats, with the Social Democrat Karl Schiller as the new minister of economics, led to a late entry of Keynesian ideas into German economic policy. The period from December 1966 to 1974, widely regarded as the high years of Keynesianism in Germany, will be discussed in section 3.4. Finally, some further developments are sketched briefly.[2]

3.2. Ordoliberalism and the Freiburg School

"It is very difficult to establish explicit and direct links between the Freiburg School and Erhard," although "there is no doubt that the Freiburg School *did* influence Erhard," Goldschmidt and Wohlgemuth (2008b, 267) have rightly stated. The closest direct personal link was Leonhard Miksch (1901–1950), whose habilitation was titled *Competition as Task: Foundations of a Competitive Order* (Miksch 1937) and was an important contribution to the four-volume set *Die Ordnung der Wirtschaft*. Miksch, like Eucken, emphasized the theoretical concept of "perfect" competition, even arguing that the state should not only safeguard but organize competition (Miksch 1947, 11). Together with Franz Böhm, the leading jurist of the Freiburg school, Eucken, and Müller-Armack, Miksch became a close adviser to Erhard as a member of a group of academic economists who were appointed to the Independent Advisory Council of the Bizonal Economic Administration in January 1948.[3] Miksch died as professor at the University of Freiburg in September 1950, only half a year after his admired mentor Eucken passed away during a lecture series at the London School of Economics. Adolf Lampe (1897–1948), another core member of the Freiburg circle, had already died, shortly after being appointed professor at the University of Bonn. These deaths contributed to the fact that ordoliberalism did not become the dominant position at German universities in the following decades.

There is no doubt that Walter Eucken (1891–1950),[4] professor at Freiburg University since 1927, was the founder and intellectual leader of the Freiburg school and ordoliberalism, together with the congenial Franz Böhm (1895–1977) in law, who later was politically active for the CDU as a member of the German parliament from 1953 to 1965. The ideas of the Freiburg school were established and became known to a wider audience through the publication of a four volume-set *Die Ordnung der Wirtschaft* (*The Economic Order*) in 1936–37. Eucken's main theoretical ideas are worked out in his *Foundations of Economics* (Eucken 1940) which can be considered the economic basis of ordoliberalism, later elaborated after the war in his posthumously published *Principles of Economic Policy* (Eucken 1952). The anchor and fundamental principle in Eucken's ordoliberal design is the functional price mechanism of full competition (*vollständiger Wettbewerb*), which became the "Freiburg imperative." The essential features of a permanent order guaranteeing individual freedom and economic efficiency are already worked out in his fundamental essay "Competition as the Basic Principle of Economic Order" (Eucken 1942), published in the middle of World War II. In contrast to Lampe and other economists, Eucken put less weight on the problems of the transition from a wartime to a peacetime economy than on designing the principles of an ideal economic order balanced between laissez-faire liberalism and central planning.[5] Eucken considered the shaping of the economic order to be a central task of government. In sectors with many small suppliers and a high degree of competition, such as in agriculture, the state should restrict itself to setting the legal framework. In many industrial sectors with a high degree of concentration, however, monopolies should be eliminated or, if possible, at least controlled to ensure that firms would act as if they were in a situation of perfect (free) competition. With the historical experience of a cartelization of heavy industries that resisted downsizing after benefiting from World War I, Eucken favored strongly a liquidation and decartelization in his 1947 report *Konzernentflechtung und Konzernauflösung*. This point well illustrates a decisive difference between "ordoliberalism" on the one hand, and the classical liberalism of Adam Smith or the more evolutionary perspective of Hayek, who came from Chicago to Freiburg in 1962, on the other hand. In Latin *ordo* refers to a natural order, but the ordoliberals did not believe that such a natural order would come about by itself. The "invisible hand" works within the institutions that reconcile individual and public interests, but does not create those institutions (Eucken [1952] 2004, 356–68). In other words, the state must play an active role in constructing and maintaining the proper legal framework and the required institutions for an efficient economy.

A functioning price system of full competition is the fundamental principle of the ordoliberal economic constitution, as most elaborated by Eucken (1952).[6] A well-functioning price mechanism plays the central role for all other constituent principles of the competitive order:

- *Monetary stability* to ensure that the system of relative prices is not distorted by inflation or deflation
- *Open markets*, that is free market entry for new firms and for foreign products to increase competitive pressure and to avoid monopoly rents
- *Private property* to stimulate an efficient use of resources. In that context any form of socialism or a centrally planned economy is explicitly

rejected: "Private property *may* lead to grievances, collective property *must* do so" (Eucken 1952, 317). In the German constitution, the Grundgesetz, no concrete economic order is fixed. However, Article 14 guarantees private property and mentions the social responsibility deriving therefrom. Article 20, 1 refers to the *Sozialstaatsprinzip*, that is, the obligation of the state to form a social order.

- *Freedom of contract* to enable the individual agents to make their own choices
- *Liability* for economic decisions. This liability principle, as developed by Eucken, is intended to link individual interests to the commonweal. In the aftermath of the post-2007 financial and economic crises, it has to be emphasized that it clearly implies cogent arguments against excessive leverage effects, that is, much higher own-capital quotas for banks to avoid taxpayers having to cover losses caused by excessive speculation. The internalization of external effects, for example in cases of pollution, also follows from the liability principle.
- *Constancy of economic policy* to make government behavior predictable for individual agents and thereby avoid misallocation of resources due to fluctuating discretionary policies. In view of modern macroeconomic debates on "rules versus discretion" and "time (in-)consistency," it is interesting to note Eucken's early emphasis on the constancy of economic policy directed against discretionary interventionism of any kind.

This allegiance to a price system made the ordoliberals strong opponents of Keynesian economic policies in subsequent debates. They share with Mises the argument for the impossibility of rational economic calculation under socialism, and with Hayek the double opposition against a wooden insistence on laissez-faire and against unforeseen governmental interferences, expressed in *The Road to Serfdom* (Hayek [1944] 2001, 18, 84).

On the other side, the state plays a substantially stronger role in the competitive order conceived by Eucken than in Hayek. This is particularly visible in the *regulating principles*[7] that have the main task of keeping the competitive order functioning. They require a strong democratic state that has primacy over the economy and not only takes responsibility for establishing the rules constituting the market process but also, in case of need, intervenes to maintain the competitive order. With regard to these regulating principles it is evident that Eucken and ordoliberalism firmly remain in the German tradition of *Staatswissenschaften* (state sciences).

The regulating principles include

- *Monopoly controls*, which are most important to contain and correct market power and thereby forces and tendencies damaging free competition

- *Income policy*, that is, some redistribution of income by progressive taxation with regard to social justice and as an acceptable means of social policy while considering repercussive effects on investment
- *Corrections of negative external effects*, in particular with regard to protection of the environment and the health of the workers
- *Corrections of abnormal supply behaviour*. Eucken (1952, 303–4) even made a plea for minimum wages set by the government in recession periods if the labor supply should increase and thereby react "perversely" to a reduction in the wage rate.

From the constitutive principles it is clear that the government should not directly interfere with market processes by fixing prices or quantities. Interventions according to the regulating principles can change the primary income distribution via progressive taxation, transfer payments, or subsidies. In addition to the constitutive and regulating principles, Eucken also discusses potential additional principles and principles of the state itself. The first include moderation in business cycle measures and encouragement of self-help, but, most importantly, the integration of the competitive order, legislation, jurisdiction, and administration and the avoidance of isolated application of measures. The second demands the limitation of the power of interest groups and the *subsidiarity principle*, that is, that the lowest possible territorial authority should take care of a problem. The subsidiarity principle is highly topical in current debates in the European Union, ordoliberals (and not just ordoliberals) strongly oppose "Brussels centralism."

Thinking in terms of an economic order comes out very clearly in the *conformity principle*, which was formulated first by Wilhelm Röpke (1899–1966) in *The Social Crisis of the Present* (Röpke 1942, 252ff.).[8] Economic measures should be conformable with their goal (means-end appropriateness), the working of the market mechanism, and the competitive order as a whole; that is, of all possible instruments the one most compatible with a market economy and a free society, unlikely to require further intervention, should be chosen.

One final comment has to be made with regard to current international debates and controversies on the appropriate monetary and fiscal policies to overcome the financial and economic crisis. The German monetary trauma that remains in memory is the hyperinflation Germany and Austria had to face after World War I, which caused a far-reaching expropriation of money wealth owners (this also had a great effect on the writings of Mises and Hayek). Since then monetary stability as an essential prerequisite for economic and political stability has been deeply engraved in German minds. Inflationary fears were a major barrier to more expansionary economic policies and the launching of employment programs in 1930–32, the years of the Great Depression when they would have been most appropriate. This historical trauma also contributed to the fact that, decades later, price stability became the decisive macroeconomic goal in the constitution of the Bundesbank (and again several decades later in the constitution of the European Central Bank), deeply affecting the Bank's monetary policies.[9]

Monetary and currency stability, which became a constituent principle in German ordoliberalism, alongside the fundamental principle of a functioning price system of full competition, reflects this historical background. Eucken himself got his habilitation from the University of Berlin in 1921 when hyperinflation, which was ended by currency reform in late 1923, was rampant. It led to his distancing from the younger historical school, in whose research tradition he had grown up. In his *Critical Considerations of the German Monetary Problem* Eucken (1923) put forward a penetrating criticism of the then quite prominent balance-of-payments explanation, as represented by Karl Helfferich, who, as state secretary in the Treasury Office, had been co-responsible for war financing. In his *Principles of Economic Policy* Eucken (1952), discussing the positive principles constituting a competitive order, opens his elaboration of the primacy of currency stability with reference to Lenin's famous dictum that to destroy civil society one only has to ravage the monetary order, and points out that all efforts to establish a competitive order are useless as long as a certain stability of the value of money is not secured.

Friedrich A. Lutz (1901–1975), Eucken's most outstanding and internationally renowned student, who, after making a career at Princeton from 1938 to 1953, declined the offer to succeed his former teacher (whose chair he had occupied in the academic year 1951–52) at Freiburg and instead moved to Zurich, made the decisive theoretical contributions on the monetary and currency order to the *Ordnungsökonomik* of the Freiburg school.[10] He had already written *The Basic Problem of the Monetary Constitution* (Lutz 1936), volume 2 of *The Economic Order*, before leaving Nazi Germany. In 1948 Lutz was one of the cofounders of *ORDO*, the journal that became the flagship of German ordoliberalism. There he published "Monetary Policy and Economic Order" (Lutz 1949), elucidating their mutual interdependencies. In this basic article Lutz emphasizes not only the role of money in enabling freedom of choice for consumers, which fades away in centrally planned economies, but also the gold standard as the proper monetary system for a competitive order, since it is based on a similar principle of an ingeniously constructed mechanism: "As the price mechanism dictates the actions of individuals, so the gold mechanism dictates actions by the chiefs of central banks and make 'their' monetary policy a more or less automatic reaction to the influx or drain of gold" (Lutz 1949, 207, my translation).

Lutz later engaged in the construction and stabilization of a functioning international currency order as an adviser to the Bank for International Settlements and as an activist in the Bellagio Group and the Mont Pelerin Society, which he presided over between 1964 and 1967. In the early period of the Bretton Woods system, which was still characterized by controls on international capital markets, Lutz became an early advocate of full convertibility of currencies and flexible exchange rates (Lutz 1954), pointing out that neither the gold standard nor flexible exchange rates are compatible with a centrally planned economy.

3.3. The Social-Market Economy

Terence W. Hutchison concludes his "Notes on the Effects of Economic Ideas on Policy: the Example of the German Social Market Economy" with the statement that "in 1948 there were German economists who ensured that 'the right ideas' were on hand to meet 'the right circumstances,' and that the 'effect' was not slow in manifesting itself" (Hutchison 1979, 440).

Among the academics who accomplished the transformation of these ideas into politics, besides Ludwig Erhard, Alfred Müller-Armack (1901–1978) was the main protagonist. Müller-Armack had been professor for economics and cultural sociology at the University of Münster from 1938 to 1950 and professor and director of the Institute of Economic Policy at the University of Cologne since 1950 before in 1952 he became the closest adviser to Erhard as director of Core Department 1 on economic policy in the German Ministry of Economics and in 1958 secretary for European affairs.[11]

Although one can say that the conception of the social-market economy has many parents, it was Müller-Armack who coined the brand name for an economic and social order that was a third way between laissez-faire economic liberalism and a socialist or planned economy (Müller-Armack 1956). Müller-Armack first used the very term "social-market economy" in his book *Economic Planning and Market Economy* (1946), in which the second chapter is entitled "Soziale Marktwirtschaft." However, the origins of the term date back to his earlier analysis of business cycles and Max Weber's sociology of religion and can be categorized as an "economic style" (Schefold 2004a). This comes to the fore as early as his *Genealogie der Wirtschaftsstile* (1941), in which Müller-Armack considers the economic process as a complement to the cultural and ethical development of societies, and points out the openness of the competitive order for social questions. Thus the social-market economy is less an ideal-type economic constitution than an economic style, developed as a synthesis of liberal ideas, Christian values and ethics, and a *freiheitlicher Sozialismus* (liberal socialism), with liberty and social justice as fundamental maxims. These ethical values, such as social justice, although established outside the market, have to be achieved by market-conforming means. Müller-Armack's interest in economic development and business cycles is also expressed in his assertion that a policy in support of a "social-market economy requires a conscious policy of economic growth" (1956, 391). Within a secure monetary order and a stable budget policy, he explicitly favored business-cycle policy measures to attain a high employment level. In contrast to ordoliberalism, his more pragmatic conception is not restricted to qualitative economic policy but also allows process policy. The social-market economy is a shifting compromise between efficiency and redistribution. As Müller-Armack (1978) emphasized: "It would be a calamitous error to give the task of creating a final social order to the automatism of the market." It is no surprise that Hayek distanced himself from the concept of the social-market economy since the adjective "social" and its concrete meaning remained obscure for him, whereas Ludwig Mises already identified ordoliberalism with ordointerventionism.

Although the conception of the social-market economy evolved from ordoliberalism, its rationale is not identical and, in its greater emphasis on the state's responsibility to actively pursue a social balance, has the character of an integration formula. It pleased the Western Allies in the Cold War to demonstrate the superiority of the Western over the Soviet model, as well as the majority of contemporary West German voters, who were enjoying strong economic growth and increasing real wages during a catching-up process. Müller-Armack's ideas, in their cultural and ethical embeddedness and more outcome-oriented approach to income distribution, have roots in the younger historical school, in particular Schmoller's ethical solution of social questions and the state's responsibility for social cohesion. On the other hand, Eucken and the Freiburg ordoliberals saw little need for a more active social policy of the government that went beyond some basic welfare provisions and a limited redistribution of primary (market) income by a moderately progressive income tax.

There can be no doubt that Müller-Armack's conception of a social-market economy is much more vague than the ordoliberalism of the Freiburg school or Buchanan's constitutional economics. This holds even more for the works of Röpke and Alexander Rüstow (1885–1963), who succeeded Alfred Weber at the University of Heidelberg in 1949 when he came back from Turkish exile. Rüstow had been the main organizer of the so-called German Ricardians in the Weimar Republic. In that period he came into closer intellectual contact with Eucken and Röpke and mutated from a moderate socialist to a social liberal. Rüstow was a participant in the famous 1938 Colloque Walter Lippmann in Paris, where he played a decisive role in the creation of the term "neoliberalism," which he later used as synonymous with social-market economy or social liberalism. He considered Hayek and in particular Mises as outdated old liberals, and favored a stronger role for the state. Like Erhard, he was inspired by the liberal socialism of Oppenheimer, and favored a high legacy tax in the spirit of John Stuart Mill to achieve equality of opportunities and to reduce taxes on income and value added. Rüstow also created the term *Vitalpolitik*, which was elaborated by Röpke, a holistic approach favoring conservative values such as strengthening the family and rural life. Müller-Armack's foundation of his economic theory on the sociology of religion, Rüstow's universal-historical cultural critique in his voluminous *Ortsbestimmung der Gegenwart* (1950–57), and Röpke's critique of mass society and pessimistic diagnosis of the crisis of Western civilization show in various ways how much this group of neoliberal thinkers stood in the tradition of the older German approach of economics with its linkages to history and sociology. Müller-Armack, however, did not share the cultural pessimism of Röpke and was much more pragmatically minded than the later Rüstow and the more fundamental Röpke, who remained in Switzerland but took part in the German debates, preferably via articles in the leading newspaper *Frankfurter Allgemeine Zeitung* (FAZ), which, in its economic and political sections, remains today a leading travel agent of ordoliberal ideas.[12]

Ordoliberal ideas and the conception of the social-market economy were engraved on economic policy in the reconstruction phase of West Germany after World War II. A full internal liberalization took place with the currency reform of June 20, 1948. The replacement of the Reichsmark by the new Deutschemark was combined with a drastic contraction of the money supply and other institutional safeguards against inflationary dangers and a restructuring and consolidation of existing public and private debt. However, not until the *Außenwirtschaftsgesetz* of 1961 did a complete external liberalization as a legal norm take place. (This marks a major difference from the currency union on July 1, 1990, when, with the introduction of the DM, a full internal *and* external liberalization happened in East Germany for which the economy was not prepared.) In 1958, after several years of controversial debates, the Gesetz gegen Wettbewerbsbeschränkungen, that is, the law against restrictions of competition, became effective. It is easy to speculate that this law, with its watered-down controls on monopoly and many exceptions to the prohibition of cartels—all due to the pressure and influence of interest groups—would have faced heavy criticism by Eucken. It was a major defeat for ordoliberals, in whose approach uncompromising antitrust and anticartel legislation had a central place. This is also indicated by the fact that, in the law finally enacted in 1957, control of company mergers was eliminated. Furthermore, a cartel could be permitted by the minister of economics if major public interests were at stake.

In a social-market economy the two principles of freedom and social justice require an institutional anchoring in the economic order. Economic policy has to conform to free markets. The reconciliation of the potentially antagonistic ideals of free-market competition and social cohesion makes it necessary to "search for new forms of property formation through profit-sharing and management-labor relationship" (Müller-Armack 1978, 330). As such elements we can regard the Codetermination Law (Mitbestimmungsgesetz) of February 1951 and the Company Statute Law (Betriebsverfassungsgesetz) of October 1952. The first labor management relation act promulgated, for the iron and steel industry, the "parity" model (a supervisory board comprising 11 members: five representatives from capital, five from labor, plus one "neutral" member nominated by directors other than the one for personnel, who could only be nominated in agreement with the works council and the proper trade unions), which had been introduced in the British zone (including the important Ruhr area) in 1948. Whereas objections to this Codetermination Law were raised by the liberal Free Democratic Party (FDP), the Company Statute Law was strongly opposed by trade unions because it did not satisfy their far-reaching claims for "industrial democracy." Instead of extending the parity model from the iron and steel industry to other industries, the representatives of labor got only one-third of the seats on the supervisory board, and the competences of the works council were restricted to personnel matters. Nevertheless, in retrospective it can be concluded that this German model of compromise between capital and labor has worked much better than labor relations in neighbouring France and many other countries. On the distribution side Erhard introduced the *Volksaktie* (people's share) with the partial privatization of the Volkswagen company on the eve of the 1961 elections to the Bundestag.

Four years earlier two other decisions were made that were important for long-run development. With the Bundesbankgesetz of July 1957 the independence of the decisions of the central bank from political influences by the government became part of the constitution. With the Rentenreformgesetz (Pension Reform Law), well timed before the 1957 September elections to the Bundestag, and without doubt contributing to the great success of Chancellor Adenauer and the CDU, pensions were "dynamized," that is, increases were linked to average annual increases in gross wages. The pension reform was associated with an initial strong increase in the pension level, reducing poverty in old age significantly. Although the oppositional Social Democrats, in contrast to Adenauer's coalition partner from the FDP, supported the pension reform, which also raised trust in the young German democracy, they did not benefit from it in the elections.

3.4. Keynesianism in Theory and Policy

In the well-known collection *The Political Power of Economic Ideas: Keynesianism across Nations*, edited by Peter Hall (1989), Christopher Allen, in "The Underdevelopment of Keynesianism in the Federal Republic of Germany," states that of the three gateways through which economic ideas make their way into policy—the economics profession, the civil service, and the political arena—the most important one, the economics profession, was most hostile to Keynesian ideas and policies (Allen 1989, 279–80). However, this is simply not true of postwar Germany.

The Keynesianism of the Hicks-Samuelson neoclassical synthesis evolved into the dominant position at German faculties of economics, outside Freiburg,

Cologne, and a very few other places, in the 1950s. This can largely be attributed to Erich Schneider, whose three-volume *Introduction into Economic Theory* (vol. 1, *National Income Accounting*, vol. 2, *Microeconomics*, vol. 3, *Monetary Macroeconomics*), originally published between 1947 and 1952, became the dominant textbook, going in double-digit editions in the late 1960s. Schneider's textbook set the canon for two decades, and was widely called the "bible" in economics.[13] Ironically, it was a protégé of Schumpeter, who had been the supervisor of Schneider's habilitation at the University of Bonn in 1932, who was instrumental in installing a moderate Keynesianism in Germany. In 1936 Schneider obtained a full professorship in Aarhus, Denmark, moving to Kiel in January 1946.[14] Soon after the Verein für Socialpolitik was refounded in 1948, Schneider became the driving force in the reconstitution of its Committee for Theory in 1949, which started its regular scientific meetings in 1953.[15] Schneider, who became the chairman of this influential committee until 1962, used his role to guide his peers to a more mathematically oriented approach, which at the beginning had to overcome strong resistance. From 1961 to 1969 he directed the Institute of World Economics in Kiel, an internationally recognized institution and powerful think tank in the German economic debates, and from 1963 to 1966 he was chairman of the Verein für Socialpolitik. In the early 1950s Schneider, who was an ardent Keynesian in its neoclassical synthesis, to which, as a great admirer of the works of Ragnar Frisch and the Stockholm school, he added a Scandinavian flavor, was involved in a controversy with the fierce anti-Keynesian Röpke.

Another economist worthy of note in this context is Andreas Paulsen, who had held the chair of economic theory at the Free University of Berlin since 1949. Paulsen considered Keynes's *General Theory* the most important work in economics in the twentieth century. In his *Neue Wirtschaftslehre* (*New Economics*, 1950), Paulsen gave a condensed summary of the ideas of Keynes in the spirit of Alvin Hansen in the United States and not only made the label of Keynesianism popular in Germany but also contributed significantly to the dissemination of Keynesian doctrines. This was supported by his textbook (Paulsen 1956), which was available in a cheap paperback edition and widely used by students. Furthermore, the dominance of the neoclassical synthesis of Keynesianism at German universities was enhanced by the fact that Paul Samuelson's successful textbook was published in a German translation as early as January 1952 by the Bund Verlag, the publishing house of the German trade unions, which published a number of revised editions and sold several tens of thousands of copies.

There can, however, be no doubt that, in international comparison, Keynesianism gained a late entry into economic policy in Germany. One reason was that the main carriers of Keynesian ideas in modern Western societies, the Social Democratic Party (SPD) and the trade unions, with their chief economist Viktor Agartz, in the early 1950s were more drawn toward Marxist ideas, nationalization, and industrial democracy than toward Keynesianism. It took two severe defeats in the Bundestag elections of 1953 and 1957 before the SPD, under the influence of Heinrich Deist, Alex Möller, and Karl Schiller, finally abandoned Marxism and with the 1959 Godesberg program accepted the concept of the social-market economy with the addition of a greater dose of Keynesianism, emphasizing the government's responsibility for growth and employment.[16] The trade unions followed with their Düsseldorf program of 1963.

It was not until the 1966–67 recession that this economic reform program could be put into practice. The old conservative-liberal coalition government collapsed over controversies over how to balance the budget. Kurt Georg Kiesinger replaced Ludwig Erhard as chancellor, with Willy Brandt as vice chancellor and foreign minister, in the new grand coalition of Christian and Social Democrats, in which the charismatic Karl Schiller (1911–1994) became minister of economics until 1972. With the entry of the SPD into government, Keynesianism found a late entry into German economic policies, which had its best years until the end of the center-left (SPD/FDP) government under Chancellor Willy Brandt (1969–74). The new grand coalition launched two public investment programs in January and July 1967, and in June 1967 the Bundestag ratified the Law for the Promotion of Economic Stability and Growth, referred to as the Stability and Growth Act. According to Article 1 of the act, the federal and state governments had "to respect the requirement of macroeconomic equilibrium in their economic and financial policy measures, which have to be undertaken in a way so as to contribute, within the scope of a market economy, to simultaneously achieve stability of prices, a high level of employment, and external equilibrium, together with steady and appropriate growth." These four macroeconomic goals, the so-called magic quadrangle, had appeared already in the statutes of the Sachverständigenrat zur Begutachtung der gesamtwirtschaftlichen Entwicklung (SVR), the German Council of Economic Advisers. The SVR was founded in 1963, Ludwig Erhard's last year as minister of economics. The German SVR differs from the American Council of Economic Advisers in being an external and independent committee for policy consultation rather than being part of the government. The five members are appointed for five years, with one new appointment or reappointment every year. The industrialists' organization and the trade unions can propose one member each. The SVR has to deliver an annual report on macroeconomic development of the economy by November 15, and the government has to respond in the annual economic report (*Jahreswirtschaftsbericht*) by the end of January, which leads to intensive economic debates in the German parliament. The constitutive five members presented their first report in fall 1964.[17]

The German economy recovered from the 1966–67 recession in the following year, not least through strong growth in exports, supported by moderate wage settlements made in the recession. In the public eye, the Stability and Growth Act, which was considered the "Magna Charta" of Keynesianism and the new government's economic policy, won the day. Karl Schiller's term of office as economics minister is widely remembered as the heyday of Keynesian economic policy in Germany. This is due to his remarkable ability to communicate with the public, reflected in his coining such terms as *Globalsteuerung* (macroeconomic demand management) and *Konzertierte Aktion* (concerted action) between the government, the Bundesbank, employers' associations, trade unions, and the economics profession to coordinate information and expectations in various fields of economic policy, not least to help bargaining partners to agree on adequate wage increases. Schiller's charismatic interpretation of economic policy contributed to a widespread faith in the government's management power over macro variables, before the first oil price shock and the new phenomenon of stagflation shook that confidence.

Two aspects of this economic story should not be overlooked. In the political sphere there never existed an option for an unrestricted Keynesianism because the SPD never had an absolute majority but was the junior partner in the coalition with the CDU/CSU from 1966 to 1969, and thereafter from 1969 to 1982 needed the liberal FDP, which finally left the government over controversies on economic policy in the recession after the second oil price shock. Furthermore, with the Bundesbank there was an important player in the field of monetary policy, which with its restrictive monetary policy in the early 1980s contributed to the overthrow of Chancellor Helmut Schmidt. In the economic sphere Schiller himself always propagated a moderate Keynesianism striving for a synthesis with ordoliberalism. This is very clearly expressed in his influential contribution "Economic Policy" to the *Handbook of Social Sciences* (Schiller 1962) in which he made a plea for a synthesis of the Keynesian message with the Freiburg imperative, paying tribute to Eucken. Schiller's leitmotiv was "competition to the extent possible, planning to the extent necessary," with "planning" understood in the sense of Keynesian demand management. In supplementing macroeconomic policies with *Ordnungspolitik*, Keynesian economic policies thus took on a specific German tinge.

In the late 1960s the German mark was increasingly undervalued. Exports and the surplus in the current account rose steadily. This enhanced the danger of imported inflation. Under these circumstances the majority of the SVR, under the dominating influence of Herbert Giersch, who succeeded Schneider as director of the Kiel Institute of World Economics in 1969, pointed out the trade-off between growth and price stability and strongly favored a massive revaluation of the DM and a greater flexibility in exchange rates (at a time when the Bretton Woods system still existed) to dampen inflation. Beginning in spring 1969 Schiller also publicly advocated a revaluation of the DM, which was heavily opposed by West German industry, Chancellor Kiesinger, and his CDU, as well as by Franz-Josef Strauß, the finance minister and forceful leader of the Bavarian CSU.

The issue of a greater flexibility of exchange rates, and the substantial revaluation of the DM associated with it, became the main controversial theme within the government on the eve of the parliamentary elections in September 1969. Schiller's aura of competence in this controversy contributed to the success of the SPD, which now, and for the first time, appeared more competent on economic issues to greater parts of the middle class, which before Godesberg had been repelled by Marxian rhetoric. Schiller also contributed to efforts to reorganize the international currency system, such as the ratification of the Smithsonian Agreement in December 1971.

3.5. Epilogue

With mounting inflationary pressures in the 1970s and a strong increase in unemployment in the 1974–75 recession following the first oil price shock, Keynesian ideas lost ground against the new monetarism launched by Milton Friedman. In Germany the Constance summer seminar on monetary theory and policy, initiated by Karl Brunner and taking place for the first time in June 1970, was the primary vehicle for a breakthrough of monetarist ideas among academics, (central) bankers, and policymakers. The rising influence of monetarist ideas is indicated by the fact that the SVR for the first time opted for control of the quantity of money by the Bundesbank in its 1972–73 report, and that the Bundesbank in December 1974 for the first time formulated a money supply target for the following year, moving from central bank money (*Zentralbankgeld*) as the main indicator to M3 only in 1987–88. However, the well-known statement by Helmut Schmidt, Germany's "super" minister for economics (since summer 1972, as the successor of Schiller) and finance, during the election campaign to the Bundestag in 1972, "Better 5 percent inflation than 5 percent unemployment," demonstrates very well that on the side of the government initially there existed strong resistance to the implementation of monetarist policies. The idea of a Phillips curve trade-off between inflation and unemployment had gained ground in the political sphere, in particular among social democrats and trade unionists.

After the late and triumphant rise of a moderate Keynesianism in German economic policy in 1967, the mid-1970s marked the fall of Keynesianism (until the global financial and economic crisis of 2007–9 caused a certain comeback). With the worsening stagflation after the first oil price shock monetarist ideas and supply-side approaches gained ground. This is clearly visible in the annual reports of the SVR, which now emphasized the trade-off between high employment and price stability. In the 1974–75 report the SVR pointed out that it is not the task of monetary policy to solve unemployment problems, and in the subsequent report a too high wage level was held responsible for low profit expectations and a resulting low investment activity and strong rise in unemployment. This became the dominant theme for the next decade, including the second oil price shock and its aftermath. After that it became almost a rule that the SVR member proposed by the unions wrote a minority report. The strong anti-Keynesian position of the majority also caused a permanent conflict of the trade unions with the SVR, which since the 1976–77 report explicitly favored a supply-side-oriented policy (*Angebotspolitik*). Sometimes the demand side was ignored completely and the arguments sounded like a very orthodox defense of Say's law (see 1977–78 Report, 26, 48, 241, 337). However, in the 1980s neoliberal economic policymaking by the Kohl government in Germany was relatively moderate compared to Reagan's policy in the United States or Thatcher's in the United Kingdom.

References

Allen, C. S. 1989. "The Underdevelopment of Keynesianism in the Federal Republic of Germany." In P. A. Hall, ed., *The Political Power of Economic Ideas: Keynesianism across Nations*, 263–89. Princeton, NJ: Princeton University Press.

Colm, G., J. M. Dodge, and R. W. Goldsmith. 1955. "Plan für Liquidation der Kriegsfinanzierung und die finanzielle Rehabilitierung Deutschlands." *Zeitschrift für die gesamte Staatswissenschaft* 111:244–84.

Deutsche Bundesbank, ed. 1998. *Fünfzig Jahre Deutsche Mark: Notenbank und Währung in Deutschland seit 1948*. Munich: C. H. Beck.

Erhard, L. 1957. *Wohlstand für Alle*. Düsseldorf: Econ Verlag.

Eucken, W. 1923. *Kritische Betrachtungen zum deutschen Geldproblem*. Jena: Gustav Fischer.

Eucken, W. 1940. *Die Grundlagen der Nationalökonomie*. Jena: Gustav Fischer. Translated by T. W. Hutchison as *The Foundations of Economics* (London: William Hodge, 1950; Chicago: University of Chicago Press, 1951).

Eucken, W. 1942. "Wettbewerb als Grundprinzip der Wirtschaftsverfassung." In G. Schmölders, ed., *Der Wettbewerb als Mittel volkswirtschaftlicher Leistungssteigerung und Leistungsauslese*, 29–49. Berlin: Duncker & Humblot.

Eucken, W. 1952. *Grundsätze der Wirtschaftspolitik*. Edited by Edith Eucken and K. Paul Hensel. 7th ed. 2004. Tübingen: Mohr Siebeck.

Goldschmidt, N. 2002. *Entstehung und Vermächtnis ordoliberalen Denkens: Walter Eucken und die Notwendigkeit einer kulturellen Ökonomik*. Münster: LIT.

Goldschmidt, N., and A. Berndt. 2005. "Leonhard Miksch (1901–1950): A Forgotten Member of the Freiburg School." *American Journal of Economics and Sociology* 64 (1): 973–98.

Goldschmidt, N., and M. Wohlgemuth, eds. 2008a. *Grundtexte zur Freiburger Tradition der Ordnungsökonomik*. Tübingen: Mohr Siebeck.

Goldschmidt, N., and M. Wohlgemuth. 2008b. "Social Market Economy: origins, meanings and interpretations." *Constitutional Political Economy* 19:261–76.

Hagemann, H. 2013. "Germany after World War II: Ordoliberalism, the Social Market Economy and Keynesianism." *History of Economic Thought and Policy* 1 (1): 37–51.

Hall, P. A., ed. 1989. *The Political Power of Economic Ideas: Keynesianism across Nations*. Princeton, NJ: Princeton University Press.

Haselbach, D. 1991. *Autoritärer Liberalismus und Soziale Marktwirtschaft: Gesellschaft und Politik im Ordoliberalismus*. Baden-Baden: Nomos.

Häuser, K. 2010. "Erich Schneider und die deutsche Nationalökonomie nach dem Zweiten Weltkrieg." In C. Scheer, ed., *Die deutschsprachige Wirtschaftswissenschaft in den ersten Jahrzehnten nach 1945*, 235–90. Berlin: Duncker & Humblot.

Hayek, F. A. 1944. *The Road to Serfdom*. London: Routledge; repr. New York: Routledge Classics, 2001.

Hutchison, T. W. 1979. "Notes on the Effects of Economic Ideas on Policy: The Example of the German Social Market Economy." *Zeitschrift für die gesamte Staatswissenschaft* 135:426–41.

Lutz, F. A. 1936. *Das Grundproblem der Geldverfassung*. Vol. 2 of *Die Ordnung der Wirtschaft*. Stuttgart: Kohlhammer.

Lutz, F. A. 1949. "Geldpolitik und Wirtschaftsordnung." *ORDO* 2:207–28.

Lutz, F. A. 1954. "The Case for Flexible Exchange Rates." *Banca Nazionale del Lavoro Quarterly Review* 7 (31): 175–85.

Miksch, L. 1937. *Wettbewerb als Aufgabe: Grundsätze einer Wettbewerbsordnung*. Vol. 4 of *Die Ordnung der Wirtschaft*. Stuttgart: Kohlhammer. 2nd ed., Godesberg, 1947.

Müller-Armack, A. 1941. *Genealogie der Wirtschaftsstile: Die geistesgeschichtlichen Ursprünge der Staats- und Wirtschaftsformen bis zum Ausgang des 18. Jahrhunderts*. Stuttgart: Kohlhammer.

Müller-Armack, A. 1946. *Wirtschaftslenkung und Marktwirtschaft*. Hamburg: Verlag für Wirtschafts- und Sozialpolitik.

Müller-Armack, A. 1956. "Soziale Marktwirtschaft." In *Handwörterbuch der Sozialwissenschaften*, 9:390–92. Göttingen: Vandenhoeck & Ruprecht.

Müller-Armack, A. 1978. "The Social Market Economy as an Economic and Social Order." *Review of Social Economy* 36 (3): 325–31.

Nützenadel, A. 2005. *Stunde der Ökonomen: Wissenschaft, Politik und Expertenkultur in der Bundesrepublik 1949–1974*. Göttingen: Vandenhoeck & Ruprecht.

Paulsen, A. 1950. *Neue Wirtschaftslehre: Einführung in die Wirtschaftstheorie von John Maynard Keynes und die Wirtschaftspolitik der Vollbeschäftigung*. Berlin: Franz Vahlen Verlag.

Paulsen, A. 1956. *Allgemeine Volkswirtschaftslehre*. 2 vols. Berlin: de Gruyter.

Peacock A., and H. Willgerodt, eds. 1989. *German Neo-liberals and the Social Market Economy*. London: Macmillan.

Plehwe, D. 2006. "Soziale Marktwirtschaft als Steinbruch? Zur Neuvermessung der Grenzen zwischen Markt und Staat in der aktuellen Debatte über wirtschaftspolitische Leitbilder." In A. Berthoin Antal and S. Quack, eds., *Grenzüberschreitungen—Grenzziehungen: Implikationen für Innovation und Identität*, 353–88. Berlin: edition sigma.

Ptak, R. 2004. *Vom Ordoliberalismus zur Sozialen Marktwirtschaft, Stationen des Neoliberalismus in Deutschland*. Opladen: Leske + Budrich.

Rieter, H., and M. Schmolz. 1993. "The Ideas of German Ordoliberalism 1938–45: Pointing the Way to a New Economic Order." *European Journal of the History of Economic Thought* 1:87–114.

Röpke, W. 1942. *Die Gesellschaftskrisis der Gegenwart*. Zurich: Rentsch.

Rothschild, K. 1964. "The Old and the New—Some Recent Trends in the Literature of German Economics." *American Economic Review* 54 (2.2): 1–33.

Rüstow, A. 1950–57. *Ortsbestimmung der Gegenwart: Eine universalgeschichtliche Kulturkritik.* 3 vols. Zurich: Rentsch. Abbreviated and translated by S. Attanasio as *Freedom and Domination: A Historical Critique of Civilization*, ed. Dankwart A. Rüstow (Princeton, NJ: Princeton University Press, 1980).

Samuelson, P. A. 1952. *Volkswirtschaftslehre: Grundlagen der Makro- und Mikroökonomie.* Cologne: Bund-Verlag.

Schefold, B. 2004a. "Der Weg Alfred Müller-Armacks: Vom Interventionsstaat zur Sozialen Marktwirtschaft." In *Beiträge zur ökonomischen Dogmengeschichte*, 505–28. Düsseldorf: Verlag Wirtschaft und Finanzen.

Schefold, B. 2004b. "Wissenschaft als Gegengabe—Neugründung und Aktivitäten des Theoretischen Ausschusses im Verein für Socialpolitik von 1949–1973." *Schmollers Jahrbuch* 124 (4): 579–608.

Schiller, K. 1962. "Wirtschaftspolitik." In *Handwörterbuch der Sozialwissen-schaften*, 12:210–31. Stuttgart: Mohr-Siebeck.

Schneider, E. 1947–62. *Einführung in die Wirtschaftstheorie.* Tübingen: Mohr-Siebeck, Vol. 1: *Theorie des Wirtschaftskreislaufs*, 1947, 14th ed., 1969. Vol. 2: *Wirtschaftspläne und Wirtschaftliches Gleichgewicht in der Verkehrswirtschaft*, 1949, 12th ed. 1969. Vol. 3: *Geld, Kredit, Volkseinkommen und Beschäftigung*, 1952, 12th ed. 1973.

Simons, H. C. 1948. *Economic Policy for a Free Society.* Chicago: University of Chicago Press.

Watrin, C. 1979. "The Principles of the Social Market Economy: Its Origins and Early History." *Zeitschrift für die gesamte Staatswissenschaft* 135 (3): 405–25.

4 | From New Liberalism to Neoliberalism

JAPANESE ECONOMISTS AND THE WELFARE STATE BEFORE THE 1980S

TAMOTSU NISHIZAWA AND YUKIHIRO IKEDA

4.1. Introduction

This chapter explores the historical and intellectual background of the shift toward neoliberal policymaking in Japan. The first signs of it appeared in the 1980s, and it became more explicit after the 1990s, culminating in the Koizumi reforms in 2001–6 (see Teranishi in this volume). It is widely held that, until this turn toward neoliberalism, Japanese economic and welfare thinking had been primarily social democratic and developmental, neoliberalism being considered alien to Japan until the expansion of Hayek studies after the 1970s. However, this interpretation has obscured the variety of liberal and neoliberal traditions in Japanese economic thought, which date back to the interwar years. The existence of these Japanese varieties of liberalism and neoliberalism means that the retrenchment of the welfare state did not necessarily need to rest on imported or externally imposed ideas.

Japan's intellectual landscape before World War II was strongly shaped by the German historical school, Marxism, and ideas of state capitalism. But there were economists who explicitly proposed new liberalism (e.g., Ishibashi Tanzan and Ueda Teijiro) and more interventionist varieties of new (social) liberalism and liberal idealism (e.g., Fukuda Tokuzo and Kawai Eijiro). Japan was also home to Yamamoto Katsuichi, who opposed collectivism and the welfare state throughout his life and became active in politics after the war. After the war, both Marxism and liberalism, suppressed in wartime, were revived by Japanese economists in the process of democratization with American support.

Under American occupation and the turn toward the Cold War, liberal frameworks moved to center stage in the national debate. The Japanese Liberal Party was founded in 1950, and, after merging with the Democratic Party, it came to power in 1955 as the Liberal Democratic Party (LDP). It has ruled the country ever since, with only brief interruptions.[1] The opposition Socialist Party, being based on Marxism, was very different from West Germany's Social Democrat Party or Britain's Labour Party. The result was that shifts from New Liberal, social democratic ideas, and social-market economic policies to neoliberalism took place within the LDP leadership.

Under strong American influence, the postwar Japanese version of developmental state capitalism focused on democratization, modernization, economic growth, and social welfare. Its intellectual foundations were New Liberalism and social liberalism, social democracy, Keynesianism, and to a certain extent Marxism. Policy was implemented by the LDP but rested on social democratic ideas. When the Advisory Board of the Social Security System (which was to play a crucial role in the making of welfare system) was founded in 1949 on the basis of the "Wandel Report" of the American Social Security Research Mission of 1947, a well-known Marxist, Ouchi Hyoe, was appointed as president. Its recommendations, made in 1950, were called the "Beveridge Plan" in Japan.[2]

Neoliberalism first received public attention in Japan in 1974 when Hayek was awarded the Nobel Prize in Economics. Yamamoto Katsuichi's *Fukushikokka Bokoku-ron* (*The Welfare State Decays the Nation: The Limits of Welfare in a Free Society*) was published in 1975, based on his work dating back to the 1950s. Nishiyama Chiaki's long interviews with Hayek on neoliberalism were published in 1976.[3] This reinforced existing pockets of neoliberal thought in academia and in the business world. Japanese neoliberals were already active in the Mont Pelerin Society, which held its first regional meeting in Japan in 1966.

This chapter will trace the different streams of liberal intellectual thought in Japan. It is organized as follows. Section 4.2 covers the prewar roots of Japanese liberal thought. It discusses the social liberal and social democratic ideas of Fukuda Tokuzo and his disciples, which provided a strong intellectual basis for the postwar welfare regime. It also covers the "New Liberalism" and "practical idealism" of Ishibashi Tanzan (a journalist and politician, dubbed "Keynes in Japan"), who paved the way to the policy of high-speed economic growth. Section 4.3 covers Ueda Teijiro's different brand of New Liberalism, important in the Japanese corporate sector; we extend our investigation to Ueda's disciples and a few business people (mostly members of the Mont Pelerin Society). This displays considerable overlap with ordoliberal ideas and the Austrian school, which helps to explain the rise of neoliberal ideas in Japan from the 1970s onward. Section 4.4 traces the rise of neoliberalism by focusing on Yamamoto, whose ideas were close to those of Mises and Hayek, and remained active in the LDP until the 1970s. Section 4.5 briefly examines the work of Nishiyama Chiaki and others. The conclusions point to a revisionist perspective on the history of Japan as a nonliberal variety of capitalism.

4.2. Social Liberalism and New Liberalism between the Wars and After

Japanese academics in the Meiji-Taisho eras were in general strongly influenced by the German historical school—the ethical and historical economics of social reform (as represented by the Verein für Sozialpolitik), which had much in common with the Oxford approach to the welfare state and social policy.[4] In addition to German influence, a form of the "English Renaissance" flourished among Japanese intellectuals in Taisho and early Showa periods (1910s and 1920s), which seems to have prompted a turn to more liberal thinking. The Webbs, Lowes Dickinson, Bertrand Russell, and Seebohm Rowntree came to Japan, and William Morris and John Ruskin were widely read.[5] In 1923 the 150th anniversary of Adam Smith's birth was enthusiastically celebrated in academic circles.[6] While the Japanese Verein für Sozialpolitik virtually collapsed because of conflict with rising Marxism,[7] the Japanese Fabian Society was founded in the same year, 1924, as the first Labour government in Britain. The big wave of social reform inspired by the British approach to the welfare state or welfare society was the background to Ueda's and Kawai's intellectual formation and activities, and their development in the postwar period by their disciples and associates. Ueda's colleague Fukuda (who had studied under Lujo Brentano) pursued the foundations of a third way (by means of welfare economy or social policy) between state capitalism and Bolshevik socialism along the contemporary lines of the British welfare state thinking. The postwar welfare regime in Japan was partly due to the impact of the intellectual legacies of prewar figures like Fukuda and Kawai and their disciples.

4.2.1. Fukuda's Middle Way (Social Democratic Liberalism) and After: The Roots of Welfare State Ideas

A major British New Liberal, J. A. Hobson, was favorably received not only in the progressive United States, but also in a backward Japan because of his economics of social reform and ethical economics of welfare. Unlike Ishibashi (discussed below), Fukuda was inspired by Hobson's welfare economic studies and his ideas on the distribution of wealth and unearned income. Fukuda proposed reform of capitalist society through social policy or welfare economy (practical welfare economics): inspired by the Liberal reforms of old-age pensions and unemployment insurance, he pursued a third way between capitalism and socialism, comparable to the British welfare state thinking.[8]

Social policy to ensure the right to a normal life was at the root of Fukuda's welfare economic studies and virtually provided the basis for Japanese welfare policymaking from the 1950s onward.[9] Article 25 of the Japanese constitution of 1946 states that "all Japanese people have the right to a minimum healthy and cultural life," which accords with Fukuda's ideas, although there seems to be no direct link between the text of the constitution and his position. Fukuda's disciples, particularly Nakayama Ichiro and Yamada Yuzo, developed and elaborated his ideas in theory and in practice. Nakayama tackled the issue of labor disputes, playing the leading role in the Central Labour Committee and Japan Productivity Centre for institutionalization of the Japanese approach to industrial management. His "Proposal for Doubling Wages" (*Yomiuri*, January 1, 1959),[10] probably inspired by Fukuda's ideas, provided an intellectual basis for Ikeda's national income-doubling plan. Nakayama was also responsible for the Minimum Wages Act (1959).[11] National insurance and national pensions were also institutionalized in Japan at this time. Yamada was instrumental in these developments and was chairman of the income-doubling plan section of the Economic Advisory Council. He was also responsible for retranslation of the Beveridge report for the Health Ministry.[12]

Fukuda discussed the struggle for the socialization of surplus value through class struggle, labor disputes, minimum wages, workers' insurance, and public unemployment insurance—ideas developed by people such as Tsuru Shigeto (at Hitotsubashi). Fukuda's ideas of welfare, close to those of Ruskin and Hobson, were largely qualitative and concerned the basic needs and the quality of life. This was also true of Tsuru, who praised Ruskin's critical acumen, arguing for human welfare rather than economic growth, to enhance people's quality of life. He insisted repeatedly that these aspirations should be the focus of economic policy.[13] Tsuru was active in calling for "welfare rather than growth."

Universal national insurance and national pension systems started in 1961 (the Minimum Wages Act had been introduced in 1959), the culmination of the recommendations of 1950 by the Advisory Board of the Social Security System. It gave substance to Article 25 of the constitution. The policy was promoted by the LDP, the program of which made explicit reference to "the fulfillment of a welfare society." It fitted with the income-doubling and high-speed economic growth policies of the governments of Kishi, Ikeda, and after. The system was developed further after 1973, called "the first year under the welfare system." The phrase "from (economic) growth to (social) welfare" was repeated by Tsuru. This was also around the time when *Limits to Growth* (1972) appeared. However, after the oil crisis policies began to change.

While Nakayama and Yamada developed Fukuda's social philosophy, they were on the borderline between social liberalism and neoliberal thinking. The neoliberal Yamamoto's book *Economic Calculation: Fundamental Problems of Economic Planning* (1932, revised ed. 1939) had been submitted as his Ph.D. thesis at Hitotsubashi University (though he graduated from Kyoto), and was examined by Nakayama (and probably Yamada). Yamada's graduation dissertation was on Carl Menger, and he studied with Morgenstern in Vienna in 1935–36 and later wrote on *Ordo*, Eucken, and Röpke, as well as Myrdal.

Yamada inspired people like Koga Katsujiro (Waseda University), who published some pioneering studies on Hayek in Japan, as we will discuss below. Koga was a leading scholar of Hayek studies together with Nishiyama Chiaki (Rikkyo University) and Kiga Kenzo (Keio University and a member of the Mont Pelerin Society). Nakayama's connection was much broader; he studied with Schumpeter, recruited Tsuru to Hitotsubashi, and reviewed Röpke's *Civitas Humana* in 1946. It was he who made possible Japanese Mont Pelerin Society founder Nishiyama's long interviews with Hayek.

4.2.2. Ishibashi Tanzan, "Keynes in Japan"

While Marxist socialism and the controlled economy arguments were looming larger in the late 1920s, liberal and New Liberal traditions were strong in prewar Japan. One of the outstanding figures was Ishibashi, who argued for "little Japanism." An influential journalist, working mainly for *Toyo Keizai Shinpo*, he was sometimes called "Keynes in Japan" because of his opposition to reestablishment of the gold standard at the old rate and to the austerity policy of the Hamaguchi government (see Teranishi in this volume). *Toyo Keizai Shinpo*, a weekly journal, had been founded just after the Sino-Japanese War (1894–95), during Japan's first period of industrialization. Its editors were sympathetic to L. T. Hobhouse and J. A. Hobson—in particular to their ideas of New (social) Liberalism and anti-imperialism—and the journal propagated the ideas and policies implemented under Britain's "New Liberalism."[14] It was even said that *Toyo Keizai Shinpo* was the Japanese version of the British journal *The Nation and Athenaeum*. Ishibashi became its editor in 1924, and the journal played a significant role in forming opinion in the business world.[15]

In the postwar turmoil, Ishibashi took an active part in politics, arguing that Japan could become a great nation by moving on from imperialism to pacifism. He was finance minister in the first Yoshida Shigeru (Liberal) government in 1946–47, and came up with an expansionary monetary policy to support the priority production (Keishaseisan) system (emphasizing the production, for example, of coal and iron) for postwar economic reconstruction. After a period out of office, Ishibashi became the minister of industry and trade of the Hatoyama Ichiro (Democratic) governments in 1954–56, and subsequently, after Hatoyama had fallen ill, he became prime minister in 1956–57. Though Ishibashi's term as prime minister was only sixty-five days, his electoral defeat of Kishi was significant in Japan's democratic political history, for he represented the New Liberal, practically idealistic, intellectual journalist from private Waseda University, while Kishi was a bureaucrat from Imperial Tokyo University.[16]

There was a prototype of the high-speed economic growth policy in the core of Ishibashi's economic policies; his "positive finance" and "expansive balanced finance" aimed at achieving full employment and raising income through expansion of investment. He believed that positive investment in plant and equipment was the only way to absorb the population of superfluous workers after the war. This was to develop into Ikeda's income-doubling and rapid growth policies[17] and was a major basis of fast postwar economic growth, on which welfare policy was grounded. Ishibashi's Keynesian ideas have something in common with those of Nakayama Ichiro and Yamada Yuzo, who were then close to Keynesian ideas and involved in the national income-doubling policies.

4.3. Ueda's New Liberalism and Beyond: Business and Society

Now we turn to Ueda Teijiro's "New Liberalism" in ideas and practice, relating much more to business, trade, and society. Ueda launched his pioneering journal *Enterprise and Society* (*Kigyo to Shakai*) with the statement that "we should view society from the perspective of enterprise and watch the corporations from the perspective of society . . . then we should search for principles on which to construct the new, globalizing Japan."[18] Like Alfred Marshall, Ueda saw business and corporations as the crucial elements in social reform, and when he produced a volume of his essays, he gave it the title *New Liberalism* (*Shin Jiyushugi*, 1927). He argued for a "practical idealism" that was critical of state-run corporations and protectionist policies, and which emphasized the importance of private (free) business enterprise. He viewed statism and socialism as failing to promote independence, creativity, and individual responsibility (Ueda 1976b, 171).

Ueda was a strong advocate of free trade, representing Japan at League of Nations congresses in Geneva (1927) and Prague (1928) and establishing the Free Trade Association and its monthly journal. He believed that Japan, with its dense population and poor natural resources, had to depend on free trade.

Ueda had studied "business policy" under W. J. Ashley at Birmingham in 1906 and introduced the discipline of "business economics and administration" in Japan. The Japanese Society of Business Administration was founded in 1926 with a membership of 342. He published *Economic Discourse of Joint Stock Companies* (*Kabushikigaisha Keizairon*) in 1912, discussing the role of joint stock companies in capitalist evolution and the importance of managerial efficiency in organizations.[19] He continued with a second period of study abroad in London and Cambridge (1912–13), and he learned from the New Liberal and social democratic movements. Subsequently, in Japan in the period of the Taisho democracy and "reconstruction" after World War I he published *Social Reconstruction and Enterprise* (*Shakai-kaizo to Kigyo*) in 1922, stressing the social importance of business corporations and "the duty-role of managers in social reconstruction"; he also wrote two different books on "History of the English Industrial Revolution" in 1923–24, which sold very well at a time of rapid industrialization and the development of the labor movement after World War I. He wrote these works after returning from the first meeting of the International Labour Organization in Washington in 1919 (he went there as an adviser to the government representative). (Fukuda regarded the ILO's international labor regulations as the "official recognition of labor as a noncommodity" and as the "great gospel of the road to the betterment of economic life" [Fukuda 1926b, 1370].)

Despite his commitment to free trade, Ueda was greatly influenced by the reformist tradition of the Oxford economists. At the beginning of *History of the English Industrial Revolution*, he made particular reference to the "enthusiastic social reformer" Arnold Toynbee, and he was also influenced by Ashley, the Webbs, and R. H. Tawney. He stated that Tawney's *The Acquisitive Society* (1921) best expressed what he himself wanted to advocate, which was a "functional society" wherein people would perform their "duty-role" (Ueda 1975b, 101–2).

In these works Ueda stressed the role of managerial personnel and the middle management classes in the large corporations of the acquisitive society: he wrote an article entitled "The Social Significance of the New Middle Classes" in *Enterprise and Society*. Their role, he stated, was not that of mere businessmen seeking profit; instead they ought to become "public men of the country" (*tenka no koujin*), working for the best interests of society, like *bushi* (samurai). Ueda praised their high administrative and managerial efficiency, differentiating mere profit-making from business, and expressed his opposition to nationalization and bureaucratic statism, upholding managerial efficiency (something akin to economic chivalry). Ueda read Marshall deeply and extensively.

In 1920 Ueda wrote "Socialism and the Duty-Role of Managers," stating that "as the age of socialism advanced, the capability of managers and their 'duty-role' would be increasingly important." "Even if we could eliminate profit-making and business, as long as production remained necessary, we could never eliminate administration or management of the organization," as evidenced by the fact that even Lenin had started to study American scientific management. Ueda went on to state that business corporations had already become major structures handling domestic production and that their success or failure would have a great impact on the lives of thousands of people. Therefore, the role of management personnel was not that of mere businessmen, but that of "public men of the country"; this suggests a spirit of "Bushido" like Marshall's "Kishido (economic chivalry)," which had a strong influence on Ueda and various other Japanese intellectuals. Ueda's ideas constituted the "bold opposition of liberalism against the tide of socialism," "well-socialized liberalism," or "New Liberalism," which accepts innovation, dedication, and honor as incentives for economic activities, and proposes the development of these occupational ethics. This became his prescription for the age of social reconstruction.[20]

Ueda's stress on the role of managers in social reconstruction, business enterprise, and society had considerable impact at that time, as did some pioneering arguments for CSR (corporate social responsibility). Indeed, a later, great entrepreneur, Mori Taikichiro, founder of the Mori Building Group, recollected his teacher Ueda's insistence on the social responsibility of business enterprise. This also seems to echo in the voices of postwar business leaders like Nakayama Sohei (Japan Industrial Bank), Sakurada Takeshi (Nisshinbo Cotton Spinning), and Kikawada Kazutaka (TEPCO), all of the organization Keizai-doyukai, founded in 1946, who made a public proposal on "the social responsibility of the corporations" and asserted in the 1950s that enterprises were "public organs," pursuing their activities for economic recovery and business democratization.[21] These three eminent business leaders became members of the Mont Pelerin Society (MPS).

In the journal *Enterprise and Society* (1926–28), Ueda advocated "New Liberalism" and was critical both of state protectionism and intervention and of collectivist socialism, stressing the importance of ideas based on individual liberalism and responsibility. "The efficiency of government officials and local government civil servants was much less than that of the company servants of joint stock companies." He was critical of state-run corporations and emphasized the importance of private business, arguing for reduction of industrial protectionist policies, cutting down the number of state-run businesses, and even arguing for the privatization of higher education. The government should concentrate more on basic education; and even state schools should gradually become financially independent.[22] A similar line was echoed after the 1990s.

Reviewing Keynes's *End of Laissez-Faire* (1926), Ueda praised Keynes's arguments for rationalizing the capitalist market without following escape routes to socialism while attributing importance to the evolution of capitalistic institutions. "It was nonsense to argue for the nationalization of railways; they were already being socialized" ("Mr. Keynes on Social Reconstruction," Ueda 1976b, 290). Ueda made his stance clear in "Keynes vs. Webb"; Webb being tolerant of bureaucracy and rather cool toward private independent actions, addressed the issue of bank nationalization, without specific attention to the idea of the Bank of England being socialized itself, as Keynes argued. In this sense, Webb was a socialist (Ueda 1976b, 295). In a review of Norman Angell's *Must Britain Travel the Moscow Road?* Ueda confirmed his view that Marxism did not pay adequate attention to the significance of the managerial middle classes and their role in the process of social reconstruction.

4.3.1. New Liberalism and Neoliberalism in the Postwar Business World

Ueda died in 1940 and left a profound intellectual legacy in the postwar period. An important disciple, active across business, academia, and politics, was Aoba Fumio (later a member of the MPS). His book *Aiming at New Liberalism* (*Shinjiyushugi wo Mezashite*, 1989) contained a preface by Fukuda Takeo, prime minister 1976–78, and also a member of the MPS.[23] Aoba worked for Fuji Bank and, beginning in 1956, for more than a quarter of a century produced a spate of papers in favor of liberalizing interest rates. After Fuji Bank he worked for the Japan Economic Research Institute (JERI, Nihon Keizaichosa Kyogikai), the economic research institute in the business world, which performed an important role as a sort of think tank, connecting business leaders and academia and diffusing New Liberalism and neoliberalism in the business world. Both the big business organizations and the JERI played a crucial role in diffusing New Liberalism and neoliberalism under the radar. JERI was founded in 1962, on the promotion of Iwasa Yoshizane (affiliated with Fuji Bank and Keizai-doyukai, later a member of the MPS), and other leaders of big business organizations, that is, Keidanren (Confederation of Japanese Industry), Shokokaigisho (Chamber of Commerce and Industry), and Nihon Boekikai (Japan Society for Trade), with General Secretary Aoba and with the academic collaboration of Nakayama Ichiro and Shinohara Miyohei (both from Hitotsubashi University.)

Marxist economics had a considerable following in the academic world, whereas in the business world leaders were eager to promote liberalism and modern non-Marxian economics. Keizai-doyukai brought out the *History of Modern Economics* (*Kindaikeizaigaku no Keifu*) in 1949, covering Walras, Pigou, Keynes, Hayek, Hicks, and so on, initiated by Nakayama.[24] Keizai-doyukai, with a number of leaders like Kikawada, was in due course to echo the ideas of Hayek and Milton Friedman, pursuing liberalism between business and social considerations. Under Kikawada's leadership it was then close to ordoliberalism.[25]

Kikawada Kazutaka, a major figure in the electric power industry and in the broader Japanese business community, was enchanted by Kawai Eijiro, in particular his *Studies in Labour Problems* (1922). In "Free-Market Economy and Order" (1969) Kikawada argued that business firms should behave like individuals in civil society: firms and their managers should have "social responsibility." After 1955, CSR was also a major emphasis of the Keizai-doyukai under Kikawada's leadership. Otherwise, the state authorities would intervene. Kikawada was sympathetic to the social-market economy, reading Röpke, and coming close to Erich Gutenberg and Hayek.[26]

The JERI asked to organize various special committees, with liberalist businessman organizers like Ohara Soichiro and Kikawada Kazutaka (both MPS members); Kikawada's committee was chaired by Kimura Takeyasu, both being the former pupils of Kawai Eijiro at Tokyo University. In 1966 this committee started work on the theme of "the free-market economy and business" and based its final report, *The Forward March of Liberalism* (1977), on a philosophy of ordered liberalism (the first of the two volumes was entitled *Liberalism as It Should Be: Principles of Ordered Liberalism*).[27] Nishiyama Chiaki was also a committee member and wrote a part of this report drawing upon Hayek's ideas. The JERI also organized the informal meeting on New Liberalism, which was actually a gathering to study the works of Hayek. Nishiyama and Kiuchi Nobutane (1899–1993) organized a regional meeting of the Mont Pelerin Society in Japan in 1966 with the financial support of Kikawada and Iwasa (of Fuji Bank), and on this occasion Hayek came to Japan. (Hayek first came to Japan in March 1964, formally invited by the president of Rikkyo University, Matsushita Masayoshi, another member of the MPS.)

The Mont Pelerin Society of Japan seems to have been set up and promoted by Kiuchi Nobutane (the first Japanese member of MPS) of the Sekai Keizai Chosakai (Institute of World Economy) and Nishiyama.[28] Kiuchi received a letter of invitation to the MPS from Hayek in the summer of 1958; Kiuchi then attended the MPS general meeting at Princeton University that September. After that Kiuchi attended MPS meetings regularly and gave papers. After the regional meeting in Tokyo in 1966, the MPS general meeting in Japan (Tokyo and Kyoto) was held in 1988, which was quite successful; some 170 people gathered for the occasion. The Institute of World Economy under Kiuchi's presidency, which began in 1955, was the major institute in the shadow of Hayek and neoliberalism. Its house organ, *World Economy* (*Sekai Keizai*), regularly published full reports of MPS meetings and many articles on Hayek and neoliberalism: it is said that the Institute of World Economy virtually played the role of a Japanese MPS. In this institute, when Hayek visited, hung a framed tablet displaying his words: "FREEDOM UNDER THE LAW = THE ABSENCE OF ARBITRARY COERCION."[29]

4.4. Yamamoto Katsuichi and Neoliberalism: The Limits of Welfare in a Free Society

Yamamoto's *The Welfare State Decays the Nation* appeared in 1975.[30] Yamamoto argued that insofar as the aim of policy was establishment of a welfare state based on social security and full employment, the budget and the number of bureaucrats would increase. The nation would become dependent on government and lose the spirit of self-help and mutual aid; consequently, the nation of freedom and prosperity must decay. The book was a culmination of warnings that he had been making since 1955, when he opposed the inclusion of the phrase "fulfilment of the welfare state" in the LDP program. As an LDP MP he questioned the government's general policy and expressed his concern about the "limits of social security in a free society," fearing the Kishi government's promotion of national insurance, a minimum wage, and other measures under the slogan of eliminating poverty from Japan. He published a leaflet called *A Warning on the Preference for Social Security: The Limits of Social Security in a Free Society* in 1961;[31] it was, incidentally, the year when Wilhelm Röpke first visited Japan to give a number of lectures.[32] In 1958 Erhard visited Japan as a guest of the state, and the Japanese translation of his book *Wohlstand für Alle* (1957) came out in 1960. Having read Röpke's works, Yamamoto inserted Röpke's critical comments on the Beveridge Plan from *Civitas Humana* as the appendix of this leaflet (Yamamoto 1961b, 18–26; 1975, 116–28). Röpke's writings were introduced and translated into Japanese in the 1940s and early 1950s.[33] Röpke and social-market economy, Eucken and ordoliberalism, and then Hayek were already attracting interest in Japan in the 1940s–1950s, but under the radar, as it were.[34]

Here we will outline Yamamoto's earlier career. Yamamoto Katsuichi graduated from Kyoto University and first taught at Wakayama Higher Commercial School. Yamamoto wrote a book titled *Economic Calculation: Fundamental Problems of Economic Planning* (*Keizai Keisan: Keikakukeizai no Kihonmondai*, 1932), one of the earliest books on this topic. The socialist economic calculation debate was a great debate on the possibility of economic calculation under the planned economy, or the possibility of a socialist planned economy from 1920s to 1940s. Yamamoto revised his earlier work, a revision that was published as *Fundamental Problems of Planned Economy: Considerations on the Possibility of Economic Calculation*, in 1939 (this was submitted as a Ph.D. thesis to Tokyo University of Commerce [Hitotsubashi]). Here he came close to the ideas of Hayek and Mises.[35] Yamamoto, deeply moved by *A Tale of Poverty* (*Binbo Monogatari*, 1917), a bestseller by Kawakami Hajime, studied economics at Kyoto University under Kawakami, a well-known Marxist economist. However, Yamamoto was suspicious of socialism and became critical of Marxism. After having got a job at Wakayama, he went abroad to study. He began by studying physiocracy in France, which changed his way of thinking. Its basic concept of "natural order" had a strong impact on Yamamoto: under the invisible hand, he believed, social organization would never be deadlocked, thanks to its spontaneous internal integrity, driven by free competition.

Yamamoto went on to write "Doubting the Realization of Socialism" (1928), observing that in contemporary mass society it is impossible for the central authority to manage the economy. He studied abroad again in 1931–32, then went to Germany via Moscow, and studied with Boris Brutzkus and Georg Halm, who were exiled from the Soviet Union. Back in Japan, he published *Economic Calculation: Fundamental Problems of Economic Planning* (1932). This was the period that saw general equilibrium theory introduced by Nakayama and a few others and, at the same time, a debate on Japanese capitalism in the Marxist economics camp. Economic calculation received scant attention from academics.

Yamamoto questioned how output and input were to be compared, and how economic calculation was performed under socialism. In his book he agreed with Mises's arguments that, under socialism, economic calculation of output and input cannot be performed, so it is not possible to determine if production is economical or not; therefore, economical and efficient management of socialism is impossible. Yamamoto believed that the market mechanism, whereby the price results from real transactions, and production is managed by making the price the basis of calculation, is the only viable option.

Yamamoto's ideas were welcomed by the Education Ministry, eager to suppress socialist ideas. In 1932 he was invited to the Institute of National Spirit and Culture to help shield the students from left-wing thought. Yamamoto criticized the controlled economy and the new economic system movement propelled by reformist bureaucrats (*kakushin kanryo*) in the Planning Agency, which the industry and commerce minister, Kobayashi Ichizo (1940–41), fiercely opposed. He asked Yamamoto to draft a critique of the "Guidelines of the new economic system," which was for the controlled economy by reformist bureaucrats, and Yamamoto also criticized the plan for state control of electric power. People like the young Kikawada in the electric power business world were also critical of the state control plan. Yamamoto's attitudes attracted the attention of the business world and leading Liberal politicians like Hatoyama Ichiro. Yamamoto was invited by Hatoyama to become a founding member of Japanese Liberal Party and became a Liberal Party MP. He served as parliamentary vice-minister of trade and industry in the Hatoyama government. In the postwar turmoil Yamamoto also came close to Ishibashi Tanzan, and shared some economic policy ideas of market liberalization and free-market tendencies.[36]

Yamamoto was active as an MP under the Kishi government (1957–60). He believed that the welfare and social security policy had come to represent the mood of the country, even "the myth of the age"; it was accepted uncritically, even beyond the limits of practical considerations. The social security budget increased more than two and half times from 1950 to 1956, albeit from a low basis. It was driven by both the Socialist Party and the LDP; the two parties appeared to compete in advancing social security policy. It was said that the old way of thinking, in terms of mere subsistence, should be discarded and that people must change their ideas "from mere subsistence (livelihood) to life itself (quality of life)"—it would be necessary to catch up quickly with progress in the general cultural standard, as announced by the president of the LDP social security investigation committee (Yamamoto 1961b, 3–4).

It was around then (in 1958) that Yamamoto questioned the government's welfare and full-employment policy, addressing "a warning on the preference for social security: the limits of social security in a free society." He questioned the welfare minister about "the limits of social security," expressing his fear of signs that Japan's welfare policy reflected the Beveridge Plan "from cradle to grave," although the UK itself was troubled by the alleged excesses of welfare. Yamamoto feared a crisis would result as the welfare policy led to a breakdown of the basis of free society. He believed that only those who could not live by their own means should be secured a minimum living through state relief; in principle, this was the idea of poor relief characterizing the Meiji era, and close to the English Poor Law of the nineteenth century. But the current conception of social security appeared to extend to the universal level. He insisted that in a free society there should be limits to collective social responsibility for securing the nation's living standards. Yamamoto feared two things: that the expansion of the social security budget would lead to chronic inflation; and that overbroad eligibility for payments would destroy the foundations of a healthy free society of self-responsibility and the sense of family and neighborhood solidarity (Yamamoto 1961b, 4–6; 1975, 95, 99). Here his views recall Mrs. Thatcher's return to Victorian values and "self-help."

Yamamoto went on to argue that the national social security system should not compete with voluntary self-help support by the family or community; the more social security was expanded beyond narrow limits, the less family and community self-support and self-help there would be. Yamamoto believed that a free society should be sustained, which meant that the principle of self-responsibility needed to be maintained and that state benefits should be disbursed only where self-support and voluntary support by the family or community proved inadequate. For Yamamoto, the Beveridge Plan clashed with the values of self-responsibility and spontaneous support offered by the family or community. Only if state benefits were kept within limits, as in Switzerland and Germany, would the state supplement for minimum needs not weaken this spirit of support. In the United Kingdom and the Scandinavian countries, on the other hand, the family and community spirit of self-responsibility and self-support had been weakened (Yamamoto 1961b, 9–11).

Yamamoto concluded his paper with a final section called "Views of Erhard," the champion of the social-market economy. He quoted phrases from Erhard's *Wohlstand für Alle*: "Economic freedom and forced national insurance are as irreconcilable as water and fire." Erhard expressed his surprise at the clamor for collective security in public spheres. He asked, if we do not take on responsibility for ourselves and look to the collective body for our security, how can the progress be maintained? These temptations and tendencies would gradually but steadily annihilate true human values and morality—the spirit of responsibility, human love, and love of neighbors (Yamamoto 1961b, 12–13).

Erhard's ideals were these: "I would try my strength by myself. I would bear the risk of life by myself and take on responsibility for my fortune by myself. The state should create the conditions for us (the people) to be able to act in this way." "Leave me alone, let me free from the state; give me freedom to make my existence and my fortune by myself" (see Yamamoto 1961b, 14).

The idea is more or less that the state should only create the conditions for "invisible hand" to work.

As Yamamoto summarized his argument, there must be limits to social security; otherwise we will lose our free society. The limits mean that we should not extend social security to a point that weakens the people's will and power to take on responsibility by themselves, and weaken the family and community spirit of voluntary relief. Therefore, state assistance or state benefits should not exceed these limits (Yamamoto 1961b, 16). Yamamoto, like Erhard, was fighting a losing battle at the time because the mainstream was far more pragmatic about the provision of welfare than the highly principled neoliberals (compare Hagemann and Plehwe in this volume).

In 1959 Yamamoto published "Ludwig Erhard—Man and Policy," with subtitle "My Respected Economist," which came out in the journal *Keizai-jidai*. Erhard came to Japan in 1958 as a guest of the state, Yamamoto praised him on this occasion: the ideas behind Erhard's economic policy were those of the social-market economy. The ideal economic system should have two conditions: one is the realization of maximum productivity, the other that improvement in productivity should result in benefit for the whole nation, welfare for everybody, or *Wohlstand für Alle*. There is no way other than business competition to achieve these conditions: competition itself raises productivity, improves quality and services, brings down the prices, and consequently benefits all the people, particularly as consumers. "Social" means aiming at prosperity for the whole nation; since it stresses business competition as an indispensable condition, the social-market economy is sometimes called a "competitive economy." In order to realize and maintain competition, the state should not only set limits to competition but also prevent any interference with fair competition, such as monopolies; strong state intervention will be needed to keep competition fair. One of the most important duties of the state is to secure free competition. Unlike classical liberalism or laissez-faire, a social-market economy needs the strong intervention of the state to exclude forces that disturb competition, like monopolies. Through competition, progress and the socialization of profit will be realized. The prescription sounds like Mrs. Thatcher's "free-market economy and strong state."

Röpke, responsible for ideas on which Erhard drew, was invited to Japan in March 1961 by the publishing house Keizai-ouraisha. It was then that Yamamoto wrote a short article, "Professor Röpke and the LDP," for the journal *Keizai-ourai* (1961a), relating to the impact of Röpke's ideas on LDP policymaking. Yamamoto wrote that, while Japanese academia was full of Marx and Keynes and almost ignored Röpke, the LDP, responsible for policy and defending freedom and the market economy, was looking to Röpke's economics and social philosophy for its policy pillar, passing over Japanese academics. LDP MP Hayakawa Takashi was also very sympathetic to Röpke's ideas and arranged a meeting between Röpke and the LDP Policy Research

Committee. They also organized a Röpke study group in the LDP with some 20 members; they read the Japanese translation of Röpke's *Civitas Humana*. Yamamoto wrote articles on wages, small industries, agricultural problems, and so on, following Röpke's arguments, in the LDP house organ, providing encouragement for future prime minister Ohira Masayoshi. Yamamoto promoted Röpke's ideas in Ikeda's brain trust called the Kochikai, which was the founding and supporting body of the income-doubling plan, and its leader, Maeo Shigesaburo, was deeply impressed by Röpke. Not only Ohira but Kurogane Yasumi, also close to Ikeda, was deeply influenced by Röpke's ideas.

According to Yamamoto, Röpke's influence on the LDP was not small. The LDP had based its policy on a free-market economy since its foundation; Yamamoto was then attracted to Hayek and Mises but, having made the acquaintance of Röpke, he turned to his ideas. Though Röpke's policy ideas were generally adopted by the LDP, Yamamoto argued that Röpke's influence was working because the LDP kept in check a bias toward a Keynes-Beveridge consensus that some economic bureaucrats might yield to, while resisting the planned economy and rejecting the *kolkhozy* (collective farm).

While we need to examine Yamamoto's arguments on Röpke and the LDP carefully, in the 1950s not only Röpke but also Eucken and ordoliberalism, thanks to his works and the annual journal *Ordo*, seem to have been fairly well known in Japan. Examples are to be seen in Yamada Yuzo's paper on *Ordo* (Yamada called it "neoliberalism" in Japanese)[37] and Oizumi Yukio's many works and translations of Eucken (Oizumi studied under Ueda Teijiro in 1920s), and other works on a social-market economy such as those by Naniwada Haruo (Yamada, Oizumi, Naniwada were from academia).[38] All this was probably inspired by the German economic miracle; *Deutschlands Rückkehr zum Weltmarkt* was translated by a well-known Marxist economist and economic adviser, Arisawa Hiromi, as Erhard's *Miracle of the German Economy* (*Doitsu-keizai no Kiseki*) in 1954. This was retranslated by Suga Takashi (of MITI) in 1958; Suga also translated Erhard's *Wohlstand für Alle* in 1960. Some other translations and works on the German social-market economy were brought out, mainly by people from the Bank of Japan, the Treasury, and the MITI. It is not hard to see why Kikawada and some business people came closer to New Liberalism and neoliberalism.

4.5. The Revival of Neoliberalism from the 1970s onward

It is indeed difficult to locate Yamamoto in the tradition of social sciences in Japanese academia; he seemed to be almost completely independent from other scholars of the same age.[39] After World War II, although the main tendency of the Japanese economists remained more or less interventionist, there emerged some scholars who contributed to the diffusion of neoliberalism in Japan. In this section we examine two such scholars whose roles were important in the dissemination of a neoliberalist way of thinking in Japan. First, we will take the case of Nishiyama Chiaki.

When he left Japan in 1950, Marxian economics was still being taught at the leading universities in Japan as an indispensable subject. Another major trend was Keynesian economics. The age of stagflation had yet to come; Keynesian economics was thought to be reliable, including the econometric models based on it. Thus, Nishiyama's decision to go to Chicago was quite exceptional, considering the political milieu in general and the academic atmosphere in particular at that time in Japan.

After a fairly long stay in Chicago, Nishiyama submitted a thesis entitled "The Theory of Self-Love: An Essay in the Methodology of the Social Sciences, and Especially of Economics with Special Reference to Bernard Mandeville." Although Mandeville appears in the title, Nishiyama's aim was to "elucidate some aspects of the methodology of the social sciences, and especially of economics." As is the case with Hayek, Nishiyama's interest in Mandeville was not purely historical; rather he approached him from a methodological point of view. On the whole, Nishiyama's thesis is an attempt to continue and enhance Hayek's methodological inquiry.

After returning to Japan, Nishiyama in 1974 published a monumental work with Asakura Kokichi, entitled *Monetary Analysis and History of the Japanese Economy: 1868–1970* (*Nihon Keizai no Kahei teki Bunseki: 1868–1970*). The title itself reveals that the work was an application of Friedman's long-term analysis of the US economy from the monetary point of view in his monumental work with Schwartz. In the introduction, Nishiyama explains how he came to publish this huge book: "The publication of this book is based on suggestions by Arthur F. Burns, who was a professor at Columbia University and the director of the National Bureau of Economic Research. Professor Burns served as the head of the international advisory board of the Center for Modern Economics, Rikkyo University. Professor Burns, who together with W. C. Mitchell promoted research at NBER, strongly asserted that economic analysis of the Japanese economy must be accomplished through the spontaneous efforts in the private sector and suggested some research programs. One of them was a monetary analysis of the Japanese economy" (Asakura and Nishiyama 1974, 3).

The quotation from the introduction clearly shows the origin and the main purpose of the book. Nishiyama founded the Center for Modern Economics at Rikkyo University, where Marxian economics was still predominant in the 1970s. Nishiyama asked Burns for his opinions for research at the Center. As pointed out in the passage quoted, both Burns and Mitchell were active members of the NBER, a private organization for economic research in the United States. The basic idea of the NBER is to promote economic research based on empirical, statistical findings, as represented by Friedman's joint work with Schwartz, a historical analysis of the US economy from a monetary point of view. Nishiyama was confident that their analysis could be applied to Japan and other nations as well, independently of the differences in economic institutions and historical backgrounds.

Two years after the publication of his joint work with Asakura, he published *Monetarism*, an introduction to monetarism for the general reader. His 1974 book, coedited with Asakura, was purely academic; *Monetarism* (*Monetarizumu*) gave laymen an overview of the discipline without relying upon heavily technical terms.

Almost at the same time, Nishiyama was attempting to popularize Hayek's thought. For this purpose, he edited *What Is Neoliberalism?* (*Shinjiyu Shugi towa Nanika?*, 1976b). As the title implies, Nishiyama wanted to proclaim Hayek's importance and to popularize his ideas. Few Japanese scholars were interested in Hayek; in the heyday of Keynesian economics after World War II, within the country and abroad, the name of Hayek soon began to fall out of circulation.

The book's introductory remarks were written by Nakayama Ichiro, a prestigious economist at Hitotsubashi University; he had already retired from the university when the book was published. The following remark by Nakayama aptly captures the differences between earlier and later Hayek: "Before World War II, Professor Hayek was known as a trade cycle theoretician, being the author of the renowned book *Prices and Production*. He continued to write in the field of economic theories until the publication of *Pure Theory of Capital* in 1941. However, he abruptly stopped publishing articles in economic theories after that. He went to the United States to avoid the turmoil caused by the war. It is said that he is now interested in the problem of freedom, social laws, and the fundamental problems of ethics and philosophy. He was more or less out of my mind for years" (Hayek and Nishiyama 1976b, 2).

Chapter 1 reproduced conversations between Nishiyama and Hayek. Hayek's far-reaching project of the denationalization of money was a topic in the conversations. It is now widely accepted among scholars, at least those seriously concerned with Hayek and Friedman, that they had completely different stances when it came to monetary policies.[40] After listening to and summarizing Hayek's arguments on the bold project of denationalization of money, Nishiyama argued that "it would be impossible for each government to increase the money supply without constraint," and posed the following question: "How is it possible for each country to know the amount of money supply that is running the whole economy? I would like to pose this question, since I am of the opinion that it is important to know exactly the rate of change of money supply. I think I am influenced by the doctrine of monetarism proposed by Milton Friedman of the University of Chicago, which emphasizes the importance of money supply among the various economic indicators" (Nishiyama 1976b, 68–69).

While this certainly was an embarrassing question for Hayek, it aptly captures the crux of the matter. If the scheme of denationalization of money were realized, it would be difficult to control the money supply. Hayek was perfectly confident that it was neither necessary nor possible to control the money supply, which boils down to his belief that it is not easy to discriminate nonmoney from money. Further discussions included in the book clearly show that Nishiyama and his *Doktorvater* have different concepts of monetary policy. Or, to put it another way, in the Hayekian scheme there would be no need for monetary policy, at least in the monetarist sense of the term, a point obviously not shared by Nishiyama.

Nishiyama seems to have been working in complete isolation from the rest of academia. However, after Nishiyama, a few scholars of the younger generation began to be interested in neoliberalism.

We now turn to Koga Katsujiro, another key figure in the diffusion and popularization of neoliberalism in Japan.[41] Koga, born in 1947, was a student of Waseda University. He attended the summer school of the Study Group of National Culture (Kokuminbunka Kenkyukai) and was inspired by the lectures of Yamamoto Katsuichi and Kiuchi Nobutane. Koga also worked for the Institute of World Economy with Kiuchi and wrote many articles for *World Economy*; Koga wrote that it was not possible to publish papers on Hayek in other journals at that time (Koga 1985, 333–40). His first book on Hayek appeared as early as 1981. Entitled *The Political Economy of Hayek* (*Haieku no Seiji Keizaigaku*), it was published by Shin-Hyoron. He seemed to be working in isolation from the few other scholars sharing the same interest in Hayek. Koga thought that the basic confrontation after the demise of Marxian thought was to be the ideological differences between the welfare state and neoliberalism. Koga, who was interested in comparing different economic systems, read Röpke and Eucken and the works of Koizumi Shinzo, a dominant thinker in the field of liberalism, as a young scholar. Comparison of various economic systems was the focus of interest in his youth.

As Koga pointed out, Hayek was no longer a leading figure in the field of economics when he, together with Gunnar Myrdal, was awarded the Nobel Prize in Economics in 1974. "Oh, Hayek, is he still alive?" was the common refrain at that time in Japan. As is often the case with Japanese daily newspapers, when the two were awarded the prize, *Mainichi* attempted to find scholars who were able to comment briefly on them. Myrdal was no problem. However, *Mainichi* could find scholars interested in Hayek only with difficulty. It is hard to say to what extent one can generalize these impressions and situations in the earlier 1970s, but it can be safely said that Hayek was virtually forgotten in Japan, at least among general readers and laymen interested in the social sciences.

In this sense the book by Koga was a new starting point in Hayek studies in Japan. It was followed by *Hayek and Neoliberalism* (*Haieku to Shinjiyushugi*,

1983) by the same author. These works, along with other smaller works by Koga, contributed to the understanding of Hayek among Japanese readers, extending far beyond the narrow scope of monetary economics per se to his later works, such as *Constitution of Liberty* and *Law, Legislation and Liberty*.

Nishiyama and Koga were deeply involved in the publication of Hayek's works in Japanese. The first series of translations included such works as *Constitution of Liberty* (three volumes in the Japanese edition), *Law, Legislation and Liberty*, *Individualism and Economic Order*, and *Sensory Order*, among others, while relatively new contributions were included in the second series, such as *Fatal Conceit*. The Japanese edition of the *Constitution of Liberty* was published as early as the 1980s—the first volume in 1986, the second and third in 1987. Thus, it was possible for the Japanese to read this classical work in their language even before the turn of the century. After a long interval, publication of the second series began with the *Fatal Conceit* in 2009. Both series were published by Shunju-sha, a publisher dealing especially with books on Buddhism and musical scores.

Many younger Hayek scholars (in a broader sense) contributed to making this long-run translation project possible. Thanks to this Japanese edition of Hayek's works and new contributions on Hayek by scholars of various fields, lay readers can now access a wide range of Hayekian scholarship.

4.6. Concluding Remarks and Some Suggestions

In the 1880s the Japanese academic world opened up to the ideas of the German historical school, and later Marxism. In the interwar period the idea of a controlled economy become dominant as war loomed closer. At the same time, various strands of liberalism can be also seen in the interwar period. Later in the 1930s, Marxism and liberalism were suppressed under fascism, but with democratization after World War II saw both flourishing.

Thus, the history of liberalism reveals many versions of Japanese liberalism. We will summarize the arguments of the previous sections in what follows. Fukuda's "Middle Way" can certainly be interpreted as his welfare state manifesto. His emphasis on the right to normal life had a forerunner in the Weimar Constitution and found expression in Article 25 of the Japanese constitution after World War II. Ueda's stance is slightly different. As we saw in section 4.3, he placed his confidence in the important role of managers and those eager to promote the figure of the middle manager. Amid the general atmosphere of this political trend, Yamamoto's point of view deserves special attention. The title of his book clearly shows that he was a fierce opponent of the concept of a welfare state. However, Yamamoto came close to Ishibashi's views after World War II, thus showing a convergence of two different types of liberalism: neoliberalism, with its emphasis on the market order, and liberalism, with some emphasis on state activities. With perhaps the one exception of

Yamamoto, it can safely be stated that the basic politico-economic ideas of the prewar period were forged in the interventionist framework.

Because the influential political ideology among intellectuals in Japan continued to be center-left long after World War II, the purest economic liberalism is hard to find in Japanese politics. Within the LDP there are many different attitudes toward economic policy: some members of the LDP still believe in the importance of public spending and Keynesian economics, while others are reluctant to employ this tool because of the huge state deficit. Broadly speaking, however, in the 1970s, along with the alleged demise of Keynesian economics, the political scene had begun to change. As we saw above, new political and economic discourses began to be introduced, read, and digested thanks to the efforts of scholars including Nishiyama and Koga.

In this long period we find scholars divided between two different camps. On the one hand, there are scholars faithful to their single political ideology. A typical example is Nishiyama, who went to the United States to write a dissertation under Hayek in the heyday of Keynesian economics and Marxian ideology in Japan. He has remained a staunch supporter of neoliberalism to this day. On the other hand, we have those who are interested in various political and economic doctrines without any one of them excluding another. To the second category belongs Nakayama. He was a well-known pupil of Fukuda, attempting to introduce Walrasian economics to Japan. At the same time he tried to expand the field of economics, à la Fukuda, one might say. As we have seen, Nakayama was one of those who supported Yamamoto's dissertation, without perhaps implying sympathy with his political ideology. Furthermore, he was generous enough to write a preface to the book consisting of conversations between Nishiyama and Hayek. In this way Nakayama was an all-round player in economics. Before the take-off of Japanese economics, such scholars were needed, as were popularizing writers able to publish readily comprehensible books.

The Japanese version of liberalism was not only for scholars, but was shared by some businessmen as well. As we saw in the previous sections, Keizai-doyukai was actively engaged in various problems of economic policies. However, after scrutinizing the views of some representative entrepreneurs of that time, we are compelled to conclude that their liberalism was a curious mixture of almost all the economic thinking available. The basic stance can be characterized as economic liberalism, without implying rejection of governmental intervention if necessary. They attempted to combine economic liberalism based on the strong initiative of each firm with some version of the welfare state.

It is interesting to note that some of the leading Japanese businessmen at that time proposed and addressed the message of "corporate social responsibility." Among them we find Nakayama, Sakurada, and Kikawada, all of whom were representative businessmen of leading firms. While the topic was discussed in the earlier 1970s after the oil crisis and during environmental disruptions, it was in the 1950s that Keizai-doyukai, led by the above three businessmen, officially and repeatedly announced this message of CSR to fend off government intervention.

References

Aoba, Fumio. 1989. *Aiming at New Liberalism* (*Shinjiyushugi wo Mezashite*). Tokyo: Gakubunsha.

Backhouse, Roger E., and Tamotsu Nishizawa, eds. 2010. *No Wealth but Life: Welfare Economics and the Welfare State in Britain, 1880–1945*. Cambridge: Cambridge University Press.

Daniels, Gordon, and Chushichi Tsuzuki, eds. 2002. *The History of Anglo-Japanese Relations*. Vol. 5: *Social and Cultural Perspectives*. London: Palgrave Macmillan.

Doi, Ikuma. 2001. "The Economics of Liberalism in Prewar Days and 'The Socialist Calculation Debate' (1) (2)" (*Senzenki no Jiyushugikeizairon to "Shakaishugi Keizaikeisanronso"*). *Seijikeizaishigaku*, 23–48, 27–49, 416–17.

Erhard, Ludwig. 1953. *Deutschlands Rückkehr zum Weltmarkt*. Düsseldorf: Econ-Verlag. Translated by Arisawa Hiromi as *Doitsu Keizai no Kiseki* (Tokyo: Jiji Shinposha, 1954).

Erhard, Ludwig. 1957. *Wohlstand für Alle*. Düsseldorf: Econ-Verlag. Translated by Suga Takashi as *Shakaiteki Shijo Keizai no Shori* (Tokyo: Jiji Shinposha, 1960).

Fukuda, Tokuzo. 1926a. *Fukuda's Collected Works in Economics*. Vol 5: *Studies on Social Policy* (*Shakai Seisaku Kenkyu*). Tokyo: Dobunkan.

Fukuda, Tokuzo. 1926b. *Fukuda's Collected Works in Economics*. Vol. 6: *Economic Policy and Topical Problems* (*Keizai Seisaku oyobi Jiji Mondai*). Tokyo: Dobunkan.

Hayek, Friedrich. 1986–90. *Collected Works of Friedrich Hayek*. 1st series, edited by Chiaki Nishiyama et. al. Tokyo: Shunjusha.

Hayek, Friedrich. 2009–12. *Collected Works of Friedrich Hayek*. 2nd series. Tokyo: Shunjusha.

Kaji, Sayo. 1994. "Mr. Kiuchi and the MPS" ("Kiuchi-san to the MPS"). Memorial issue of Kiuchi Nobutane, *World Economy* (*Sekai Keizai*), 49 (4): 84–89.

Kawakami, Hajime. 1917 [1947]. *A Tale of Poverty* (*Binbo Monogatari*). Tokyo: Iwanami Shoten.

Koga, Katsujiro. 1981. *Political Economy of Hayek* (*Haieku no Seiji Keizaigaku*). Tokyo: Shin-Hyoron.

Koga, Katsujiro. 1983. *Hayek and Neoliberalism* (*Haieku to Shinjiyushugi*). Tokyo: Kojinsha.

Koga, Katsujiro. 1985. *Economics of Hayek and Surrounding Topics* (*Haieku Keizaigaku no Shuhen*). Tokyo: Kojinsha.

Kresge, Stephen, and Leif Wenar, eds. 1994. *Hayek on Hayek*. Indianapolis: Liberty Fund.

Makino, Kuniaki. 2010. *Economists during the War* (*Senjika no Keizaigakusha*). Tokyo: Chuokoronsha.

Minoguchi, Takeo and Tadashi Hayasaka, eds. 1978. *Modern Economics and Japan* (*Kindaikeizaigaku to Nihon*). Tokyo: Nihonkeizai-shinbunsha.

Miyamoto, Moritaro. 1986. *Japanese Views of Britain* (*Nihonjin no Igirisukan*). Tokyo: Ochanomizushobo.

Nishiyama, Chiaki. "The Theory of Self-love: An Essay in the Methodology of the Social Sciences, and Especially of Economics with Special Reference to Bernard Mandeville." Ph.D. dissertation, University of Chicago.

Nishiyama, Chiaki. 1976a. *Monetarism* (*Monetarizumu*). Tokyo: Toyo Keizai Shinposha.

Nishiyama, Chiaki. 1976b. *What Is Neoliberalism?* (*Shinjiyu Shugi towa Nanika?*). Tokyo: Tokyo Shinbun Shuppankyoku.

Nishiyama, Chiaki, and Kokichi Asakura, eds. 1974. *Monetary Analysis and History of the Japanese Economy: 1868–1970* (*Nihon Keizai no Kahei teki Bunseki: 1868–1970*). Tokyo: Sobunsha.

Nishizawa, Tamotsu. 2001. "Ueda Teijiro's New Liberalism and His Views on the Japanese Economy" ("Ueda Teijiro no Shinjiyushugi-Nihonkeizairon"). In C. Tsuzuki, et al. eds., *History of Anglo-Japanese Relations*, vol. 5, *Social and Cultural Perspectives* (*Nichiei Koryushi. Shakai to Bunka*), 150–65. Tokyo: Tokyo University Press.

Nishizawa, Tamotsu. 2002. "Ichiro Nakayama and the Stabilization of Industrial Relations in Postwar Japan," *Hitotsubashi Journal of Economics* 43 (1): 1–17.

Nishizawa, Tamotsu. 2007. *Marshall and Economic Thought of the Historical School* (*Marshall to Rekishigakuha no Keizaishiso*). Tokyo: Iwanami Shoten.

Nishizawa, Tamotsu. 2010. "The Ethico-Historical Approach: The Case of Fukuda." in R. Backhouse and T. Nishizawa, eds., *No Wealth but Life: Welfare Economics and the Welfare State in Britain, 1880–1945*, 136–58. Cambridge: Cambridge University Press.

Nishizawa, Tamotsu. 2014. "The Economics of Social Reform across Borders: Fukuda's Welfare Economic Studies in International Perspective," *Journal of Global History* 9 (2): 232–53.

Okazaki, Tetsuji, et al. 1996. *Postwar Japanese Economy and Keizai-doyukai* (*Sengo Nihon Keizai to Keizai Doyukai*). Tokyo: Iwanami Shoten.

Okon, Hiroyuki. 1997. "Yamamoto Katsuichi: The Life of a Freedom Fighter (1)" ("Yamamoto Katsuichi: Jiyushugi no Toushi (1)"). *Wakayama University, Economics Faculty, Annual Bulletin* 1:63–103.

Ouchi, Hyoe. 1970. *50 Years in Economics* (*Keizaigaku 50 Nen).* Tokyo: Tokyo University Press.

Röpke, Wilhelm. 1944. *Civitas Humana.* Zurich: E. Rentsch. Translated by Kitamura Hiroshi as *Hyumanizumu no Keizaigaku.* Tokyo: Keiso Shobo. 1952–54.

Röpke, Wilhelm. 1947. *Die Krise des Kollektivismus* and *das Kulturideal des Liberalismus.* Zurich: E. Rentsch. Translated by Kitamura Hiroshi as *Gendai Keizai no Kiki* (Aoya Shoten, 1949).

Shakaihoshoseido Shingikai Jimukyoku, ed. 1971. *Twenty Years of the Advisory Board of Social Security System* (Shakaihoshoseido Shingikai 20 Nen no Ayumi). Tokyo: Shakai Hoken Hoki Kenkyukai.

Takamiya, Susumu, ed. 1978. *Business Ideas of Kikawada Kazutaka* (*Kikawada Kazutaka no Keiei-rinen*). Tokyo: Denryoku-shinpo-sha.

Tamai, Kingo. 1992. *Creation of the Destitution Prevention* (*Bohin no Sozo*). Kyoto: Keibunsha.

Tezuka, Makoto. 2015. "Economic Ideas of Naniwada Haruo: In Particular Reference to His Studies on the German Social-Market Economy" ("Naniwada Haruo no Keizai Shiso: Doitsu Shakaiteki Shijo Keizai Kenkyu wo Chushin ni"). *Essays on Foreign Literature* (Teikyo University) 21, 67–111.

Tsuru, Shigeto. 1971. "In Place of GNP." In *Collected Works of Tsuru Shigeto*, vol. 13, 73–93. Tokyo: Kodansha, 1976.

Tsuru, Shigeto. 1976. *Collected Works of Tsuru Shigeto*. Vol. 13: *Towards a New Political Economy*. Tokyo: Kodansha.

Tsutsui, Kiyotada. 1986. *Ishibashi Tanzan: Tracks of a Liberalist Politician* (*Ishibashi Tanzan: Jiyushugi-seijika no Kiseki*). Tokyo: Chuokoron-sha.

Ueda, Tatsunosuke. 1942. "Dr. Ueda's Views on Duty-Role of Managers" ("Ueda-hakushi no Kigyosha-shokubun-ron)". In *Memorial Essays for Dr. Ueda Teijiro* (*Ueda Teijiro-hakushi Kinen-ronbunshu*), vol. 1, 13–40. Tokyo: Kagakushugikogyosha.

Ueda, Teijiro. 1975a. *Collected Works of Ueda Teijiro*. Vol. 2: *Economic Discourse on Joint Stock Companies* (*Kabushikigaisha Keizairon*). Tokyo: Daisan Shuppan.

Ueda, Teijiro. 1975b. *Collected Works of Ueda Teijiro*. Vol. 4: *Social Reconstruction and Enterprise* (*Shakai Kaizo to Kigyo*). Tokyo: Daisan Shuppan.

Ueda, Teijiro. 1976a. *Collected Works of Ueda Teijiro*. Vol. 3: *Industrial Revolution* (*Sangyo Kakumei*). Tokyo: Daisan Shuppan.

Ueda, Teijiro. 1976b. *Collected Works of Ueda Teijiro*. Vol. 7: *New Liberalism* (*Shin Jiyushugi*). Tokyo: Daisan Shuppan.

Yamada, Yuzo. 1954. "On the Annual Journal *Ordo* in West Germany" ("Nishi Doitsu ni okeru Nenkanshi *Orudo* ni tsuite"). *Hitotsubashi Review*, 32–32, 140–58.

Yamada, Yuzo. 1961. "The Neoliberalism of Professor Röpke" ("Repuke Kyoju no Shinjiyushugi"). *Keizai Ourai*, April, 108–10.

Yamamoto, Katsuichi. 1932. *Economic Calculation: Fundamental Problems of Economic Planning* (*Keizai Keisan: Keikakukeizai no Kihonmondai*). Tokyo: Chikura Shobo. Rev. ed., *Fundamental Problems of Planned Economy: Considerations on the Possibility of Economic Calculation* (*Keikakukeizai no Konponmondai: Keizaikeisan no Kanosei no Ginmi*). Tokyo: Riso-sha, 1939.

Yamamoto, Katsuichi. 1959. "Ludwig Erhard—Man and Policy: My Respected Economist" ("Ludwig Erhard—Sono Hito to Seisaku: Watashino Sonkeisuru Keizaigakusha"). *Keizai-jidai* 24 (6): 101–05.

Yamamoto, Katsuichi. 1961a. "Professor Röpke and the LDP." *Keizai-ourai*, May, 95–98.

Yamamoto, Katsuichi. 1961b. *A Warning on the Preference for Social Security: The Limits of Social Security in a Free Society* (*Shakaihosho Mood eno Keikoku: Jiyushakai ni okeru Shakaihosho no Genkai*). Tokyo: Yamamoto kai. In *The Welfare State Decays the Nation: The Limits of Welfare in a Free Society* (*Fukushikokka Bokoku-ron: Jiyushakai ni okeru Fukushi no Genkai*) (Tokyo: Hokenhukushi Kaihatsu Kenkyu Zaidan, 1975).

Yamamoto, Katsuichi. 1980. *Battle with the Socialist Theories: Selected Essays of Yamamoto Katsuichi* (*Shakaishugi-riron to no Tatakai*). Edited by Y. Kano and T. Miura. Tokyo: Kokuminbunka Kenkyukai.

II | Neoliberalism and the Changing Understanding of the Welfare State

5 | Between Business and Academia in Postwar Britain

THREE ADVOCATES OF NEOLIBERALISM AT THE HEART OF THE BRITISH BUSINESS COMMUNITY

NEIL ROLLINGS

5.1. Introduction

The conventional account of the rise of neoliberalism in Britain is familiar and frequently reproduced. It begins with the creation of the Mont Pelerin Society (MPS) by Friedrich Hayek in 1947.[1] This long-term intellectual project deliberately stayed out of the mainstream until it was gradually given a higher public profile by right-wing think tanks, notably, in Britain, the Institute of Economic Affairs. Following the crisis of the 1970s and the growing discontent with the Keynesian approach to economic policy, it culminated in the election of Margaret Thatcher in 1979.[2] Thus Thatcherism is seen as "the political embodiment of an intellectual counterrevolution against the Keynesian consensus" (Prasad 2006, 101). Moreover, this intellectual counterrevolution was carried out in Britain by a very small group of individuals—Maurice Cowling suggests as few as about 50 people (Cockett 1994, 3). Many accounts detail and elaborate on elements of this conventional account (e.g., Hayek 1967; Hobsbawm, quoted in Cassidy 2000; Oliver 1997, chap. 3; Oliver 1996, 80–86). Similarly, there is a wealth of literature exploring the interaction of ideas, interests, institutions, and economic circumstances in explaining this paradigm shift to neoliberalism (e.g., Marquand and Seldon 1996; Hall 1992, 1993; Hay 2001; more generally, see Middleton 1996).

On the other hand, there is also an emerging literature illustrating that this conventional account is a caricature: it is flawed, inconsistent, and contested in many respects. Recent work has rejected the previous contested attempts to define neoliberalism in detail. Instead, there has been an acceptance that, while there may be certain core beliefs (Turner) or groups of individuals (the

Mont Pelerin Society as a "thought collective") (Plehwe), no single grand narrative of neoliberalism is possible: it should be seen as "a complex and varied ideology," an umbrella concept that has evolved over time.[3] Plehwe has also shown that social network analysis of the attendees of the MPS conferences "helps to shed light on the group of less well-known neoliberal activists, who all too frequently have remained hidden in the shadow of the official leaders and prominent neoliberals" but who were active in attending MPS conferences (Plehwe 2009, 17). In Britain the role of think tanks has also come under scrutiny (Kandiah and Seldon 1996; Denham and Garnett 1998; Denham 1996). More generally, contemporary historians have begun to unpick the historical background to the emergence of Thatcherism (Green 1999; Jackson 2010; Jackson and Saunders 2012).

This chapter extends and develops such recent work on the MPS and on the rise of neoliberalism in Britain by exploring the activities and writings of three British business economists who acted as advisers at the heart of the business community but were members of the MPS and active in the IEA. Hayek tended to be cautious in protecting the Mont Pelerin Society from undue influence from business. For him the MPS was a long-term intellectual movement where too much interaction with business would muddy and confuse any desire for intellectual clarity. Thus, the main relationship of the MPS with business, it is commonly understood, was as a provider of finance (Plehwe 2009, 6–7). Similarly, Jackson has shown the growth of business funding of the IEA in Britain (2012, 47). While individual business people and individual companies supported the IEA, the peak-level representative bodies of business in Britain, the Federation of British Industries (FBI), and its successor from 1965, the Confederation of British Industry (CBI), play no part in accounts of the rise of neoliberalism in Britain.[4] Indeed, organized business in the form of the CBI is conventionally viewed to have lost out with the election of Margaret Thatcher, as it was tainted with 1970s corporatism. Instead she consulted ideologically sympathetic businessmen directly or used the overtly free-market Institute of Directors as her route to business opinion (Grant 1980; Mitchell 1990; Baggott 1995; May, McHugh, and Taylor 1998). The CBI has been presented as an obstacle to the rise of neoliberalism.

The focus in this chapter is to illuminate the versions of neoliberalism of three business economists giving advice to leading businessmen at the heart of the business community, in particular through their critique of the postwar Keynesian welfare state in Britain. Each was also to some degree an academic economist as well as a business adviser. One, John Jewkes, is reasonably well known as an academic economist and would meet the definition used by Peden in this volume to define an economist. The other two, Arthur Shenfield and Barry Bracewell-Milnes, have received virtually no attention to date. Shenfield, having been a lecturer in economics during World War II, was the economic director to the FBI and its successor organization, the CBI, between 1955 and 1967. In 1967 he then was seconded from the CBI to be director of a new body, the Industrial Policy Group (IPG), whose membership was made up of representatives of big business. Jewkes, on retiring from his chair at Oxford, became Shenfield's replacement at the IPG in 1969, a position he held until the IPG was wound up in 1974. Similarly, the third individual here, Barry Bracewell-Milnes, became the CBI's new economic director within months of Shenfield's departure to the IPG. Bracewell-Milnes had a Ph.D. in agricultural economics from Cambridge (Rollings 2013). It is their critical views of the welfare state espoused as advisers to business that are illustrated in the chapter and that culminated in an ideological split within the CBI. Crucial here is the row between Bracewell-Milnes and Campbell Adamson, the director general of the CBI, which ended with the former's forced resignation in 1973.[5] This episode highlights the contested nature of economic advice at the heart of the British business community—one strand linked to neoliberalism, the other corporatist.

Incorporating the advice of these business economists has significant ramifications for our understanding of the process by which neoliberal ideas came to the fore in Britain. Given that this advice was being presented to leading businessmen, and supported by some, we need to accept that the rise of these ideas was not limited to a small isolated group but found some support more widely. Moreover, these views were being presented throughout the 1950s and 1960s. The chapter also highlights the role of business economists, a group growing rapidly in number in the postwar period but, to date, rather ignored. This group may have been an important conduit for the spread of neoliberal economic policies from the MPS and IEA to wider society.

5.2. Public Advocates of Neoliberalism within Leading Business Organizations

With this in mind it is now possible to turn attention to the three individuals who it is argued question this conventional account. Below the director general in the FBI and the CBI were various directors who were responsible for particular subject areas (directorates). The director general and the directors would draft most of the papers, which then went to the committees for discussion. They also tended to work closely with the chairmen of the committees in their area of responsibility. Thus they played an important role in setting the direction of internal discussions and external policy statements of the FBI and CBI (Blank 1973, chap. 3; Grant and Marsh 1977, chap. 5). Two of the three individuals considered here were economic directors of the FBI and CBI, covering the period from 1955 to 1973. The third, John Jewkes, replaced Shenfield as director of the IPG in 1969. Although it was formally separate from the CBI and a frequent cause of contention in the CBI leadership, there were close links between the CBI and the IPG: the CBI president and the director general were ex officio members of the IPG, the IPG's office was in the CBI's building and its papers were commented upon by CBI staff prior to publication. All three individuals, therefore, provided economic advice and expertise at the heart of organized business in Britain. Each also critiqued the postwar welfare state in his personal and representative positions on lines almost identical to those emanating from the IEA; indeed they were directly involved in the IEA's efforts in this field.

5.2.1. Arthur Asher Shenfield

Arthur Shenfield was appointed as the FBI's economic director in 1955. Shenfield is noteworthy because he lies close to the center of the network of frequent participants in MPS meetings (Plehwe 2009, 20). Only those who attended at least half of the 26 conferences between 1947 and 1986 are included in Plehwe's analysis and Shenfield's proximity to the center means he attended significantly more and can be regarded as highly active in the MPS. Indeed, he was president of the society 1972–74, succeeding Milton Friedman. Yet little seems to be known about Shenfield (Plehwe 2009, 18; Tribe 2009, 87, 96). He came to Britain in the 1920s with his father, a Russian émigré and Jewish rabbi, and his brother.[6] They settled in Cardiff, becoming naturalized British in 1927, and Asher Sheinfield, as he was called at that time, studied economics and politics at the local university. Sheinfield got a position at the London School of Economics as assistant editor of the London and Cambridge Economic Service in 1939. It was at this point that he changed his name by deed poll to Arthur Asher Shenfield and began associating with other British neoliberals at LSE, including Arthur Seldon, later one of the two leading lights in the IEA (Cockett 1994, 136).

Shenfield was active in the Mont Pelerin Society soon after the war, giving a paper at the 1953 British regional meeting and two at the full meeting the following year in Venice, "Democracy, Socialism and the Rule of Law" and "Trade Union Legislation: Situation in Britain."[7] Shenfield's neoliberal credentials were, therefore, firmly established prior to his appointment as the FBI's economic director in 1955. He also remained active in the MPS, as shown in table 5.1. He had various key administrative roles in the MPS, but his role peaked with his presidency of the MPS, giving his presidential address on "The English disease."[8] In the early years of the war, like Arthur Seldon and many of the economists examined in chapters 2 and 3 in this volume, he was active in the Liberal Party.

Stephen Blank suggests that Shenfield's appointment as the FBI's economic director marked a significant change in the organization. First, he was much more active and dynamic than his predecessor, and the FBI's Economic Policy Committee became more independent and authoritative under his influence. Second, his approach was more theoretical and neoliberal in nature. Blank believes that this "did not essentially alter the Federation's position on

TABLE 5.1 Papers to the Mont Pelerin Society Meetings by Arthur Shenfield

YEAR	TITLE
1954	Democracy, Socialism and the Rule of Law
	Trade Union Legislation: Situation in Britain
1957	Liberalism and Colonialism
1959	No title (session on industry)
1961	Small and Big Business
1962	The Return to Economic Planning in Britain
1964	Economic Planning in the UK: Note on the Case of the National Incomes Commission
1967	Fundamental Constitutional Problems
1968	Omissions of Government: The Emancipation of Labour
1970	The Businessman and the Politician
1974	Presidential Address: The English Disease
1978	The Political Order of a Free Society
1984	Unionised Australia: Is It Still "The Lucky Country"
	The International Labour Organisation: A Tale of Superstition and Prestige
1986	The Legacy of Bruno Leoni

SOURCE: www.liberaalarchief.be/MPS2005.pdf, inventory of MPS General Meetings.

economic policy . . . but he shaped and stated [it] in a more abstract and dogmatic fashion," adding that Norman Kipping, then the director general, "generally agreed with Shenfield's views" and that the Federation's policies after 1955 "strongly reflected Shenfield's influence" (Blank 1973, 129, 159).

He was the lead author of a number of key publications by the FBI in this period and his views are discernible in such publications, notably the Federation's March 1957 statement *Britain's Economic Problems and Policies* (FBI 1957; Peters 1997, 216 n. 38). As the foreword put it:

> Much of the blame rests on successive governments for taking too large a portion of the national output. It [the report] shows how attempts by budgetary manipulation to limit the inflation thus generated have produced a level of taxation harmful to thrift, efficiency and enterprise. . . .
>
> There must be a radical reduction in government and local authority expenditure in order to pave the way for reductions in taxation designed to encourage enterprise, efficiency and thrift, and also to make room for the necessary expansion in investment and exports. To end inflation the government must use its power over the monetary system with a firm hand, and it must seek ways of improving the technique of monetary management. (FBI 1957, iii)

It was thus forthright in its argument and its anti-Keynesian approach, arguing that the way to reduce demand was to operate stricter control over the money supply (FBI 1957, 14). Its argument is similar to the IEA publication

Not Unanimous, produced in 1960 as a critique of the *Report of the Radcliffe Committee on the Working of the Monetary System.*[9] The FBI report concluded:

> For expansion we must produce an atmosphere of opportunity; we must put a premium on risk-taking and adaptability; we must stimulate investment and give it an opportunity to reap high reward. For stability we need the power and skill of the state in the field of monetary management and control; but we must reduce its power and scope as a spender and as a direct participant in economic activity. (FBI 1957, 34)

For Shenfield, Britain had an unhealthy obsession with full employment rather than with the competitive power of the economy (Shenfield 1960, 163, 166).

In 1963 Shenfield took leave from the FBI to be the Ford Foundation Visiting Professor of Business Economics at the Graduate School of Business, headed by George Stigler, at the University of Chicago, that stronghold of neoliberal ideas (Shenfield 1963). However, he returned to the FBI and stayed on as economic director of the newly created CBI in 1965, a time when a number of staff retired or left. In 1967, as business criticism of government policy grew, he was seconded from the CBI to the newly created IPG (Sampson 1971, 571, 612). The group, led by Sir Paul Chambers, the chairman of ICI, consisted of about 20 heads of large British companies and aimed to study "the fundamental causes of the malaise of the British economy" and to increase attention to these issues in popular debate (Corina 1967, 17). The Chancellor of the Exchequer, James Callaghan, dubbed the group "potentially sinister" and led by "dubious people." Opinion in the group was diverse, but there was a clear neoliberal dimension to it (Jewkes 1966).

The IPG gave Shenfield more freedom to defend the role of private enterprise and to attack the Labour government and, indeed, postwar economic policy with renewed vigor.[10] The culprits behind the rise of such flawed economic policy were clear to him:

> Post-war policies have been principally guided by the ideas propounded a generation ago by Keynes, Beveridge and by the authors of the 1944 White Paper on Employment Policy (Cmd. 6527). . . .
>
> In attributing the tendencies of post-war policies, whether under Conservative or Labour Governments, to Keynes, Beveridge and the 1944 White Paper, we do not at all wish to imply that these sources were exactly similar in character or inspiration. The aim of full employment, regardless of other vital purposes of policy, is attributable to Beveridge only.[11]

As he saw it the errors of policy were the takeover by the state of economic activity; the erosion of the market and the weakening of its disciplines; the failure to apply state power efficiently where it was needed; and the application of state power where it was unnecessary and damaging.

In arguing against "the penal taxation of higher incomes" he often focused on the welfare state and the National Health Service (NHS).[12] His arguments often mirrored those of his friend at the IEA, Arthur Seldon, who was engaged in a fierce debate with Richard Titmuss and others over the welfare state (Fontaine 2002; Jackson, forthcoming). In 1961 Shenfield wrote a piece that, in turn, criticized the Conservative government for failing to control the growth of public expenditure, and experts and their biases in favor of increased expenditure, in particular, those in the field of social administration (i.e., Titmuss and his supporters), "in which it is possible to erect an academic reputation on a foundation of snippets of descriptive work, law, statistics, and general guesswork" (Shenfield 1962). He went on to outline an archetypal neoliberal view of the welfare state:

> The Welfare State rests on humbug because it was ostensibly established to relieve poverty while what in fact it does is something else. Beveridge's four giants—Want, Disease, Squalor and Ignorance—were to be banished from the land and minimum standards were to be secured for everybody. In fact the true purpose of the welfare state is to socialise the provision of certain services, whereby it actually reduces standards below what they might be. . . .
>
> The method of the welfare state is to require that everyone must pay for and be free to take state-provided services in order that those that cannot provide them for themselves shall have them. Thus it raises taxation to a level which reduces the nation's wealth by weakening the incentive to produce and save. . . . It undermines both the personal responsibilities which are the warp and woof of freedom and the family responsibilities on which the wholesomeness of society rests. It teaches the electorate to vote for things that most of them do not intend to pay for. Above all, by providing services for all it fails to provide fully effective services for those that are really in need. (Shenfield 1962, 52)

To turn things around, means testing needed to be used for all state social services, private supply of these services promoted and developed, and charging used more widely in the interim before private supply took over.

Shenfield reiterated these views on various occasions within the CBI and the IPG, but more explicitly in the IPG, as he felt rather constrained by the day-to-day grind of CBI work.[13] In the IPG's second report on public expenditure, drafted by Shenfield, he set out his position: there were two great causes of concern underpinning the upward trend of public expenditure. They were "the provision of services to all consumers free of charge, or at a charge far below cost" and "the subsidisation of persons or business activities with a view to directing the economy away from the impress of free-market forces, and therefore away from maximum productivity."[14] Curtailing, but not completely abandoning, these positions would allow provision for the genuinely underprivileged to expand as resources would be focused on those in most need.

Turning to specific policy changes, he noted, "The history of the National Health Service has been one of progressive disappointment of expectations. It is almost a classic example of the counter-productive effects of the principle of universality, financed by taxation, and supply [*sic*] free of charge."[15] He proposed a three-tier medical service, consisting of freedom to contract out whereby those making no national health service contributions would pay for the full cost of any treatment; a National Health Service run on a part-cost basis; and selective "and *generous*" aid for those on incomes below that required for treatment on a part-cost basis. Turning to education, he argued for loans for students in higher education and that it should not be compulsory for children to stay at school from 15 to 16, while, in housing policy, rent controls and subsidies needed to be removed. On pensions, while "people like Titmuss, Townsend and Abel Smith" criticized occupational pension schemes, Shenfield "would not accept them as authorities on anything."[16] He continued to expound such a neoliberal critique of the welfare state after his 1969 retirement from the IPG.[17]

Thus both in published papers and in internal papers for leading businessmen, Shenfield propounded and elaborated a position during the 1950s and 1960s that was clearly neoliberal and reflected his active engagement with the Mont Pelerin Society and his close friendship with Arthur Seldon, who was saying many of the same things via the IEA. Shenfield was clearly at odds with what has subsequently become known as the postwar consensus.

5.2.2. John Jewkes

John Jewkes, like Shenfield, was active in the MPS, being its president in 1962–64. Of the three, he was the one who most clearly had an academic presence and whose work has been more widely read. Jewkes returned from wartime service to Manchester in 1946 as Stanley Jevons Professor of Political Economy before moving to Oxford in 1948 to a chair in economic organization, where he stayed until he retired in 1969.[18] Jewkes came to popular attention for his coruscating attack on postwar controls and planning in *Ordeal by Planning*, published in 1948. With the revival of planning in the 1960s Jewkes reprinted the essay with a new section on planning in the sixties (Jewkes 1968). He also wrote more widely at the time of his distaste for nationalization. Indeed, Jewkes played a leading role in the IEA-led assault on the welfare state in the early 1960s. *The Genesis of the British National Health Service*, written with his wife, was presented as the first of a series of planned works on the subject and opened by explaining why the book "may seem unduly critical of the British National Health Service."[19] The pair went on to provide one of the first critiques of Titmuss's defense of the National Health Service, "a medical system," Jewkes believed, that "seemed doomed to remain second- or third-rate" (subsequently published in IEA 1964, 29–35, and Jewkes 1978, 139–69, 77–88, quote from 87).

In 1969, following his retirement from Oxford, it was Jewkes who replaced Shenfield as director of the IPG. Jewkes commented, "[I] gladly accepted [the post] because I sympathised with the aims of the Group and because my academic studies had always led me towards conclusions, concerning the sure foundation of a vigorous system of private enterprise, similar to those held by the members of the Group."[20] He was a known critic of the government's prices and incomes policies and, with that, of the CBI's voluntary price control.[21] However, Jewkes was less critical than Shenfield of the 1944 white paper *Employment Policy* (Jewkes 1978, 39–52). While he accepted that it was "a 'Keynesian' document," Jewkes refuted the argument that the white paper was a source of Britain's postwar problems: "The Paper was a cautious statement, promulgated by the famous wartime coalition government, thought out and written by a group of middle-of-the-road economists, accepted by Keynes himself and formulating a way of maintaining rough stability of employment and prices through the manipulation of aggregate demand but also embodying a set of clear warnings of the conditions to be satisfied if adverse reactions, and especially inflation, were to be avoided" (Jewkes 1978, 42, 46). In his view, those that disputed this were either ignorant of the white paper's contents or misunderstood it. If there was blame for the obsession with full employment, then here he agreed with Shenfield that Beveridge and his colleagues were the real culprits (Jewkes 1978, 49). Thus Jewkes held views broadly similar to Shenfield's on the desirable framework for economic and social policy but did not always agree on the actual nature of policy implemented. Likewise he held a more nuanced view of monetarism, in which he was willing to compromise with the Keynesian position (Jewkes 1978, 49).

5.2.3. Barry Bracewell-Milnes

Shenfield's departure to the IPG did not mark a rejection of neoliberal economic advice in the CBI. For a matter of months the CBI's next economic director was D. Taylor, but in 1968 he was in turn replaced by Dr. J. Barry Bracewell-Milnes. After completing a Ph.D. at King's College Cambridge on the marketing of milk in Western Europe, he acted as an economic adviser in the iron and steel industry and was then appointed by the FBI in 1964. In 1965 he was given the title of assistant economic director in the CBI, promoted to deputy economic director on Shenfield's departure, and then to economic director in 1968. He left the CBI in 1973 to become economic adviser to the more right-wing Institute of Directors, a post he held until 1996 (Bracewell-Milnes 2002, 9). Like Shenfield, after leaving the CBI Bracewell-Milnes published widely, mainly in the area of taxation, and on neoliberal lines for many neoliberal and libertarian organizations.[22]

Though never as central to the MPS as Shenfield or Jewkes, Bracewell-Milnes was a member of the society.[23] He also moved in the same circles as Shenfield and Jewkes: the IEA, the Adam Smith Institute, the Libertarian

Alliance, and other neoliberal groups. He became chairman of the Adam Smith Club. In 1974 he was one of 11 signatories to an open letter to the prime minister, Harold Wilson, arguing that the only cure for inflation was increasing unemployment (Tanzi, Bracewell-Milnes, and Myddleton 1970; Jay 1974, 1). Among the other signatories were Harry Johnson, E. V. Morgan, David Laidler, Brian Griffiths, and S. H. Frankel.

While he was CBI economic director Bracewell-Milnes made clear his neoliberal outlook. His line of argument typically stressed the need for a reduction in tax levels and a shift in the burden of taxation from direct to indirect taxation (Bracewell-Milnes 1970, 1971, 1967, 1972). Bracewell-Milnes was known "to take a classical view of private enterprise and market economics," and this can be discerned in CBI publications and internal discussions at this time (Grant and Marsh 1977, 104). His influence can be seen, in particular, in the CBI's representations during the annual pre-budget lobbying of government. In 1968 the CBI budget representation, the first drafted by Bracewell-Milnes as the CBI's economic director, was much more comprehensive than previously and called for a program of tax reform not just for that budget but for the longer term on the grounds that the principal way the budget could help the economy was by "re-creating confidence at home and abroad" and that the tax system "penalises effort and thrift and favours consumption."[24] Accordingly, the CBI proposed a broad shift from direct to indirect taxation, including reductions in corporation tax, income tax, surtax, capital gains tax, betterment levy, and estate duty. The CBI's 1969 budget representations restated the long-term program of tax reform and this also formed the basis of the 1970 representations.[25]

Bracewell-Milnes's policy preferences on the welfare state were made explicit in a row within the CBI between himself and the director general, the corporatist Campbell Adamson. There were long-standing "differences of opinion about certain aspects of the CBI's affairs" between Bracewell-Milnes and Adamson (Grant and Marsh 1977, 104). These differences festered from 1970 until bursting out into a full-scale argument in 1973, resulting in Bracewell-Milnes's forced resignation that year. At the CBI's Economic Committee in November 1970, Adamson, supported by Sir Hugh Weeks, the committee's chairman, proposed that the budget representations should contain some proposals for tax relief for "the poorer sections of society."[26] At the committee's next meeting, unhappy that this point had not been taken on board sufficiently by Bracewell-Milnes, Adamson suggested that the representations "should give greater attention to measures which would afford some immediate relief to poorer sections of the community."[27] More than this, he suggested the money to fund this could come from modifying the reductions called for in surtax, estates duty, and capital gains tax, all consistently at the heart of Bracewell-Milnes's recommendations.

As a sign of the distance between the two positions, a rare and special joint meeting of the Taxation Panel and the Economic Committee was called at short notice to try to resolve this difference.[28] Again Adamson opened by calling for proposals helping the lower paid. Alun Davies, chair of the Taxation Panel, responded by urging caution against such changes. Davies "saw eye to eye on almost every matter" with Bracewell-Milnes and, like Bracewell-Milnes, was at odds with Adamson's "middle-of-the-road, consensus approach," believing it was impossible to have egalitarianism and growth.[29] Several others present called for a significant reduction in surtax in line with Bracewell-Milnes's suggestion, but Adamson refused to budge.[30] Adamson wanted to propose raising the threshold for liability to income tax to remove one million lower-paid workers from that tax liability and to extend family income supplements. Again there was resistance with one member questioning whether it was appropriate for this to come from the CBI, but Adamson once more won the argument.

This clear split between Bracewell-Milnes and Adamson was renewed over the content of the 1973 budget representations. At the CBI's Taxation Panel meeting in December 1972, Bracewell-Milnes outlined the guidance from a Special Budget Committee that had noted but ignored the Taxation Panel's view that the CBI should "not concern itself with detailed recommendations on behalf of the lower income earners."[31] From the other side of the argument, Adamson explained to the CBI Council on January 17, 1973, why the Taxation Committee's budget representations, drafted by Bracewell-Milnes, had been amended.[32] First, he suggested, "because of the need for as much cooperation as possible between the two sides of industry at the present stage of the battle against inflation, the CBI's representations ought not to advocate in too strong and general terms the reduction of estate duty." Second, Adamson, supported by Sir John Partridge, soon to be the CBI president, explained that since the CBI had been emphasizing the importance of food prices in the cost of living, a new proposal had been added asking for the zero-rating of foods subject to purchase tax, the main form of indirect taxation at this time in Britain.[33] Members of the Taxation Committee and the Taxation Panel on the CBI Council questioned these changes, emphasizing the amount of work carried out by CBI staff, Bracewell-Milnes, and his colleagues, in formulating the budget representations and arguing that the zero-rating of food should be withdrawn—this was an issue for the food industry, not the CBI. Nevertheless, Adamson then read out revised versions of part of the budget representations for approval, which was given.[34] Pointedly, Adamson's report for the March Council meeting "applauded" the zero-rating of food and young children's clothing in the budget.[35]

In the meantime Bracewell-Milnes was forced to resign. As a leading article in the *Times* put it, this was not a clash of personalities but "a clash of ideologies."[36] Adamson himself explained that "the direction the CBI is moving in was not to his [Bracewell-Milnes's] liking."[37] From the other side of the argument, Bracewell-Milnes referred to his intellectual opponents as "the enemy."[38] Having left the CBI, Bracewell-Milnes was quickly appointed to a similar role at the neoliberal-inclined Institute of Directors. One IEA publication turned Bracewell-Milnes into a neoliberal martyr: he was sacked "for supporting capitalism, free enterprise and the market economy" (Bracewell-Milnes 2002, 9). There was even a party organized by the IEA to mark the 30th anniversary of the sacking. And, as noted above, Mrs. Thatcher appeared to favor the Institute of Directors over the CBI for business advice once she became prime minister.

All three of these business economists at the heart of the business community had a similar view of the economy and of the role of the government in it. Bracewell-Milnes typified this position, redolent of Shenfield's 1957 FBI paper: "There is no one cause [of Britain's economic problems] but major causes may well be the system of taxation, public expenditure and restrictions on overseas direct investment . . . and to these might be added our industrial relations and our social security systems."[39] He added, "Historically government intervention has failed lamentably as a means to maintain industrial efficiency." But it is also important to note that while their outlook was supported by parts of the business community others, favoring a more corporatist outlook, contested this position. Indeed, attitudes to the welfare state lay at the heart of this division.

5.3. Conclusion

Highlighting the views and roles of these three advocates of neoliberalism adds to our understanding of this intellectual movement and its rise from the creation of the Mont Pelerin Society in 1947 to Margaret Thatcher's election victory in 1979. Four points in particular can be made. First, these three individuals were neoliberals, both as part of the thought collective of the MPS and in terms of their stated values. Each endorsed the four generic principles that Turner has highlighted as being at the heart of neoliberalism—the importance of market order; the role of the state in preserving individual liberties; the advocacy of minimal state intervention; and the importance of private property. However, on certain issues or details the three were at odds with each other, and this illustrates the complex and disputed nature of neoliberalism.

Second, they were all economists, though not necessarily academic economists. There is a danger in focusing narrowly on academic economists when looking at post–World War II economic opinion, particularly with regard to a movement like neoliberalism. Since 1945 there has been an enormous growth in the number of economists employed outside of academia, be it in government, business, or the City (see, e.g., Coats 1978, 1981). These may not be academically "eminent," but their incorporation into the story of the rise of neoliberalism in Britain adds to our understanding of the process that occurred. Conventional accounts highlight the role of American economists, particularly those at Chicago, and the close links that these American economists had with the IEA.[40] These links were crucial, but there was still the need for their ideas to become accepted into wider British society just at the time that academic economics was becoming highly mathematical and abstracted from the real world and where the vast majority of British academic economists were unsympathetic to the neoliberal message. Economists working in the City or any sort of business environment were potentially more sympathetic to that message.[41] These were not only a growing group but an increasingly organized one too (Anderson 2003).

Third, and related to the second point, the chapter confirms and develops Plehwe's contention that to understand the MPS, and hence neoliberalism, it is necessary to look beyond the Nobel Prize winners. All three individuals—Shenfield, Bracewell-Milnes, and Jewkes—were members of the MPS, two even became presidents, yet only Jewkes could be described as an academic economist. The other two would have regarded themselves as intellectuals but worked in the applied world of giving economic advice to organized business. Hayek's focus on the MPS as a long-term intellectual movement needs some qualification, and the emphasis on this aspect may be a reflection of reading back from the neoliberal turn taken in the last few decades. Clearly, it was an intellectual movement, but that was only part of the story: it was also about getting those ideas implemented by governments and accepted by society. Although Hayek discounted the short-term political and practical tasks of gaining popular support, it was necessary to "raise and train an army of fighters for freedom," and this tends to get forgotten when focusing on those most famous (quoted in Cockett 1994, 104). On this basis it becomes imperative to understand the activities of individuals like Shenfield, Bracewell-Milnes, Jewkes, and others of that ilk if we are to comprehend fully the process by which neoliberalism became a dominant paradigm of thought. MPS members like these can be seen as brokers who bridged the gap between the intellectual ideas and debate of the MPS and the rest of society. Such brokers are now often presented as key players, with significant social capital, in the diffusion of ideas from one network to another (Burt 2007). To date, that brokerage role has focused on the IEA and other right-wing think tanks, but it is important to start to consider alternative or supportive links as well.

Finally, the chapter alters our understanding of the rise of neoliberal ideas in Britain. The existing emphasis on the isolation of a small coterie of neoliberal outsiders in Britain during the dominant period of Keynesianism seems overstated. All three individuals had clear links to the heart of organized business and big business, and each acted as an advocate for neoliberal ideas in that arena. This took place for virtually the whole of the era associated with the postwar Keynesian consensus. Thus we need to be careful not to exaggerate the strength and spread of support for the key elements of that consensus—the mixed economy, the welfare state, and full employment. All three elements were strongly and consistently critiqued by Shenfield, Bracewell-Milnes, and Jewkes and these critiques found support and endorsement for their views at the heart of the business community. As Boswell and Peters have argued, over the postwar period British business remained split over its attitude to Keynesian-style policies and to corporatism (Boswell and Peters 1997). This split in opinion within the business community was shown in its starkest form in the open warfare within the CBI between Adamson and Bracewell-Milnes. Thus, business support for neoliberalism was not restricted to marginalized maverick businessmen outside mainstream opinion: within this mainstream there were some important businessmen, like Sir Paul Chambers, supportive of neoliberal ideas for much of the postwar period. The paradigm shift, therefore, from Keynesianism to neoliberalism, so often presented as revolutionary, had wider roots in British society than conventionally depicted.

References

Anderson, Donald. 2003. "Fifty Years of the Society of Business Economists." In Jim Hirst, ed., *The Challenge of Change: Fifty Years of Business Economics*, 180–203. London: Profile Books.

Baggott, Rob. 1995. "From Confrontation to Consultation? Pressure Group Relations from Thatcher to Major." *Parliamentary Affairs* 48 (3): 484–502.

Barry, Norman, ed. 1998. *Limited Government, Individual Liberty and the Rule of Law: Selected Works of Arthur Asher Shenfield*. Cheltenham: Edward Elgar.

Blank, Stephen. 1973. *Industry and Government in Britain: The Federation of British Industries in Politics, 1945–65*. Farnborough: Saxon House.

Boswell, Jonathan, and James Peters. 1997. *Capitalism in Contention: Business Leaders and Political Economy in Modern Britain*. Cambridge: Cambridge University Press.

Bracewell-Milnes, Barry. 1967. "Bias against Investors Condemned." *Financial Times*, February 9.

Bracewell-Milnes, Barry. 1970. "Cutting Taxes without Cutting Expenditure." In Vito Tanzi, Barry Bracewell-Milnes, and D. R. Myddleton, eds., *Taxation: A Radical Approach. A Reassessment of the High Level of British Taxation and the Scope for Its Reduction*. London: IEA.

Bracewell-Milnes, Barry. 1971. *The Measurement of Fiscal Policy: An Analysis of Tax Systems in Terms of the Political Distinction between "Right" and "Left."* London: CBI.

Bracewell-Milnes, Barry. 1972. "Short-Term Regulation of Economy Crucial." *Financial Times*, July 6.

Bracewell-Milnes, Barry. 1974. *Is Capital Taxation Fair? The Tradition and the Truth*. London: Institute of Directors.

Bracewell-Milnes, Barry. 1976a. *The Camel's Back: An International Comparison of Tax Burdens*. London: Centre for Policy Studies.

Bracewell-Milnes, Barry. 1976b. *Economic Integration in East and West*. London: Croom Helm.

Bracewell-Milnes, Barry. 1979. *Tax Avoidance and Evasion: The Individual and Society*. London: Panopticum Press.

Bracewell-Milnes, Barry. 1980. *The Economics of International Tax Avoidance: Political Power versus Economic Law*. Deventer: Kluwer.

Bracewell-Milnes, Barry. 1982. *Land and Heritage: The Public Interest in Personal Ownership*. London: IEA.

Bracewell-Milnes, Barry. 2002. *Euthanasia for Death Duties: Putting Inheritance Tax Out of Its Misery*. London: IEA.

Bracewell-Milnes, Barry, and J. C. L. Huiskamp. 1977. *Investment Incentives: A Comparative Analysis of the Systems in the EEC, the USA and Sweden*. Deventer: Kluwer.

Bracewell-Milnes, Barry, and Ranjit Teja. 1991. *The Case for Earmarked Taxes: Government Spending and Public Choic*e. London: IEA.

Brittan, Samuel. 1973. *Is There an Economic Consensus: An Attitude Survey*. London: Macmillan.

Burt, Ronald. 2007. *Brokerage and Closure: An Introduction to Social Capital*. Oxford: Oxford University Press.

Cassidy, John. 2000. "The Price Prophet." *New Yorker*, February 7, 44–47.

Coats, A. W. 1978. "Economists in Government: A Research Field for the Historian of Economics." *History of Political Economy* 10 (2): 298–314.

Coats, A. W. 1981. "Britain: The Rise of the Specialists." *History of Political Economy* 13 (3): 365–404.

Cockett, Richard. 1994. *Thinking the Unthinkable: Think-Tanks and the Economic Counter-revolution, 1931–1983*. London: HarperCollins.

Corina, Maurice. 1967. "Industrialists Form Policy Group to Study Economy." *Times*, October 12, 17.

Denham, Andrew. 1996 *Think-Tanks of the New Right*. Aldershot: Dartmouth.

Denham, Andrew, and Mark Garnett, 1998. *British Think-Tanks and the Climate of Opinion*. London: UCL Press.

Federation of British Industries (FBI). 1957. *Britain's Economic Problems and Policies*. London: FBI.

Fontaine, Philippe. 2002. "Blood, Politics, and Social Science: Richard Titmuss and the Institute of Economic Affairs, 1957–1973." *Isis* 93 (3): 401–34.

Grant, Wyn. 1980. "Business Interests and the British Conservative Party." *Government and Opposition* 18 (2): 143–61.

Grant, Wyn, and David Marsh. 1977. *The Confederation of British Industry*. London: Hodder and Stoughton.

Green, E. H. H. 1999. "Thatcherism: An Historical Perspective." *Transactions of the Royal Historical Society* 9:17–42.

Hall, Peter A. 1992. "The Movement from Keynesianism to Monetarism: Institutional Analysis and British Economic Policy in the 1970s." In Sven Steinmo, Kathleen Thelen, and Frank Longstreth, eds., *Structuring Politics: Historical Institutionalism in Comparative Analysis*, 90–113. Cambridge: Cambridge University Press.

Hall, Peter A. 1993. "Policy Paradigms, Social Learning, and the State: The Case of Economic Policymaking in Britain." *Comparative Politics* 25 (3): 275–96.

Hartwell, Max. 1995. *A History of the Mont Pèlerin Society*. Indianapolis: Liberty Fund.

Harvey, David. 2005. *A Brief History of Neoliberalism*. Oxford: Oxford University Press.

Hay, Colin. 2001. "The 'Crisis' of Keynesianism and the Rise of Neoliberalism in Britain: An Ideational Institutionalist Approach." In John L. Campbell and Ove K. Pedersen, eds., *The Rise of Neoliberalism and Institutional Analysis*, 193–218. Princeton, NJ: Princeton University Press.

Hayek, Friedrich. 1967. *Studies in Philosophy, Politics and Economics*. London: Routledge.

Institute of Economic Affairs (IEA). 1964. *Monopoly or Choice in Health Services? Contrasting Approaches to Principles and Practice in Britain and America*. London: IEA.

Jackson, Ben. 2010. "At the Origins of Neo-liberalism: The Free Economy and the Strong State, 1930–1947." *Historical Journal* 53:129–51.

Jackson, Ben. 2012. "The Think-Tank Archipelago: Thatcherism and Neo-liberalism." In Ben Jackson and Robert Saunders, eds., *Making Thatcher's Britain*, 43–61. Cambridge: Cambridge University Press.

Jackson, Ben. Forthcoming. "Richard Titmuss versus the IEA: The Transition from Idealism to Neo-liberalism in British Social Policy." L. Goldman and S. Jones, eds., *Welfare and Social Policy in British Historical Perspective, 1850–2010: Essays in Honour of Professor Jose Harris*.

Jackson, Ben, and Robert Saunders, eds. 2012. *Making Thatcher's Britain*. Cambridge: Cambridge University Press.

Jay, Peter. 1974. "Economists Advise Mr Wilson: Act Now to Control Inflation." *Times*, July 16, 1.

Jewkes, John. 1948. *Ordeal by Planning*. London: Macmillan.

Jewkes, John. 1968. *New Ordeal by Planning*. London: Macmillan.

Jewkes, John. 1978. *A Return to Free Market Economics? Critical Essays on Government Intervention*. London: Macmillan.

Jewkes, John, Paul Chambers, and Lionel C. Robbins. 1966. *Economics, Business and Government*. IEA Occasional Paper 8. London: IEA.

Jewkes, John, and Sylvia Jewkes. 1961. *The Genesis of the British National Health Service*. Oxford: Basil Blackwell.

Kandiah, Michael, and Anthony Seldon, eds. 1996. *Ideas and Think Tanks in Contemporary Britain*. 2 vols. London: Frank Cass.

Marquand, David, and Anthony Seldon, eds. 1996. *The Ideas That Shaped Post-war Britain*. London: Fontana.

May, Timothy C., John McHugh, and Tom Taylor. 1998. "Business Representation in the UK since 1979: The Case of Trade Associations." *Political Studies* 46:260–75.

Middleton, Roger. 1996. *Government versus the Market: The Growth of the Public Sector, Economic Management and British Economic Performance, c.1890–1979*. Cheltenham: Edward Elgar.

Mirowski, Philip. 2009. "Postface: Defining Neoliberalism." In Philip Mirowski and Dieter Plehwe, eds., *The Road from Mont Pèlerin: The Making of the Neoliberal Thought Collective*, 417–55. Cambridge, MA: Harvard University Press.

Mitchell, Neil J. 1990. "The Decentralization of Business in Britain." *Journal of Politics* 52 (2): 622–37.

Oliver, Michael. 1996. "A Response to Denham and Garnett's 'The Nature and Impact of Think Tanks in Contemporary Britain.'" In Michael Kandiah and Anthony Seldon, eds., *Ideas and Think Tanks in Contemporary Britain*, 2:80–86. London: Frank Cass.

Oliver, Michael. 1997. *Whatever Happened to Monetarism?* Aldershot: Ashgate.

Plehwe, Dieter. 2009. Introduction to Philip Mirowski and Dieter Plehwe, eds., *The Road from Mont Pèlerin: The Making of the Neoliberal Thought Collective*, 1–42. Cambridge, MA: Harvard University Press.

Prasad, Monica. 2006. *The Politics of Free Markets: The Rise of Neoliberal Economic Policies in Britain, France, Germany, and the United States*. Chicago: University of Chicago Press.

Rollings, Neil. 2013. "Cracks in the Postwar Keynesian Settlement? The Role of Organised Business in Britain in the Rise of Neoliberalism before Margaret Thatcher." *Twentieth Century British History* 24 (4): 637–59.

Sampson, Anthony. 1971. *The New Anatomy of Britain*. London: Hodder and Stoughton.

Seldon, Arthur, ed. 1960. *Not Unanimous: A Rival Verdict to Radcliffe's on Money*. London: IEA.

Shenfield, Arthur A. 1960. "Britain's Economic Situation." *Journal of the Royal United Services Institution* 105 (May): 160–73.

Shenfield, Arthur A. 1962. "The Public Sector versus the Private Sector in Britain." *Modern Age* 6 (1): 43–58.

Shenfield, Arthur A. 1963. "The Two Faces of the Common Market." University of Chicago Graduate School of Business Selected Papers No. 6.

Stedman Jones, Daniel. 2012. *Masters of the Universe: Hayek, Friedman, and the Birth of Neoliberal Politics*. Princeton, NJ: Princeton University Press.

Tribe, Keith. 2009. "Liberalism and Neoliberalism in Britain, 1930–1980." In Philip Mirowski and Dieter Plehwe, eds., *The Road from Mont Pèlerin: The Making of the Neoliberal Thought Collective*, 68–97. Cambridge, MA: Harvard University Press.

Turner, Rachel. 2008. *Neo-liberal Ideology: History, Concepts and Policies*. Edinburgh: Edinburgh University Press.

6 Neoliberalism, New Labour, and the Welfare State

MATT BEECH

6.1. Introduction

The context of this chapter is the evolution of liberalism and the intellectual challenge to the welfare state. In particular, it is a story of how one variant of liberalism—neoliberalism—emerged in reaction to the postwar consensus (Addison 1975) and with what is sometimes referred to as the social democratic state. Components of that can be understood to have comprised the universal welfare state (predicated on recommendations from the Beveridge report), publicly funded goods, a mixed economy with a significant proportion of industries nationalized, a tripartite approach to industrial relations, and Keynesian demand management. In Britain, like much of Western Europe, social democratic parties both fashioned and sought to guard this consensus. However, it is more precise to term it a postwar settlement as opposed to a postwar consensus. After all, the Liberal Party and to a lesser extent the Conservative Party settled for, rather than ideologically concurred with, the reforms of Clement Attlee's governments (Pimlott 1988).

First this chapter seeks to explain the emergence of neoliberalism in British politics and more specifically within the Conservative Party of the 1970s. This is of vital importance if one wishes to trace the ebbs and flows of twentieth-century liberalism as an ideology and to discern, as best as one can with a set of fluid ideas and values, the philosophical and economic step-change within liberalism toward the welfare state. Second, the chapter addresses the controversial relationship between New Labour and neoliberalism with regards to the welfare state. The question here, in essence, is to what extent did New Labour *neoliberalize* welfare? The argument deployed asserts that the economic and social data pertaining to core public services and entitlements of the welfare state during the Blair and Brown governments points to a less cut-and-dried classification than *neoliberalization.* Third, the chapter charts the influence of *liberalisms* on the welfare state. This is valuable because it is the neoliberal reaction to the welfare state and Keynesian assumptions of managed capitalism that aided the proliferation of its ideas and reset the direction of liberalism to a pre-1945 orientation.

6.2. The Emergence of Neoliberalism in British Politics

Neoliberalism is commonly understood as a variant of classical liberalism that emerged in postwar Britain in reaction to the social democratic state. The social democratic state is predicated on a set of political ideas including positive liberty, community, greater social and economic equality, and social justice. Chief among the institutions that comprise the social democratic state is the broad range of publicly funded goods and services collectively termed the welfare state. In his book *The Neo-liberal State*, Raymond Plant suggests that "the welfare state has been seen by social democrats as an instrument of greater social justice understood as greater social equality" (2010, 116). These ideas for the need to provide welfare in a capitalist economy to protect individual liberty and to promote social justice and egalitarianism conflict and collide with the ideas that underpin neoliberalism, in particular, the idea that individual liberty can be anything other than freedom from the absence of coercion or control (Hayek 1973) and that social injustice exists in any meaningful sense (Hayek 1976). This "new" or *neo*liberalism was found in both the Liberal and Conservative Parties, and its common adversary was the Labour Party, whose collectivist ethos and radical governments of Attlee sought to transform the economy and society of Britain from 1945 to 1951 (see Peden in this volume).

Speaking of the antipathy toward liberalism in the intellectual climate in Nazi Germany and wartime Britain, Hayek says, "There is the same contempt for nineteenth century liberalism, the same spurious 'realism' and even cynicism, the same fatalistic acceptance of 'inevitable trends'" (Hayek 1944, 3). Hayek does not for one moment believe that as societies Nazi Germany and wartime Britain are morally equivalent or politically the same. He is making the point that aspects of socialist ideology that underpin Nazi fascism were present within the intellectual classes of wartime Britain because they too are inherent in democratic socialism. The ideological ingredients in both democratic and nondemocratic socialist conceptions of the ideal society are a large and active role for the state apparatus, social and economic planning, and reticence toward individualism and free-market capitalism.

Much initial intellectual work in the proliferation of free-market ideas was performed by the Institute of Economic Affairs (IEA), established in 1955 under the initial leadership of Antony Fisher and subsequently aided by Ralph Harris and Arthur Seldon (Muller 1996). To this day the IEA contains both Conservatives and Liberals, but by the 1970s its antiplanning, anti-Keynesianism, and free-market solutions to economic and social problems were more keenly embraced by a significant proportion of the parliamentary Conservative Party than the parliamentary Liberal Party. The ideological shoots of neoliberalism in British government arguably broke ground inauspiciously when Chancellor Peter Thorneycroft and his Treasury team of Enoch Powell and Nigel Birch resigned from Macmillan's government in 1958 over the issue of public expenditure in the face of rising inflation. These Conservatives, later seen as early free-marketers, lost the argument of the day, but their economic and political assumptions won some support within the Conservative Party. Evidence of what could be explained as frustration and impatience with the mixed economy approach of successive Labour and Conservative administrations is noted by E. H. H. Green, who argues that free-market views were increasing among Conservative activists by the 1960s (Green 2006, 39).

The most influential convert to neoliberalism in frontline Conservative politics was the member of Parliament for Leeds North-West from 1956 to 1987, Sir Keith Joseph. Joseph was a moderate Conservative for approximately the first half of his career, but his political conversion came during a period in opposition to the Wilson-Callaghan governments of 1974–79 and owed much to the IEA. In the face of myriad British economic and social difficulties, neoliberalism's counterarguments about the role of government in industry, the power of the trade unions, the limitations of Keynesianism concerning inflation and the pursuit of growth, and both the fiscal and social cost of comprehensive welfare provision received a wider audience, and one of its most careful listeners was Joseph. Once convinced of the need for the Conservative Party to change tack, Joseph began to proselytize the virtues of his newfound faith through the establishment in 1974 of the Centre for Policy Studies (CPS), as a research center for neoliberal public policy and, also in that year, through a series of radical speeches that sought to set out the philosophical direction that the Conservative Party ought to take (Joseph 1976). Joseph's role in the story of the emergence of neoliberalism in Britain is of central import not because he attained one of the great offices of state or rose to lead his party—though he considered challenging Edward Heath before deciding against it—but because of his direct and long-lasting influence upon Margaret Thatcher. He stood shoulder to shoulder with her as she challenged and successfully defeated Heath in 1975, and together they began to gradually change Conservative policy. Thatcher states that she had an early understanding of free trade and markets from working in her father's grocers shop: "There is no better course for understanding free-market economics than life in a corner shop" (Thatcher 1995, 566). However, the friendship and intellectual influence of Joseph many years later galvanized Thatcher's political economy and helped translate it into a political vision of Conservatism that drew in large measure from nineteenth-century liberalism and located it in debates about Britain's relative decline, the scale of bureaucracy, the trade union problem, and the growth in the size and cost of the central state. Joseph's role was to help provide the ideational framework for Thatcher's political agenda. Speaking of the neoliberal Conservative conviction that she and Joseph held, Thatcher asserts:

> The kind of Conservatism which he and I—though coming from very different backgrounds—favoured would be best described as "liberal" in the old-fashioned sense. And I mean the liberalism of Mr Gladstone not of the latter day collectivists. (Thatcher 1996, 5)

Thatcher, with President Ronald Regan, embodied the politics of neoliberalism in the democratic world. Despite their respective parties being avowedly and historically conservative, the approaches to economic and welfare policy of Thatcherism and Reaganism can be described as projects predicated on liberal assumptions of free markets and individualism. Of course, Thatcherism and Reaganism were not simply projects hijacking liberalism for an era of popular conservative rule. Both "isms" were part of the New Right conservative movement that harnessed neoliberal economics to a brand of social conservatism and an aggressive anticommunism (Levitas 1988).

In her first term the cabinet was a balance between neoliberals and One Nation Tories, but Thatcher managed to make some policy breaks with the past. For example, in 1979 her government immediately introduced monetarism to replace Keynesianism and, by ending exchange controls and wages and prices policies, supplanted economic planning with free-market mechanisms (Sked and Cook 1993). With the general election of 1983 the political expediency of balancing her cabinet was much less necessary for Thatcher. It proved to be a political watershed for neoliberalism in Britain, producing a majority of 144. This landslide electoral victory established a significant new group of Conservative MPs in to the House of Commons, MPs who could be viewed as "Mrs. Thatcher Conservatives" or "Thatcherites." In the following general election of 1987, the Conservatives under Thatcher won their third consecutive victory, and, once again, she delivered a landslide victory despite the fact that the Conservative majority was reduced to 102 seats. Thatcherism, as the dominant perspective of the parliamentary Conservative Party, had arrived and, to this day, continues to define Conservatives in British politics. The governments of Thatcher from 1983 to 1990 successfully implemented neoliberal public policy that altered the established postwar settlement of welfare capitalism. Among the most significant public policy changes in this period were industrial relations reform, privatizations of public corporations and utilities, continued reduction of income tax rates, and the "poll tax" (Sked and Cook 1993).

It is necessary in this discussion of the emergence and rise of neoliberalism in British politics to note three things that relate to neoliberalism in the period after Thatcher. First, her successor, John Major, led Conservative governments from 1990 to 1997, including winning the Conservative's fourth consecutive general election in 1992. Major continued with the party's adopted neoliberal agenda and arguably furthered its mission with the introduction of the internal market in the NHS; abolition of the National Economic Development Council and the Wages Council; and the privatization of British Rail (Dorey 1999). Second, neoliberal economics became embedded in many countries, especially within Anglo-Saxon societies (Hutton 1996). Third, and with the previous point in mind, neoliberalism affected the generation of leading Labour politicians who emerged in the early 1990s. Blair and Brown were shaped in part by the strength of neoliberal arguments advocated by the Thatcher and Major administrations, especially on the issues of trade union reform, direct taxation, the City of London, and the efficiency of markets. It is this final point that moves the discussion on to the question of the ideological provenance of New Labour in relation to neoliberalism and its approach toward the welfare state. While the Bevanite socialism of Michael Foot with its commitment to widespread nationalization of industry, corporatism, and very high rates of direct taxation has been consigned to British political history, it is quite a different thing to suggest that moderate social democratic politics—with its focus on welfare capitalism—suffered the same fate in the wake of Thatcherism.

6.3. New Labour and the Neoliberalization of Welfare

New Labour was the leading tendency within the Labour Party and the dominant player in British politics for approximately a decade and a half (Beech 2008). Comprising at first a modestly sized group of reformist Labour MPs and supporters, it arguably grew to include all those who accepted invitations to serve in the governments of Tony Blair (1997–2007) and Gordon Brown (2007–10). Some Labour MPs would resist such categorization and suggest they were serving the country through a Labour rather than a New Labour administration. Be that as it may, New Labour began as a group of party modernizers around the one-time friendship of Blair and Brown and included Labour Party workers and future MPs Peter Mandelson, Ed Balls, David Miliband, the pollster Philip Gould, and spin doctors Alastair Campbell and Charlie Whelan. Over time, two devoted factions emerged around the principal figures and their perceived distinctive approach to Labour modernization: one more enthusiastic about the use of market mechanisms in public sector reform, the law and order agenda, and the euro; the other less so. This did not amount to a stark philosophical divide as much as a difference of judgment on certain issues. Through a combination of Blair's dynamic leadership, a weary and ineffective Conservative Party, successful communication of an aspirational political narrative, and a well-organized party machine, New Labour's landslide electoral triumph in 1997 grew into the most identifiable and controversial political project—both at home and abroad—since Thatcherism.

The argument of this part of the chapter is that New Labour operated an ideologically modified welfare state when compared to previous Labour governments in the postwar era, but the ideas underpinning the management of core public services and entitlements are within the traditions of British social democracy. There is a *majority view* within the established scholarship that miscategorizes New Labour and its approach to the welfare state. The case of evaluating New Labour requires greater nuance, as the data in fact points to a blend of neoliberal and social democratic influences. This is termed the *minority view*.

Why then do many scholars consider New Labour's approach as the *neoliberalization* of welfare? Undoubtedly, the first and overarching reason is because New Labour is interpreted as a neoliberal project predicated upon economic liberalism (Hay 1999; Heffernan 2001; Hall 2003; Lee 2007; Faucher-King and Le Galès 2010). Economic liberalism gives primacy to free-market ideas and considers state intervention in the economy to be often counterproductive in terms of efficiency and bureaucracy and that an interventionist state is usually a "growing state" that, in turn, pushes entrepreneurs out of the marketplace and, by so doing, reduces the capacity for wealth creation. This "growing state" is expensive and requires increasing levels of funding through high taxes that take money from the private sector of the economy and, crucially, undermine individual liberty, preventing citizens from using their money as they see fit. The welfare state is considered to be profligate and an obstacle of liberty, both for those who receive welfare and those on whom taxes are levied to cover its cost (many citizens fall into both categories simultaneously).

Social democratic and New Liberal attitudes toward welfare are generally taken as more generous toward citizens in need of assistance than economic liberal attitudes. Within Labour circles, the role of the conditionality of specific welfare benefits divides social democrats. Those who view access to the welfare state as a right of citizenship deem tougher conditionality on unemployment assistance as unfair. Those who view access to the welfare state as part of a reciprocal relationship between state and citizen based on financial contributions over time are more likely to support conditionality for certain benefits, such as unemployment assistance. This can be loosely understood as a disagreement between liberal and communitarian social democrats.

While New Labour and its allied think tanks—Progress and Policy Network—might not advocate full-blooded economic liberalism of the like associated with Thatcherite Conservatism, the core vision of a free-market economy, as opposed to a mixed economy consisting of a large state sector and a tightly regulated profit-making sector, summarizes the economic worldview of such progressives. Economic liberal perspectives and those of its younger cousin neoliberalism sit within progressive politics in the Labour Party, but they do not cohere with the political economy of social democrats. Interestingly, Blair states in his memoirs, "I represented in office . . . liberal economic policies, market reforms in welfare and public services, and engagement and intervention abroad" (Blair 2010, 665), and in his foreword to Philip Gould's updated edition of *The Unfinished Revolution* he self-identifies his politics as progressive (Blair 2011). For the prime figure in the New Labour project, the liberal economy with its approach to welfare and public services is part and parcel of progressive politics. For the British Left, this—as much as the Iraq War—is why Blair is the most controversial Labour prime minister of the postwar era. New Labour's protagonist endorses economic liberalism, albeit by the term *liberal economics*, and therefore it is understandable why a *majority view* exists that categorizes New Labour's approach to British politics in general, and welfare in particular, as part of a continuous flow of neoliberalism from Thatcher. Colin Hay argues that British politics has experienced "the politics of conspicuous convergence" (1999, 140). Neoliberalism can be argued to have become paradigmatic in British political economy because no major party until the great financial crash was arguing for a return to Keynesian demand management or proposing to overhaul the regulation of the financial sector.

However, the nub of the issue lies in the degree to which the *majority view* provides a full account of the dominance of neoliberalism in British politics and, by implication, the extent to which New Labour abandoned social democratic ideas and policy including the welfare state. Other contemporary historians take an alternate view (Fielding 2002; Meredith 2006; Tonge 2010). The *minority view* asserted here contends that while the *majority view* is accurate with regards to New Labour's political economy in terms of finance capital, direct taxation, and the use of market mechanisms to deliver public services, the available economic and social data suggests that New Labour operated a discernible social democratic approach to welfare.

Evidence to support this claim comes in the form of several key factors that when aggregated reveal a fuller picture. First, New Labour's degree of interventionism in terms of public policy and public spending denotes an active, robust approach to state management and a belief that there is a strong role for the state in society and the economy with the exception of the financial sector (Beech 2008). Second, such state interventionism is predicated on a conception of social justice that seeks to mitigate the injustice of market outcomes and personal misfortune. The chief method of measuring how just a society is by the degree of poverty and, in particular, the degree of relative poverty. According to analysis by the Institute for Fiscal Studies evaluating New Labour's record on poverty reduction,

> Relative poverty has fallen since Labour came to power, falling most for pensioners and children. This contrasts with a rise in poverty observed under the previous period of Conservative government between 1979 and 1997. (Joyce et al. 2010, 64)

However, it ought to be stated that while significant reductions in poverty occurred, inequality between incomes increased marginally (Brewer, Phillips, and Sibieta 2010). Third, given both New Labour's interventionist statecraft and its commitment to reducing poverty, it is apparent that public expenditure was the key fiscal instrument. It is argued that this demonstrates intentionality to utilize social expenditure for collective betterment and to give priority to the poorest neighborhoods, families, and individuals (Mullard and Swaray 2010). In an international comparative study of public expenditure during the New Labour years the Institute for Fiscal Studies found the following:

> In 1997, out of the 28 countries for which we have comparable information, the UK had the 22nd largest level of public spending as a share of national income. Most countries have increased public spending as a share of national income since then but the increase in the UK has been the largest. As a result the UK is now estimated to have the 6th largest level of public spending as a proportion of national income. (Chote et al. 2010, 5)

During the governments of Blair and Brown public expenditure on healthcare rose from 6.1 percent to 7.9 percent of GDP, and education expenditure rose from 4.5 percent to 5.6 percent of GDP (Mullard and Swaray 2010, 514–15), while expenditure on social security benefits was 13.4 percent of GDP in 2010–11 (Chote et al. 2010, 3). It is therefore clear that these three factors counter the *majority view* of New Labour's *neoliberalization* of the welfare state.

6.4. The Influence of Liberalisms on the Welfare State

If we accept that neoliberalism is related to classical liberalism of the nineteenth century, we can look for family resemblances and find a strong attachment to free markets, individualism, a negative conception of liberty and the desire for a limited state. However, the family of liberalism is large and diverse and includes the strand of political and social thinking offered by J. S. Mill (Mill 1859) and then by the New Liberalism of the late nineteenth century, inspired in large part by the ideas of T. H. Green (Green 1906) and, transmitted in the Edwardian era, by the likes of J. A. Hobson (Hobson 1902) and L. T. Hobhouse (Hobhouse 1911). These liberals contended that for liberty to be meaningful in Britain's Victorian and Edwardian capitalist society, with its widespread poverty and insecurity, the state ought to be utilized as an instrument for the common good; in other words the state should seek to guarantee positive liberty for those citizens and their dependents in distress by providing them with certain economic goods and services. The governments of Henry Campbell-Bannerman (1906–8) and Herbert Henry Asquith (1908–1914) are examples of the New Liberalism, and notable policy prescriptions included free school meals, national insurance, and old-age pensions. However, with the advent of New Liberalism classical liberalism did not wither. Economically, the early twentieth century remained firmly a period of laissez-faire capitalism with more social protection for the poor on the statute books. The defining historical event that separates the eras in which New Liberalism and neoliberalism flowered in Britain is World War II. As a consequence of the war a different politics and economics occurred that was informed by New Liberal assumptions about an active state and partly, though not exclusively, coauthored by two men grounded in its particular school of thought: John Maynard Keynes and William Beveridge.

The postwar years up until the emergence of Conservative neoliberalism were shaped by the Attlee governments and the social democratic state they implemented. New Liberalism's contribution here was threefold. First, there had been much intermingling by New Liberals and Fabian socialists in the opening three decades of the twentieth century with some former Liberals joining the Labour Party and others remaining in the Liberal Party but contributing to the intellectual conversation on the moderate left of British politics (Clarke 1978). Second, the economic doctrine of Keynesian demand management was adopted in peacetime by Attlee's administration, and this provided Labour with a sophisticated political economy where previously there had been a paucity of ideas outside of orthodox precepts that the 1929–31 government led by Ramsay MacDonald followed (Beech 2006). Third, Labour implemented the Beveridge report and, in fact, built upon its recommendations to establish a more comprehensive, universal welfare state (Page 2007). Therefore, despite the Liberal Party's absence from power, the influence of the ideology of liberalism, and New Liberalism in particular, was notable for much of the postwar era in British politics (see Peden in this volume).

The emergence of neoliberalism in the mid-1970s within the Conservative Party did much to promulgate a historic liberalism in British politics. For neoliberals the practical limitations of a comprehensive welfare state relate to its sustained cost and drain on manpower; its moral limitations concern them in the form of a dependency culture for some citizens; and the philosophical stumbling block amounts to a category error advanced by "positive libertarians." In the following quotation, Hayek contrasts the classical and neoliberal view of society with the social democratic view. He implies that the demand for social justice—which drives the social democrats' approach to governance and provides their motivation for the maintenance of the welfare state—is demanded by an elite of unspecified agents who use the levers of the state to shape the lives of citizens according to their plan for social justice:

> It might indeed be said that the main difference between the order of society at which classical liberalism aimed and the sort of society into which it is now being transformed is that the former was governed by principles of just individual conduct while the new society is to satisfy the demands for "social justice" or, in other words, that the former demanded just action by the individuals while the latter more and more places the duty of justice on authorities with power to command people what to do. (Hayek 1976, 65–66)

But if neoliberals such as Hayek object to the comprehensive welfare state fashioned by social democrats, then what form of social safety net would be permissible in a society of "just individual conduct"? Plant explains what an ideal type neoliberal welfare state might look like:

> The neo-liberal welfare state is not inspired by social justice; it is limited in scope; it is not designed to change relative positions of individuals and groups within society; it embodies a view of negative liberty; it is compatible only with a set of negative rights; it does not seek the achievement of specific ends such as social justice or social solidarity and in this respect is nomocratic rather than telocratic; it operates with a modest level of bureaucracy; and it is not involved in the direct provision of welfare itself but is limited to a funding and commissioning role. (Plant 2010, 250)

On reading the quotations from Hayek and Plant about a neoliberal vision of welfare it is clear that Britain's welfare state is quite different. The welfare polices of Blair and Brown were redistributive and so sought to implement a vision of social justice and therefore were predicated on a positive conception of liberty. While conditionality was increased for unemployment benefit, the welfare state received record investment. New Labour did, however, continue the market-led reforms that encouraged a plurality of providers of public goods and services funded by the state because they had been convinced by the argument that competitive markets drive up standards, are efficient, and perpetuate consumer choice. With this marketplace came league tables, performance targets, and a less anodyne view of public sector professionals. One could see the influence of neoliberal ideas in this aspect of New Labour's welfare provision. This is distinct from traditional social democratic and New Liberal attitudes about the public provision of key services.

The Conservative-Liberal coalition of 2010–15 placed neoliberal ideas and values back at the heart of discussions over public policy. The Institute for Fiscal Studies estimated that the combined effect of the 2010 Emergency Budget and the 2010 Comprehensive Spending Review on welfare spending equated to a £20 billion reduction by 2017–18 (Emmerson and Tetlow 2012, 17).

6.5. Conclusion

The evolution of liberalism in the second half of the twentieth century profoundly influenced the Conservative Party and New Labour. Before then, New Liberal and social democratic ideas dominated the practice of interventionist government, managed capitalism, and the welfare state. In a sense, the post-war moderate Left was a victim of its own success. Old ideas and traditional emphases of English liberalism fell out of fashion except on the fringes of the Conservative and Liberal Parties. There they waited, organized and industrious. As the electorate's expectations rose, in terms of what the social democratic state could provide, the financial costs and the unintended consequence of a dependency culture seized the mind of liberal critics. With the Thatcher revolution a new form of classical liberalism emerged and has not departed frontline politics.

While New Labour contained elements of neoliberal reasoning in its attitude to welfare, it sought through its interventionist statecraft to mitigate the negative externalities of the market economy and give greatest support and priority to the poorest citizens. Therefore, it is most accurate to describe New Labour as a blend of ideological influences, and, in its management of the welfare state, the most recognizable influence was a form of moderate social democracy.

Are the main political parties all neoliberal now? The Conservative Party, the Liberal Democrats, and the Labour Party—to greater or lesser extent—have been affected by neoliberal ideas. In the case of the Conservative Party one can talk of a full-scale takeover. With the Liberal Democrats, the classically liberal right wing enjoyed a prominent position during the leadership of Nick Clegg (2007–15). Clegg's tenure provided the necessary ideological conviction—which enabled partnership through a full parliament with David Cameron's Conservative Party—for the liberal-inspired coalition (Beech 2015). For the Labour Party, New Labour continues to exist in both the Blairite and Brownite groupings of MPs. Under the leadership of Ed Miliband (2010–15) a conscious effort was made to step away from New Labour. This was evident in pronouncements on the Iraq War, immigration, taxation, and the role of markets. The future for a more economically liberal center-left offering is uncertain, as Labour Party activists are unsurprisingly to the left of where Blair and Brown were situated. The difficulty for future Labour leaders will be how to reach out to floating voters, especially in marginal constituencies, and at the same time galvanize the party base. While conservatism and democratic socialism discus ideas and values in British politics, their intellectual purchase is subordinate to neoliberalism, which continues to be one of two defining ideologies in British politics, the other being moderate social democracy. This battle for ideational pre-eminence was evident throughout the New Labour years and spilled over into the management of the welfare state. It is most likely that these two perspectives—each with an antecedent in a form of liberalism—will continue to vie for the right to reshape and reform the welfare state in their own image.

Acknowledgments

I would like to thank Dr. Matthew Francis for inviting me to present a version of this chapter at a joint Centre for British Politics (University of Nottingham) and Centre for Political Ideologies (Oxford University) workshop on June 15, 2011, in Oxford entitled "A Permanent Revolution? Neo-liberalism and British Politics." I would also like to warmly thank Professor Tamotsu Nishizawa for inviting me to the Institute of Economic Research at Hitotsubashi University to give a research seminar on this subject on February 14, 2012. I am grateful to colleagues at both events for their feedback. I would also like to acknowledge the four anonymous reviewers for their comments and suggestions on an earlier draft. Any errors are of course my own.

References

Addison, P. 1975. *The Road to 1945*. London: Quartet Books.

Beech, M. 2006. *The Political Philosophy of New Labour*. New York: IB Tauris.

Beech, M. 2008. "New Labour and the Politics of Dominance." In M. Beech and S. Lee, eds., *Ten Years of New Labour*, 1–16. Basingstoke: Palgrave Macmillan.

Beech, M. 2015. 'The Ideology of the Coalition: More Liberal Than Conservative." In M. Beech and S. Lee, eds., *The Conservative-Liberal Coalition: Examining the Cameron-Clegg Government*, 1–15. Basingstoke: Palgrave Macmillan.

Blair, T. 2006. "Our Nation's Future—Social Exclusion." Speech to the Joseph Rowntree Foundation, York, September, 5.

Blair, T. 2010. *A Journey*. London: Hutchinson.

Blair, T. 2011. Foreword to P. Gould, *The Unfinished Revolution: How New Labour Changed British Politics For Ever*, ix–xxvi. London, Abacus.

Brewer, M., D. Phillips, and L. Sibieta. 2010. *Living Standards, Inequality and Poverty: Labour's Record*. 2010 Election Briefing Note No. 2 (IFSBN89). London: Institute for Fiscal Studies.

Campbell, J. 2001. *Margaret Thatcher*. Vol. 1: *The Grocer's Daughter*. London: Pimlico.

Chote, R., R. Crawford, C. Emmerson, and G. Tetlow. 2010. *Public Spending under Labour*. 2010 Election Briefing Note No. 5 (IFS BN92). London: Institute for Fiscal Studies.

Clarke, P. 1978. *Liberals and Social Democrats*. Cambridge: Cambridge University Press.

Dorey, P. 1999. "Despair and Disillusion Abound: The Major Premiership in Perspective." In P. Dorey, ed., *The Major Premiership: Politics and Policies under John Major, 1990–1997*, 218–49. Basingstoke: Palgrave.

Emmerson, C., and G. Tetlow. 2012. *Autumn Statement 2012: More Fiscal Pain to Come?* London: Institute for Fiscal Studies.

Faucher-King, F., and P. Le Galès. 2010. *The New Labour Experiment: Change and Reform under Blair and Brown*. Stanford, CA: Stanford University Press.

Fielding, S. 2002. *The Labour Party: Continuity and Change in the Making of New Labour*. Basingstoke: Palgrave Macmillan.

Gould, P. 2011. *The Unfinished Revolution: How New Labour Changed British Politics For Ever*. London: Abacus.

Green, E. H. H. 2006. *Thatcher*. London: Hodder Arnold.

Green, T. H. 1906. *Prolegomena to Ethics*. Oxford: Clarendon Press.

Hall, S. 2003. "New Labour's Double-Shuffle." *Soundings* 24 (July): 10–24.

Hay, C. 1999. *The Political Economy of New Labour: Labouring under False Pretences*. Manchester: Manchester University Press.

Hayek, F. A. 1944. *The Road to Serfdom*. London: George Routledge and Sons.

Hayek, F. A. 1973. *Law, Legislation and Liberty*, Vol. 1: *Rules and Order*. London: Routledge and Kegan Paul.

Hayek, F. A. 1976. *Law, Legislation and Liberty*. Vol. 2: *The Mirage of Social Justice*. London: Routledge and Kegan Paul.

Heffernan, R. 2001. *New Labour and Thatcherism*. Basingstoke: Palgrave Macmillan.

Hobhouse, L. T. 1911. *Liberalism*. London: Thornton Butterworth.

Hobson, J. A. 1902. *Imperialism: A Study*. London: James Nisbet.

Hutton, W. 1996. *The State We're In*. London: Vintage.

Joseph, K. 1976. *Stranded on the Middle Ground*. London: Centre for Policy Studies.

Joyce, R., A. Muriel, D. Phillips, and L. Sibieta. 2010. *Poverty and Inequality in the UK: 2010*. IFS Commentary C116. London: Institute for Fiscal Studies.

Lee, S. 2007. *Best for Britain? The Politics and Legacy of Gordon Brown*. Oxford: OneWorld.

Levitas, R. 1988. Introduction to R. Levitas, ed., *The Ideology of the New Right*, 1–24. Cambridge: Polity Press.

Meredith, S. 2006. "Mr Crosland's Nightmare? New Labour and Equality in Historical Perspective." *British Journal of Politics and International Relations* 8 (2): 238–55.

Mill, J. S. 1859. *On Liberty*. London: John Parker & Son.

Mullard, M., and R. Swaray. 2010. "New Labour Legacy: Comparing the Labour Governments of Blair and Brown to Labour Governments since 1945." *Political Quarterly* 81 (4): 511–21.

Muller, C. 1996. "The Institute of Economic Affairs: Undermining the Post-war Consensus." *Contemporary British History* 10 (1): 88–110.

Page, R. 2007. *Revisiting the Welfare State*. Maidenheads: Open University Press.

Pimlott, B. 1988. "The Myth of Consensus." In L. M. Smith, ed., *The Making of Britain: Echoes in Greatness*, 129–41. Basingstoke: Macmillan.

Plant, R. 2010. *The Neo-liberal State*. Oxford: Oxford University Press.

Sked, A., and C. Cook. 1993. *Post-war Britain: A Political History, 1945–1992*. 4th ed. Harmondsworth: Penguin.

Thatcher, M. 1995. *The Path to Power*. London: HarperCollins.

Thatcher, M. 1996. *The Keith Joseph Memorial Lecture: Liberty and Limited Government*. London: Centre for Policy Studies.

Tonge, J. 2010. "Did Blair Advance Social Democracy?" In S. Griffiths and K. Hickson, eds., *British Party Politics and Ideology after New Labour*, 24–29. Basingstoke: Palgrave Macmillan.

7 The Initiative for a New Social-Market Economy and the Transformation of the German Welfare Regime after Unification

DANIEL KINDERMAN

7.1. Introduction

This chapter focuses on how business interests and neoliberal ideas have come together in Germany in the past two decades. It is based on a detailed analysis of the Initiative Neue Soziale Marktwirtschaft (INSM) or New Social Market Initiative, a large-scale campaign founded in 2000 and funded by the metal industry employers' association Gesamtmetall[1] to shape public opinion. Since its founding, the INSM has done much to bolster the economic reform and liberalization agenda in Germany. Gesamtmetall gave the INSM a clear mandate to propagate and popularize ordoliberal/neoliberal ideas and reforms. To date, Gesamtmetall's regional employers' associations have spent in excess of 150 million euros to fund the INSM's activities.[2] In its attempt to influence public opinion, the INSM draws on advertisements, events, scientific studies, and an extensive online presence.[3] As a business-led public relations campaign, the purpose of the INSM is to influence public opinion and policymaking rather than to develop new economic ideas. The INSM's founders, as well as many of its leading figures, are business officials and politicians pursuing market-oriented reforms. Nevertheless, as we will see, a group of economists—the core of which is associated the Mont Pèlerin Society—have also actively supported and campaigned for the INSM. And there can be no doubt regarding its main object of critique: the welfare state. During the past 17 years, the INSM has launched a systematic attack on the German welfare state while also endorsing austerity policies at the EU level, anglophone-inspired neoliberal ideas, and more ordoliberal policy prescriptions.

The evidence suggests that there are elective affinities between German ordoliberal/neoliberal economists and business interests, and that there is a lot of support for the liberalization of the welfare state and the labor market in the leading sectors of the German economy. Claims advanced by the influential varieties-of-capitalism (VofC) literature (Hall and Soskice 2001) that German employers have an overriding preference for nonliberal institutions or that their defense of traditional institutions constrains liberalization are hard to sustain. Indeed, this chapter points to a serious problem with the academic literature that characterizes Germany as an exemplar of "nonliberal" capitalism or as "a 'model' for countries unwilling to subject themselves to the rule of the market in the same way and to the same extent as Anglo-American economies" (Streeck 2009, 21): the positions of leading German business officials and economists are fundamentally and unmistakably liberal. We can call their preferred economic model the "German variety of neoliberalism" (Ptak 2009, 126).

But there are variations on this theme: the articulation of business interests through the INSM changes over time. During the initial period (2000–2006), the INSM was an outspoken and influential advocate of far-reaching institutional change. The INSM played a proactive and agenda-setting role, and many of its positions were radical and point to a shift toward an anglophone-liberal market economy-style model. This suggests that employers wanted to go further than the Agenda 2010 reforms. But since 2006 and especially 2008–9, the INSM has been forced to adapt to changes in public opinion and electoral politics. In this period, the INSM's campaigns have become more moderate and defensive. Following the discrediting of the Anglo-American model in the financial crisis, significant wage repression by German employees and the unexpected revitalization and resurgence of the German economy, employers may have rediscovered the virtues of ordoliberalism and of the (new) German model. While this suggests that the social-market economy is a versatile, flexible, and supple ideological construct, it is unclear whether this shift in the INSM's communications represents a shift in employers' underlying interests. As we will see, during these years the INSM sought to defend and consolidate the reform agenda in the domestic realm while simultaneously advocating stringent austerity measures at the EU-level.

The organization of this chapter is as follows. The second section discusses the INSM's origins in the late 1990s. The third section describes the INSM's programmatic agenda and the involvement of some key economists. The fourth section discusses the INSM's push for liberalization between 2003 and 2005. The fifth section addresses the INSM's apparent moderation after 2006 as well as its push for stringent austerity policies during the European banking and sovereign debt crises. The sixth section concludes the chapter.

7.2. The Origins of the INSM in the Late 1990s

We were at a dead end (*in einer Sackgasse*) . . . there were more and more recessive tendencies.

—*Volker Fasbender, managing director of Hessenmetall and one of the INSM's founding figures*

Political and economic considerations led Gesamtmetall to set up the INSM. By the mid-1990s, the survival of the German model was in question: Germany was mired in "a deep structural crisis" (Creutzburg, interview 2013) and a "catastrophic equilibrium" of rising unemployment and high nonwage labor costs (Dyson 2005). A climate of *Reformstau* lay over the whole country, and deteriorating economic conditions led to a growing discontentment in the business community (Streeck 2005).

According to the INSM's founders, rising levels of social protection were the underlying cause of these pathologies (Brocker and Fasbender, interviews 2013). As Brocker, founder of the INSM and former managing director of Südwestmetall and Gesamtmetall recalls, "Contributions to unemployment insurance became more expensive, competition was growing, and the pressure became harder. . . . Eventually the advantages that Germany enjoyed were used up" (interview 2013). Yet instead of taking decisive steps to address these problems, politicians implemented costly new welfare state programs to please voters. Employers failed to halt the implementation of long-term care insurance in the early 1990s, which "catalyzed [employers'] strategic reorientation from accommodation to assertiveness. . . . Employers realized that reacting to proposals by other actors was not enough to defend their interests; they had to try to define the reform agenda proactively" (Paster 2012a, 168).

For Brocker, the 1996 conflict over reductions in sick pay from 100 percent to 80 percent was clear evidence of the public's hostility to reforms (interview 2013). Unions protested, and the SPD vowed that it would reverse the cuts—which it did once in office. The public's hostility toward reforms contributed to Helmut Kohl's 1998 election loss. The views of the general population and of companies were drifting further and further apart, and discontentment within business was growing. As a result of these growing pressures, the INSM could have been founded as early as the mid-1990s (Fasbender, interview 2013); but a public opinion poll in the summer of 1999 proved decisive. The poll showed that German citizens mistrusted business and the market and supported a generous welfare state. Two-thirds of respondents viewed the prospect of upcoming economic reforms with attitudes ranging from "skepticism" to "fear," (Gesellschaft im Zwiespalt 2000, 16), and 42 percent favored a "third way" between capitalism and socialism (Speth 2004, 7).

Gesamtmetall founded the INSM to influence the broader institutional environment and public opinion climate[4] and in order to "get our fellow citizens to recognize what we see as necessary reforms as a positive reform." It was necessary to take proactive steps to inform the public and "halt the decline/demise (*Niedergang*)" (Fasbender, interview 2013) of the country that was underway:

> Beginning in the 1960s there was an increasing entitlement mentality, more and more demands on society and less and less individual responsibility. . . . The point [of the INSM] was to connect the social market economy with the essentials of entrepreneurial activity: competition, competitiveness, flexibility. All of this contradicts welfare state thinking that focuses on protection, excessive rigidity (*Betonierung*), and all that. (Brocker, interview 2013)

There was also a political dimension. Employers were concerned that Chancellor Gerhard Schröder's newly elected Red-Green government, with its left-wing finance minister, Oskar Lafontaine, would pursue an antibusiness and redistributive agenda. The INSM was founded to ensure that even under a Red-Green government, employers could pass laws that were employer- and business-friendly. Brocker's ideas had struck a chord; with the support of Südwestmetall executive Dieter Hundt and Gesamtmetall president Werner Stumpfe, Hessenmetall joined on, as did Gesamtmetall as a whole, along with many large and small firms (Engemann, interview 2013; Vajna, personal communication, January 5, 2015).[5] In 1999, the advertising company Scholz & Friends was selected to organize the public relations. The INSM began its work on June 1, 2000.

7.3. The Agenda of the INSM and the Involvement of Economists

The INSM campaign is entitled the *neue soziale Marktwirtschaft*—the "New Social Market Economy"—although its goal is to restore the "old" social-market economy (Kinderman 2005).[6] The social-market economy is the founding myth of the Federal Republic of Germany (Haselbach 1997). For ordoliberals in the 1950s, the term stood for the view that free-market competition is the best way to achieve social goals (Paster 2012a). The prominence and currency of "social-market economy" discourse in Germany is remarkable. As Haselbach emphasizes, "The tale of the 'social market economy' . . . is referred to almost every day, somewhere in a German newspaper or political statement; it has become part of the national memory" (1997, 161). The genius of the social-market economy lies in its versatility: it is both "social" (fair/just) and a "[capitalist] market." The INSM is focused on the disjuncture between the historically evolved social-market economy and its ideational origins. As Ralf Ptak points out, "Since the trade unions and the Social Democratic Party learned to use the concept in the same opportunistic way as ordoliberals, persuading governments to expand the welfare state under continuous reference to the social-market economy, the model increasingly lost its original neoliberal content" (2009, 125).

The INSM's founders have sought to move Germany's discourse, policy, and institutions closer to the social-market economy's ordoliberal origins. Just as ordoliberalism's founders "were hostile in principle towards social welfare as a state responsibility" (Haselbach 1997, 172), the INSM is suffused with a thoroughly liberal ethos. As Fasbender remarks, "Freedom is the central value of the social-market economy" (interview 2013). While many German citizens associate the social-market economy with the welfare state or *Vater Staat*, the INSM's founder, Ulrich Brocker, states that he is "for the social-market economy but against the welfare state" (interview 2013). Randolf Rodenstock concurs. As president of the Bavarian employers' and metalworking industry association, vice president of Gesamtmetall and a member of the Mont Pèlerin Society (MPS), Rodenstock writes that "the social market economy has gotten out of balance over the years. . . . Instead of promoting self-reliance," he chides, "Germany has developed into a welfare state" (Rodenstock 2009). Indeed, a common ideological orientation is not the only thing the INSM shares with early ordoliberal thought. While the INSM and its campaigns are innovative in many ways, employers' use of public relations and advertising to popularize and legitimize the economic ideas and ideology of ordoliberalism and the social-market economy is far from new: these very methods were used in the early 1950s, in the early years of the Federal Republic (see Schindelbeck and Ilgen 1999). In this sense, and given its intellectual pedigree, the INSM can also be seen as a return to the past.

Rodenstock's book *Chancen für Alle* is centered on the idea of equality of opportunity in free markets (Rodenstock 2001). Readers are introduced to the "visionary" Ludwig Erhard (Rodenstock 2001, 19)—the father of Germany's economic miracle and the undisputed hero of the book, who was also a member of the MPS—on the book's first page, and Friedrich Hayek is the most prominent and celebrated intellectual in the book (36–37). Rodenstock praises the United States and suggests that Germany should model itself on America's flexible labor and product markets and low levels of regulation (178). Because the social market relies on efficient self-regulation, it only needs a minimum of ethics and rules (28). Over time, Germany has gotten on the wrong path with higher wages, greater social benefits, more state and social protections (29). The more the state withdraws and expands the room for private initiative, the more jobs will be created (116). Market-distorting institutions are unnecessary and counterproductive because the market itself is fair and just: it rewards performance and is based on equality of opportunity (25). These views seem faithful to faithful to Erhard's. Erhard reportedly told Hayek, "I hope you don't misunderstand me when I speak of a social market economy (*Soziale*

Marktwirtschaft). I mean by that that the market economy as such as social not that it needs to be made social" (Ebenstein 2001, 242). As Ptak (2009, 108) points out, "The basic agreement of the German ordoliberals with the ideas of Hayek (and vice versa) is mostly *underestimated*."

Rodenstock emphasizes the need for flexiblization and deregulation in general, and of labor markets in particular; and the creation of jobs as the overriding goal of social policy and the principal requirement of social justice. "Badly paid jobs are better than none at all. . . . A guiding principal of the new social market economy is the motto: Just is whatever creates employment" (Rodenstock 2001, 54–55). This motto has had a significant impact on German public debate and on public policy. In 2002, the INSM made it the focus of a large-scale advertising campaign. "The purpose of this initiative was to redefine the term 'social' out of the widespread, but one-sided orientation towards government redistribution" (INSM 2009). In the fall of 2002, this motto was used by CDU/CSU and FDP political candidates before Wolfgang Clement, then minister of labor and economics, adopted it as the more or less official slogan of the Agenda 2010 labor market reforms. It is seldom recognized that the central motto of Agenda 2010 is a creation of the INSM.

Former Bundesbank president and first INSM chairperson Hans Tietmeyer's statements are also hard to reconcile with the view that German employers are opposed to liberalization. In an early INSM publication, Tietmeyer explicitly refers to a *Systemwechsel*, or change of economic model, and makes clear where the journey should go: "The New Social Market economy is equivalent with the Anglo-Saxon, the American principle." Tietmeyer stresses that the road ahead will not be easy: "The necessary reforms and cutbacks will entail social hardships" and "bitter medicine" (2001, 8, 22). In 2003, the INSM challenged trade unions with the motto "Less welfare state means more jobs," and by declaring May 1 to be the day to create jobs through supply-side reforms. In 2004, the INSM placed a sign that read: "It's high time for reforms: GERMANY" at a prominent place in the Spree river in Berlin. The sign was hung so that GERMANY was half submerged under the water, to symbolize the gravity of Germany's situation.

In 2005 the INSM provided a two-page article to the daily newspaper *Die Welt* entitled "The Greatest Job Destroyers of the Federal Republic" (Hahne and INSM 2005). This article follows a familiar INSM pattern by invoking Erhard to criticize the enemies of the new social-market economy, which include Keynesianism, the welfare state, deficit spending, codetermination, employment protection, labor market regulation, and other forms of social protection. I summarize the worst offenders and their offenses in table 7.1.

The article's criticism of deficit spending, high wage settlements, and excessive tax burdens may not raise many eyebrows, as these are the complaints one expects from a business advocacy organization. However, critiques of the

TABLE 7.1. The Greatest Job Destroyers of the Federal Republic

	CHANCELLOR	PARTIES	YEARS	PROBLEMS ACCORDING TO INSM
1.	Willy Brandt and Helmut Schmidt	SPD and FDP	1974–1982	Codetermination and deficit spending
2.	Helmut Kohl	CDU and FDP	1991–1998	Burdens of reunification, high wage settlements
3.	Kurt Georg Kiesinger	CDU and SPD	1966–1969	Federalism hinders reforms and tax competition
4.	Gerhard Schröder	SPD and Greens	1998–2002	"Strangulation" of the labor market
5.	Helmut Kohl	CDU and FDP	1982–1991	Reforms too timid
6.	Konrad Adenauer	CDU and FDP	1949–1963	Employment protection legislation, pension reforms

SOURCE: Author's compilation.

1976 codetermination law and employment protection legislation should be unsettling for scholars who believe that German employers depend on these institutions for their competitive strategies and defend them against political attacks. If that were really the case, Gesamtmetall would not spend significant amounts of money to publicize the message that "Kohl lacked the courage for radical reforms along the lines of Reagan in the United States or Thatcher in the United Kingdom" (Hahne and INSM 2005, 13). The article also criticizes West Germany's first chancellor, Konrad Adenauer (for his pension reform law), and former MPS member and Social Democratic finance minister Karl Schiller, who "propagated a moderate Keynesianism striving for a synthesis with ordoliberalism" (Hagemann in this this volume).

Many economists have been associated with the INSM, including Hans Barbier, Juergen Donges, Dominik Enste, Gerhard Fels, Otmar Issing, Karl-Heinz Paqué, Rolf Peffekoven, Bernd Raffelhüschen, Thomas Straubhaar, Ulrich van Suntum, Hans Tietmeyer, and Klaus Zimmermann. Although only two economists closely associated with the INSM are MPS members—Karl-Heinz Paqué and Randolf Rodenstock—an examination of these authors' publications reveals many critiques of welfare state intervention in the economy and a far-reaching overlap with the worldviews of neoliberal economists and MPS members. In a 1980 article, later INSM representative Donges lamented that West Germany's economy was "not so market-oriented" (Donges 1980), while Paqué (1991) criticized the structural wage rigidities and labor market regulations in the German economy. In a remark that is relevant to the ongoing eurozone crisis, Hans Barbier (1992) stated that the EU's Maastricht Treaty (which led to the establishment of the euro) was a mistake and that "what is economically wrong can't be politically right."

Furthermore, this network or "thought collective" (Mirowski and Plehwe 2009) was tightly woven around the late Herbert Giersch, who became professor at the Saarland in Saarbrücken University in 1955. From 1969 to 1989, Giersch was president of the Kiel Institute for the World Economy, and he was president of the MPS from 1986 to 1988. Giersch coined the terms *Eurosklerosis* and *Standortdebatte*, and he influenced "countless students," most of whom became staunch supply-side, free-market economists (Pieper 2006). Thus, Gerhard Fels, Juergen B. Donges, and Hans D. Barbier Paqué were students of Giersch, and Donges worked closely under his supervision while at Kiel for a decade. In addition, Giersch mentored Gerhard Fels, who served as president of the IW, the Cologne Institute for Economic Research (a think tank with close links to employers and industrial associations) from 1983 until 2004. Randolf Rodenstock explicitly thanks Fels for "intellectual sharpness" and "conclusive arguments" in the preface of his INSM manifesto book (Rodenstock 2001, 13). The next section discusses in greater detail how the INSM pressed for liberalization in the early to mid-2000s.

7.4. Pressing for Liberalization: The INSM from 2003 until 2005

From 2003 until the 2005 election, there was widespread agreement on the necessity of liberalization and welfare state reform in the German political establishment. Employers were less constrained by electoral politics during these years than at perhaps any other time in postwar German history. The INSM "had public opinion leadership," recalls Max Höfer, one of the INSM's former directors (interview 2013). According to VofC, employers should have sought to defend existing institutions upon which their competitive advantage depends. But if liberalization theorists are right, employers should press for fundamental liberalization. I find that employer positions more closely approximate the latter position than the former. Indeed, there is evidence that employers wanted to go further than the Agenda 2010 reforms.

From 2003 until the 2005 elections, employers clearly supported the CDU and FDP, which had criticized the Red-Green government for adopting too few reforms and too little liberalization. The first few months of 2003, when Schröder announced his Agenda 2010, represent "a decisive turning point in the history of the semisovereign German state" (Streeck 2005, 163). The INSM facilitated these developments; it laid the foundations for this shift:

> We in the INSM had devised the central slogan of Agenda 2010: "Sozial ist, was Arbeit schafft" ("Just/fair is whatever creates work"), and organized a broad platform of politicians that supported the slogan: Wolfgang Clement, Olaf Scholz, Fritz Kuhn, Wolfgang Schäuble, and Guido Westerwelle. . . . The credo "Sozial ist, was Arbeit schafft" redefined the word *sozial*: until then, the

> word meant that the state spent more money on students, on social assistance, on families, etc. The high unemployment forced us to rethink this: a job helps people more than social assistance. (Höfer 2013, 184)

In a 2003 newspaper column, INSM representative Tietmeyer wrote: "Germany needs far-reaching market-oriented reforms. If necessary, these need to be implemented despite disagreement with influential interest groups and parts of the [SPD's] own party" (Tietmeyer 2003). This statement was made just three weeks before Schröder's famous Agenda 2010 speech. In another column just one month later, INSM representative Oswald Metzger stated that the "necessary retrenchment of the unaffordable welfare state will take until the end of the decade" (Metzger 2003). At an INSM-organized event in the fall of 2003, Friedrich Merz of the CDU's business wing stressed the need for far-reaching reforms of the labor market, social transfer systems, the social safety net, the tax system, and the education system—"in sum, almost excessive demands for politicians and citizens. But there is no alternative" (Merz 2003, 22). These examples illustrate the tight linkages between the INSM's campaigns and Agenda 2010. In the words of Höfer, former INSM director, "We did Schröder's public relations activities" (interview 2013). There are reasons to believe that the INSM was impactful during these years. In one session of Germany's most influential talk show, *Sabine Christiansen*, three of the five guests were affiliated with the INSM; and between 2003 and 2008, over 120 media statements per day were attributable to it (INSM 2009).

The INSM also facilitated the Christian Democrats' turn toward more business- and market-friendly policies. The CDU's 2003 Leipzig party convention agenda has been characterized as "pure market culture" and as "the most market radical program in the party's history. . . . catapulting [Merkel's] party into Anglo-Saxon capitalism" (Kessler 2011). The CDU's and FDP's positions from the Leipzig party convention leading up to the 2005 Bundestag elections were radical. In the early 2000s, the INSM favored a transition to flat-rate health contributions to lower nonwage labor costs: a "paradigm shift" in Germany's social policy and a departure from the existing trajectory of the past 120 years (Merz 2003, 18). It is revealing that instead of cautioning overzealous politicians from jumping on the neoliberal bandwagon, "many top managers and entrepreneurs were enthusiastic about Merkel's 2003 Leipziger Parteitag agenda" (Balzer 2008). They wanted to go *further* than the Hartz reforms, for example by eliminating employment protection and by further reducing nonwage labor costs (Fleig, interview 2015): they were not satisfied with the extent and rate of liberalization.

In 2005, the INSM proclaimed that "Germany needs a comprehensive program of market-oriented reforms that goes considerably beyond Agenda 2010" (INSM 2005a, 8). The INSM praised Margaret Thatcher for not letting adverse circumstances or "fierce distributional conflicts" take her off the path of reforms (INSM 2005b, 47), and cited New Zealand, the United Kingdom, the United States, and Sweden as examples of successful welfare state reforms. The INSM also praised Ronald Reagan's deregulation and tax cuts and Sweden's decentralization of wage bargaining in the early 1990s (INSM 2005b, 48). In another publication, INSM-affiliated economist Ulrich van Suntum exalts Margaret Thatcher's radical reforms and laments that these would not be possible in Germany's political system (Van Suntum 2006, 132–33). Claims that "support for the welfare state is much broader, reaching deep in the business community" (Mares 2003, 265) are hard to sustain in light of this evidence. If that were really the case, Germany's business community would not fund a large-scale PR campaign that praised radical welfare state retrenchment and advocated flat-rate health insurance, a 25 percent flat-rate income tax, and other forms of the individualization of risk. Nor would they choose staff members to disseminate their ideas who, inspired by public choice theory, propagated the reduction or elimination of employment protection and the further flexibilization of labor markets (Enzweiler 2013).[7]

The mid-2000s presented employers with a larger liberalization carrot than ever before in the postwar period, and many wanted to bite. The language used by the INSM was that Agenda 2010 was no more than "a step in the right direction," and further reforms were demanded. An anonymous official close to the INSM and Gesamtmetall recalls that "according to the 'hawks' in Gesamtmetall, the INSM should attack the state and unions. Schröder's Agenda 2010 did not go far enough" (anonymous, personal communication; March 5, 2014). Shortly before the 2005 elections, the INSM launched its *Hamburger Appell* campaign, consisting of a series of slogans signed by 250 German economists. This campaign sought to support and defend market-conforming supply-side policies against deficit spending and market-correcting policies, which were receiving growing public and political support at the time. The central message of the campaign was summarized by an ad by Joachim Starbatty that read: "Those who disturb markets reduce aggregate demand" (Pühringer 2015, 38). But voters had had enough. Already by the summer of 2004, Angela Merkel's Leipziger Parteitag agenda had come under considerable pressure from *within* the CDU: 56 percent of CDU voters wanted the party to move in a more "social" or moderate direction, while 31 percent favored "radical reform." In the spring of 2005, Merkel's CDU/CSU had hit 45 percent in the polls, but in the Bundestag election on September 18, Merkel received only 35 percent of the vote—a "traumatic defeat" and just marginally more than Schröder's SPD (Clemens 2007, 234, 239). Not employers but public opinion constrained reforms.

During the preceding period of Hartz and Agenda 2010 reforms from 2003 until 2005, employers became "a force for the liberalization of the welfare state and of labor markets" (Paster 2012a, 160). Meanwhile industrial relations institutions and firms were undergoing far-reaching changes. Fleig describes advancing the reform agenda without completely undermining the existing system of social partnership as "a tightrope walk"—how far can one go?—and "like dancing on a razor's edge." Following IG Metall's defeat in the 2003 strike over working-time reduction, Fleig recalls that some employers wanted to "let the union run against the wall" and crush them (Fleig, personal communication, March 22, 2015; interview 2015). The fact that they did not do this in the end does indicate some support for traditional institutions. But almost going to the wall cannot be understood as a defense of traditional institutions in any meaningful sense. If the CDU and the FDP had won a majority in the 2005 elections, they would likely have tried to legislate further liberalization. The fact that this did not occur is a contingent result of electoral politics rather than of German employers' defense of traditional institutions.

7.5. The Moderation of the INSM and Its Push for Austerity since 2006

As the political winds shifted to the left, the INSM was forced into an increasingly defensive position. In 2003, there was an elite political consensus on the necessity of reforms (even if these were contested by the general population and the political rank and file). Through the INSM, German employers acted as motors of the liberalization process: "All important reform topics were on the table," stated former INSM chairperson and Bundesbank president Hans Tietmeyer (interview 2006). The Pforzheim collective bargaining agreement took place against the background of threats by both governing and opposition parties to legislate opening clauses in collective agreements if the social partners would not voluntarily agree to them. There was widespread mistrust in collective bargaining; Bundesverbands der Deutschen Industrie president Michael Rogowski declared that collective bargaining agreements should be burned. Within 10 years the situation underwent "a complete reversal—it's unbelievable," remarked Dietrich Creutzburg (interview 2013). The very same parties that pursued liberalization endorsed the first mandatory national minimum wage, and in 2014 the CDU-SPD coalition government adopted it.

While the 2005 election results and the resulting CDU-SPD coalition government were widely seen as a referendum against reforms, the blowback began with the so-called *Montagsdemonstrationen* protests against Hartz IV in 2004. This sentiment grew when SPD chairman Franz Müntefering described private equity firms as "locusts." The successful establishment of Die Linke, the left-wing party in the German party system, was another sign of growing resistance. Elites had failed to win over citizens' emotions for their reform agenda (Fleckenstein 2013, 74; Wolfrum 2013, 578), and many German citizens came to perceive the Agenda 2010 labor market reforms as unjust. Trade union and civil society efforts in opposition to radical neoliberal campaigning, such as the establishment of LobbyControl in 2005, also contributed to this shift. In the words of NRW Metall's Hubertus Engemann, who was present at the founding of the INSM, "Reforms were going in the right direction . . . but then the societal mainstream shifted to the left" (interview 2013). Axel Rhein, a director at IW Medien, has been involved with the INSM since its inception. Rhein likens the public sphere to a stage, on which the INSM needs a megaphone in order to be heard. From 2000 until 2005, the INSM's campaigns resonated in the media and in the CDU/FDP opposition, which, in turn, amplified the INSM's messages. This changed under the CDU-SPD grand coalition (Rhein, interview 2014).

These developments made the INSM's work more difficult, and necessitated a strategic reorientation in the domestic arena. From 2000 to 2005, the INSM's negative campaigning style greased the wheels of liberalization. Following the 2005 elections and the formation of the CDU-SPD coalition, the INSM's campaigns became more moderate. In 2006, their focus was on promoting economic growth; in 2008, it was on increasing labor market participation; and in 2009, the INSM celebrated the virtues of the social-market economy. The INSM began placing more emphasis on defending existing reform achievements than on pushing for further liberalization. An environment in which "reform politics aren't mainstream anymore," the INSM's current director, Hubertus Pellengahr, noted, demands a different approach than one in which reform proponents can play an agenda-setting role (interview 2013). Rodenstock recalled that following Agenda 2010, "The wind was taken out of our sails. The topics were no longer perceived as being so urgent and conspicuous" (interview 2013). An internal memo points toward setbacks in the battle for discursive hegemony:

> The political debate in 2007 was dominated by redistribution. The recognition that economically successful reforms are also profitable/beneficial for ordinary citizens did not prevail. In this conflict situation Die Linke, SPD, and trade unions were able to successfully set the agenda for redistributive questions (minimum wages, maximum wages, etc.) by offering solutions that appear to offer more security. All political parties, including the CDU/CSU, became involved in a debate about justice, which is mainly a debate about redistribution, as the 2009 Bundestag elections approaches. (INSM 2009)

These developments support Bruff's claim that the INSM has had limited success in "detaching a large enough portion of the social democratic and trade union opinion from their version of common sense" (Bruff 2008, 156).

The financial crisis that began in 2008 compounded the INSM's problems and threatened to terminate the INSM itself: according to insiders, it was unclear what discretionary expenditures Gesamtmetall would be able to sustain as the bottom fell out of the global economy. With the rapid recovery of Germany's export markets, these financial concerns faded into the background. While the INSM's operational budget was reduced, Gesamtmetall's willingness to sustain this expenditure even during hard times attests to the INSM's continued importance for its founders and funders.

Growing societal antipathy toward markets turned out to be a more serious problem. The financial crisis (compare Plehwe in this volume) terminated the *Reformdebatte*, the push for market-oriented reforms: "From 2000 to 2005 we had the wind of history behind us. That changed with the financial crisis. We had a new field of debate" (Höfer, interview 2012). The INSM had been pushing for comprehensive liberalization but "forgot the deregulation of financial markets" (Höfer, interview 2014). In response to the financial crisis, the INSM retreated to a more moderate ordoliberal position to prevent the market order itself from being made responsible and coming under attack: "The INSM had to react to these changed circumstances to avoid being labeled as radically neoliberal, as further demands for reforms would have been rejected as excessive and unrealistic" (Rath, interview 2014). With the financial crisis, businesses' discursive power declined, and their favored and preferred market liberal model was delegitimized.

For the INSM, the ambiguity of the ideational construct "social-market economy" turned out to be a blessing, for it could now present itself as an alternative to the very same neoliberal economic policies it had itself advocated just a few years earlier.[8] With the financial crisis, the anglophone neoliberal model lost much of its luster. In May 2009, in the midst of the US subprime crisis, the INSM hired an actor to play Ludwig Erhard, father of the social-market economy, and convey the message that Germany's social-market economy was a model for the United States. A large banner ad on Wall Street read: "Germany invented Aspirin for your headache. We also got something for depression: Social Market Economy." The message was that "American market fundamentalism can learn a great deal from the social market economy. We must return to these rules" (Höfer 2013, 25).

Meanwhile, the INSM was busy defending Schröder's Agenda 2010 against politicians clamoring to reregulate markets. My interviewees express admiration for Gerhard Schröder's reforms and a general preference for bourgeois parties. However, they have deep reservations—and in many cases overtly critical attitudes—about Angela Merkel's CDU-led governments for rolling back existing reforms and failing to pursue new ones. By 2013, for example, all German Länder had nullified university tuition fees, a policy the INSM had campaigned for. This suggests that the INSM was not supporting the CDU-FDP government in the 2013 Bundestag elections, as Speth has claimed (2013). Instead, the INSM was campaigning against *all* the major parties who were seeking to roll back Agenda 2010's market oriented reforms.

In this context, it is logical that Wolfgang Clement replaced Hans Tietmeyer at the head of the INSM's board of trustees in 2012. While

Tietmeyer's age played a role (he passed away in late 2016), Clement had become minister for business and abor in 2002 with one goal in mind: to transform Germany. Clement played a pivotal role in pushing through the Hartz labor market reforms; he was a man of conviction who remained convinced of the need for far-reaching reforms even after his political party, the SPD, abandoned this agenda. At an INSM event in September 2008, just 10 days after the bankruptcy of Lehman Brothers triggered the global financial crisis, Clement criticized the governing CDU-SPD coalition for relapses into "welfare statism" and urged a systematic continuation of the reform agenda he had begun as a federal cabinet minister six years earlier: "Agenda 2010 was just a start." Clement also emphasized the need for a constitutional balanced budget amendment (*Schuldenbremse*). The approval of this amendment in 2009 (it became legally binding as of 2011) can also be seen as an achievement of the INSM. In the 2009 Bundestag elections, Clement supported the FDP's Guido Westerwelle, who five years earlier had stated that "the Hartz reforms were just the beginning and that much deeper cuts were needed" (Wolfrum 2013, 573).

"Firms are afraid that [the Agenda 2010] reforms will be taken back," Hubertus Pellengahr, the INSM's current managing director, remarked prior to the 2013 Bundestag elections (interview 2013). These fears came to fruition with the 2013 Bundestag elections. The resulting CDU-SPD coalition government has legislated a statutory minimum wage, partially reversing a decade of labor market reforms. The INSM campaigned hard against this legislation, and its passage represents a clear defeat for the INSM. Political debates in Germany have moved more and more onto the terrain of justice—generally inhospitable territory for business because of its association with antimarket and redistributive politics. The INSM stayed true to its founding ideals, its commitment to equality of opportunity, and fought for a more nuanced and differentiated understanding that includes needs-based justice, equality of opportunity, and performance-related justice (*Leistungsgerechtigkeit*). Studies commissioned by the INSM show that Germany's performance in these areas is better than many citizens believe. The INSM has stayed true to its founding ideals, and its recent campaigns criticize the push to regulate temporary employment contract work.

Despite some setbacks, it appears that Gesamtmetall's member federations and member companies' dissatisfaction with political-economic conditions has decreased in recent years, and it's not hard to see why: during the past two decades, Germany's industrial relations system and broader institutional architecture have been subordinated to the need for "radical improvements of the 'international competitiveness of the economy' in the face of the 'imperatives of globalization'" (Lehndorff 2011, 351). Employees, works councils, and trade unions have made far-reaching concessions.[9] INSM-affiliated economist Karl-Heinz Paqué celebrates these changes:

> Germany has changed as a *Wirtschaftsstandort* during the past two decades. The country has become a production location that is not only highly innovative—it always was—but also offers a high degree of flexibility. Germany is no longer a citadel of Rhenish Capitalism in which powerful employers' associations and unions hinder adjustment to world market fluctuations. (Paqué 2011, 25)

More recently, Paqué has expressed concern that Germany may be on its way "back into the sickbed." One of his recent posts on the INSM website INSM Oekonomenblog reads: "From the 'sick man of Europe' to a model country—and back again. That is what threatens Germany with the pension and minimum wage plans of the Grand Coalition" (Paqué 2014).

It should be noted, however, that even in this phase of apparent moderation, the INSM pushed for austerity at home and especially at the EU level. At the height of the eurozone crisis in 2011, the INSM organized a lecture in the center of Berlin by European Central Bank president Mario Draghi. Central to this event was a celebration of the "breakthrough for clear fiscal rules in our monetary union" (INSM 2012, 31) and an emphasis on the need for more of the same. The INSM's director, Pellengahr, summarized the INSM's position by stating, "The only way out of the crisis is through credible fiscal discipline" (INSM 2012, 5). Gesamtmetall president Martin Kannegiesser also discussed the preferences of his member companies: "We businessmen have had limited enthusiasm for political decisions made during recent years. But the most recent decision in Brussels for a fiscal union with automatic sanctions and a clear orientation toward stability—that receives our enthusiastic applause. I have spontaneously expressed [our views] by congratulations and support to the chancellor. . . . These are also the sentiments of probably thousands of other businesspeople" (INSM 2012, 15).

In addition, the INSM commissioned a study written by Lüder Gerken and two other economists at the Centrum für Europäische Politik in Freiburg. This study (Gerken et. al. 2011) advocates balanced budget amendments (*Schuldenbremsen*) in the constitutions of eurozone member states. But the authors of this study stress that these constitutional amendments by themselves are insufficient: the political acceptance and legitimacy of austerity measures in everyday politics is no less essential. In addition, the authors advocate supply-side reforms to decrease debt levels, regulation, and bureaucracy, and to increase competitiveness. The INSM also conducted a survey of German economists, in which 60 of 96 respondents (62.5 percent) spoke out against an EU-wide economic government, while 33 respondents (34 percent) supported such a proposal. Fifty-two respondents (54 percent) opposed a fiscal union at the EU level. Instead, 81 respondents (84 percent) expressed support for legally binding or constitutionally based balanced budget amendments across the EU. Only 14 (15 percent) of the surveyed economists opposed such amendments (INSM 2011). The INSM's campaigns for austerity in these years evince a "pathological fear of government debt that sits at the heart of economic liberalism" (Blyth 2013, 114).

This discussion shows that even while the INSM has been on the defensive concerning the reform agenda in the domestic realm, it has sought to proactively define the agenda and ensure the predominance of austerity measures in German government policy and in other EU member states. In its quest to legitimate and popularize these notions within Germany, the INSM has regularly commissioned studies comparing the success of different German federal states and even cities in reducing their budget deficits and balancing their budgets.

7.6. Conclusion

The transformations surveyed in this chapter challenge the notion of Germany's economy as nonliberal capitalism. Drawing on ordoliberal thought and on the work of MPS-affiliated economists, the INSM has advocated for more market coordination in all areas of social and economic life: it has put wind in the sails of liberalization since its founding 17 years ago. By the end of 2018, Gesamtmetall will have spent approximately 160 million euros funding the INSM's activities. Despite changing campaigns and emphases over time, the INSM's overall message is clear: a celebration, legitimation, and defense of the unencumbered market, and a harsh critique of the welfare state. While the intellectual pedigree of the INSM is ordoliberal, the differences from anglophone neoliberalism should not be overstated. As Mudge points out, the "elevation of the market . . . over all other modes of organization" is neoliberalism's "ideological core" (2008, 705).

The chapter has also sought to shed light on changes in the INSM's orientation and strategy over time. In the period from 2000 to 2005, the INSM played an agenda-setting role by paving the way for the Agenda 2010 labor market reforms and by coming up with some of its central slogans. From 2003 to 2005, the INSM articulated radical critiques of the German model that point toward a *Systemwechsel* toward liberal market economy-style institutions. Many INSM representatives and employers viewed the Agenda 2010 labor market reforms as the beginning and not the terminus of liberalization. The fact that these programmatic goals were justified with explicit reference to the social-market economy suggests that neoliberalism itself is protean (Baccaro and Howell 2011, 551) and that ordoliberalism, the German variety of economic liberalism (Haselbach 1997, 169), "is substantially less different from other streams of neoliberal thought than many have thought" (Ptak 2009, 99).

Given the strength, dynamism, and renewed celebration of the German model today, it is important to recall that employer support for Germany's nonliberal institutions was by no means a foregone conclusion a decade ago.

Since 2006, and especially since 2009, the INSM's positions in the domestic arena have become more moderate. The INSM has sought to defend and consolidate existing reform achievements against retrenchment, but it has had to swim with the leftward tide of public opinion and moderate its positions in order to remain relevant. In the first period, the INSM achieved many victories. In the second period, in the context of reduced business legitimacy, the INSM has sustained some defeats in its attempt to defend market-liberal reforms against reregulation. Nevertheless, the fact that the INSM has been able to consolidate and defend the Hartz labor market reforms in a climate of hostile public opinion is a major achievement. In addition, during this phase of apparent moderation, the INSM became a forceful advocate of another liberal policy idea—austerity—at the EU level.

I have suggested that the INSM's moderation in the second period should be understood as a response to a growing antiliberalization sentiment and electoral pressures rather than as an indication of employer support for the institutional status quo. At the same time, improvements in firms' competitiveness, reductions in unit wage costs, and the crisis of the anglophone model may also help explain the INSM's moderation. This does not contradict my claim that German employers have a genuine preference for liberalization, but it suggests a nuanced and dynamic relationship between ideas and interests, as Marx and Weber have long recognized, as well as that employer strategies and interests are complex and influenced by a variety of factors.

In the end, Gesamtmetall's investment of large sums of cash in a cutting-edge professional PR campaign has been insufficient to convince German policymakers and citizens of the continued necessity of reforms in their own country. This suggests that business does not always win, and that "there is always a fighting chance" (Streeck 2009, 268) for those who seek to rein in the market. This does not imply that employers are incessantly at war with market-constraining institutions. After far-reaching institutional reforms and concessions by employees and the crisis of anglophone liberal market models, and in the face of growing societal opposition to further liberalization, German employers toned down their demands for liberalization. But "we cannot expect institutional stability as such . . . the German labour market and the economy are undergoing further remodelling" (Eichhorst 2015, 67).

Following new welfare state largesse and the reregulation of labor markets, "The discontentment of business is growing and a new *Standortdebatte* [debate on Germany as a production location] is taking place in German companies" (Hüther, interview 2014). While it is impossible to know how German employers will confront these future challenges, this chapter suggests that their responses will likely take place on the terrain of economic liberalism. In spite of the undeniable differences between different strains and streams of liberal economic thought, they have much in common.[10] Future scholarship should build on this insight.

Acknowledgments

I would especially like to thank Dieter Plehwe for helpful comments. The usual disclaimers apply.

References

Baccaro, Lucio, and Chris Howell. 2011. "A Common Neoliberal Trajectory: The Transformation of Industrial Relations in Advanced Capitalism." *Politics and Society* 39:521–63.

Balzer, A., H. Müller, and C. Rickens. 2008. "Angela Merkel: Die Abkanzlerin." *Manager Magazin*, August 29.

Bank, Max. 2013. "Stunde der Neoliberalen? Politikberatung und Wirtschaftspolitik in der Ära Adenauer." Ph.D. dissertation, University of Cologne.

Barbier, Hans D. 1992. "Was wird aus Europa? Der Irrtum von Maastricht. Was ökonomisch falsch ist, kann politisch nicht richtig sein." *Frankfurter Allgemeine Zeitung* July 31, 29.

Barry, Michael and Adrian Wilkinson. 2011. "Reconceptualising Employer Associations under Evolving Employment Relations: Countervailing Power Revisited." *Work, Employment and Society* 25(1):149–62.

Blyth, Mark. 2013. *Austerity: The History of a Dangerous Idea*. New York: Oxford University Press.

Bruff, Ian. 2008. *Culture and Consensus in European Varieties of Capitalism: A "Common Sense" Analysis*. Basingstoke: Palgrave.

Clemens, C. 2007. "Two Steps Forward, One Step Back: Merkel's CDU/CSU and the Politics of Welfare State Reform." *German Politics* 16:222–46.

Donges, Juergen B. 1980. "Industrial Policies in West Germany's Not So Market-Oriented Economy." *World Economy* 3 (2): 185–204.

Dyson, Kenneth. 2005. "Economic Policy Management: Catastrophic Equilibrium, Tipping Points and Crisis Interventions." In Simon Green and William E. Patterson, eds., *Governance in Contemporary Germany: The Semisovereign State Revisited*, 115–37. Cambridge: Cambridge University Press.

Ebenstein, Alan. 2001. *Friedrich Hayek: A Biography*. New York: Palgrave.

Eichhorst, Werner. 2015. "The Unexpected Appearance of a New German Model." *British Journal of Industrial Relations* 53(1):49–69.

Enzweiler, Tasso. 2013. *Wege aus dem Reformstau: Zentrale Determinanten bei der Akzeptanz wachstumsstärkender Strukturreformen*. Berlin: Springer.

Fleckenstein, Timo. 2013. "Learning to Depart from a Policy Path: Institutional Change and the Reform of German Labour Market Policy." *Government and Opposition* 48:55–79.

Gerken, Lüder, Bert Van Roosebeke, and Jan S. Voßwinkel. 2011. "Anforderungen an die Sanierung der Euro-Staaten: Schuldenbremse plus Nebenbedingungen." Centrum für Europäische Politik, September 19. Study ordered by and paid for by the INSM.

Gesellschaft im Zwiespalt. 2000. *Marktwirtschaft und Unternehmer im Spiegel der öffentlichen Meinung*. Cologne: Deutscher Instituts Verlag.

Giersch, Herbert. 1988. "Liberal Reform in West Germany." *Ordo* 39: 3–16.

Hahne, P., and Initiative Neue Soziale Marktwirtschaft. 2005. "Die größten Jobvernichter der Bundesrepublik." *Die Welt*, February 4, 12–13.

Hall, Peter A., and David Soskice. 2001. An Introduction to Varieties of Capitalism. In Peter A. Hall and David Soskice, eds., *Varieties of Capitalism*, 1–68. Oxford: Oxford University Press.

Haselbach, Dieter. 1991. *Authoritatärer Liberalismus und Soziale Marktwirtschaft*. Baden-Baden: Nomos Verlag.

Haselbach, Dieter. 1997. "Social Market Economy and West German Identity." In Matthias Zimmer, ed., *Germany: Phoenix in Trouble?*, 157–82. Edmonton: University of Alberta Press.

Höfer, Max. 2013. *Vielleicht will der Kapitalismus gar nicht, dass wir glücklich sind?* Munich: Knaus.

Höfer, Max. 2010. "Externalisierung der Verbandskommunikation: Die Initiative Neue Soziale Marktwirtschaft." In Olaf Hoffjan and Roland Stahl, eds., *Handbuch Verbandskommunikation*, 21–28. Wiesbaden: VS Verlag, 2010.

Initiative Neue Soziale Marktwirtschaft (INSM). 2005a. *Initiative!Direkt*. Cologne: INSM.

Initiative Neue Soziale Marktwirtschaft. 2005b. *Vision D: Der Wohlstand hat Zukunft*. Cologne: Deutscher Instituts Verlag, 2005.

Initiative Neue Soziale Marktwirtschaft. 2009. *Die Kommunikation der Initiative Neue Soziale Marktwirtschaft, 2000–2009*. Internal documentation.

Initiative Neue Soziale Marktwirtschaft. 2011. "Deutschland-Check: Eine Dauerstudie zur Beurteilung der Wirtschaftspolitik der Bundesregierung in der 17. Legislaturperiode durchgeführt vom Institut der deutschen Wirtschaft (IW) Köln im Auftrag von Initiative Neue Soziale Marktwirtschaft (INSM) und WirtschaftsWoche." Cologne: Institute for Economic Research.

Initiative Neue Soziale Marktwirtschaft. 2012. *Geldpolitische Handlungsfelder in der Sozialen Marktwirtschaft: Mario Draghi*. Initiative dokumentation, Ludwig Erhard Lectures. Cologne: IW Medien.

Kessler, M. 2011. "Die 180-Grad-Drehung der CDU." *Rheinische Post*, November 14.

Kinderman, Daniel. 2005. "Pressure from without, Subversion from within: the Two-Pronged German Employer Offensive." *Comparative European Politics* 3:432–63.

Kinderman, Daniel. 2014. "Challenging Varieties of Capitalism's Account of Business Interests: The New Social Market Initiative and German Employers' Quest for Liberalization, 2000–2014." MPIfG Discussion Paper 14/16.

Lehndorff, Steffen. 2011. "Before the Crisis, in the Crisis, and beyond: The Upheaval of Collective Bargaining in Germany." *Transfer: European Review of Labour and Research* 17 (3): 341–54.

Merz, Friedrich. 2003. Die Zeit ist reif für eine wirklich große Einkommenssteuerreform. Cologne: Chancen für alle.

Metzger, O. 2003. "Nutzt das Fenster für Reformen." *Handelsblatt*, March 21.

Mirowski, Philip, and Dieter Plehwe, eds. 2009: *The Road from Mont Pèlerin: The Making of the Neoliberal Thought Collective*. Cambridge, MA: Harvard University Press.

Mudge, Stephanie. 2008. "What Is Neo-liberalism?" *Socio-Economic Review* 6: 703–31.

Paqué, Karl-Heinz. 2014. "Back into the Sickbed: From the 'Sick Man of Europe' to a Model Country—and Back Again. That Is What Threatens Germany with the Pension and Minimum Wage Plans of the Grand Coalition." INSM Oekonomenblog, March 20. http://www.insm-oekonomenblog.de/11375-zurueck-ins-krankenlager/.

Paqué, Karl-Heinz. 1991. "Structural Wage Rigidity in West Germany 1950–1989: Some New Econometric Evidence." Kiel Working Papers No. 489.

Paster, Thomas. 2012a. *The Role of Business in the Development of the Welfare State and Labor Markets in Germany: Containing Social Reforms*. Abingdon: Routledge.

Paster, Thomas. 2012b. "Do German Employers Support Board-Level Codetermination? The Paradox of Individual Support and Collective Opposition." *Socio-Economic Review* 10:471–95.

Pieper, Nikolaus. 2006. "Der Wirtschaftsdoktor Herbert Giersch als Ökonom." Kiel: Institute for World Economics. https://www.ifw-kiel.de/konfer/2006/giersch/giersch_pieper.pdf.

Ptak, Ralf. 2009. "Neoliberalism in Germany: Revisiting the Ordoliberal Foundations of the Social Market Economy." In Philip Mirowski and Dieter Plehwe, eds., *The Road from Mont Pèlerin The Making of the Neoliberal Thought Collective*, 98–138. Cambridge, MA: Harvard University Press.

Pühringer, Stephan. 2015. "Wie wirken ÖkonomInnen und Ökonomik auf Politik und Gesellschaft?" ICAE Working Paper Series No. 35 06/2015.

Rodenstock, Randolf. 2009. "Begrüßung." Reception for the Bavarian government in Munich, May 26.

Rodenstock, Randolf. 2001. *Chancen für Alle: Die Neue Soziale Marktwirtschaft*. Cologne: Deutscher Instituts Verlag.

Schindelbeck, Dirk, and Volker Ilgen. 1999. *Haste was, biste was! Werbung für die Soziale Marktwirtschaft*. Darmstadt: Wissenschaftl.Buchgesellschaft.

Speth, Rudolf. 2013. "Gerechtigkeit a la INSM." *Mitbestimming* 9.

Speth, Rudolf. 2004. "Die politischen Strategien der Initiative Neue Soziale Marktwirtschaft." Arbeitspapier 96. Hans-Böckler-Stiftung, Düsseldorf.

Streeck, Wolfgang. 2009. *Re-forming Capitalism*. Oxford: Oxford University Press.

Streeck, Wolfgang. 2005. "Nach dem Korporatismus: Neue Eliten, neue Konflikte." MPIfG Working Paper No. 05/4, May.

Tietmeyer, Hans. 2003. "Treibt die Reformen voran!" *Handelsblatt*, February 21.

Tietmeyer, Hans. 2001. *Die soziale Marktwirtschaft erneuern*. Cologne: Chancen für alle.

Van Suntum, Ulrich. 2006. *Masterplan Deutschland: Mit dem Prinzip Einfachheit zurück zum Erfolg*. Munich: Deutscher Taschenbuch Verlag.

Wolfrum, Edgar. 2013. *Rot-Grün an der Macht: Deutschland 1998–2005*. Munich: C.H. Beck.

Interviews

Brocker, Ulrich. 2013. July 4.

Creutzburg, Dietrich. 2013. August 8.

Engemann, Hubertus. 2013. July 3.

Fasbender, Volker. 2013. July 2.

Fleig, Günther. 2015. 7 April.

Höfer, Max. 2014. July 12.

Höfer, Max. 2013. July 30.

Höfer, Max. 2012. August 8

Hüther, Michael. 2014. August 19.

Pellengahr, Hubertus. 2014. August 6.
Pellengahr, Hubertus. 2013) August 8.
Rath, Dieter. 2014. June 11.
Rhein, Axel. 2014. June 11.
Rodenstock, Randolf. 2013. July 22.

8 | Neoliberalism and Market-Disciplining Policy in the Koizumi Reform in Japan

JURO TERANISHI

THE PURPOSE OF THIS chapter is to examine the process of the diffusion of neoliberalism in postwar Japan, focusing on the Koizumi reform, deregulation, and structural reform policy carried out under the Koizumi administration (2001–6), with respect to the underlying logic that justified the reform and the reasons for the public support for the policy. Although the welfare system introduced after World War II in Japan was, arguably, less comprehensive than the systems that developed in Western Europe, the orientation of the Japanese toward a more equitable society was very strong after World War II, partly because of the recognition that distributive inequality was the main reason for the social unrest that hampered efforts to stem the move to war. The degree of income inequality measured by Gini coefficients declined drastically during the high-growth era (1955–73). This occurred partly because of income sharing among stakeholders in the Japanese-style firm system, and partly because of government interventions in the competitive conditions of industries, favoring in particular declining and weak industries. Various tools for intervention were introduced in order to shift the rents that accrued to modern and competitive industries in the direction of stagnating industries, including the small and medium-sized sectors and agriculture, although the bureaucrats claimed the policy tools were for "industrial policy" with the aim of assisting the major growing industries directly, and indirectly by mitigating the stress of industrial adjustment for the economy. Once high growth had been accomplished, government interventions were gradually attenuated so that market mechanisms could come into play more efficiently. While it is not certain to what extent the lesser degree of government intervention or deregulation contributed to growth rates, the deregulation policy definitely aggravated income maldistribution, raising Gini coefficients significantly, especially after the bubble burst in 1991. Thanks to the sharing system through the Japanese-style firm system and the equality policy implemented at the interindustrial level, class conflicts were not strong in Japan. Consequently, the neoliberal bent in economic thinking that intensified distributive conflicts among economic classes and retrenched welfare capitalism elsewhere was not strong in Japan, at least until the end of the last century. The Koizumi administration, however, which marched under the banner of drastic deregulation and liberalization, won a landslide victory in the election of 2001, and implemented radical reform policies, typical of neoliberalism. Why was Koizumi supported so widely, and why was his policy welcomed so ardently by the public? This is the question addressed in the present chapter. In other words, the issue tackled here is why neoliberalism was able to cross geopolitical boundaries and find a habitat in soil substantially different from the Western ideological world.

It will be argued that there are two main, perhaps mutually interrelated, reasons for the success of Koizumi's political strategy. First is the Japanese attitude toward global standards in the ideological and intellectual world. Growing up in a society that developed quite differently in terms of religious and philosophical background, the Japanese had ambivalent feelings about global standards. Nationalism and an indigenous mentality always generated resistance to adapting to global standards. When economic policy reaches an impasse, however, such resistance abruptly ebbs, and the turn of the tide finds substantial political support. Through comparison of the Koizumi reform with the Inoue fiscal policy (*zaisei*) of the early 1930s, it is argued that the enthusiastic public support for both policies should be attributed not to the policy per se, but to the stance of the reformers in implementing the policy as part of the policy package designed to approach the global standards of the time, the gold standard in the case of the Inoue policy and neoliberalism in the case of the Koizumi reform.

Second, there was the opposition to and weariness with the bureaucratic system reigning at the time. When Koizumi embarked on his deregulation policy, he was well aware that the public support for the bureaucratic intervention lay in the equality implications of the policy. If Koizumi had justified his policy of introducing market discipline by pointing out its affinity with neoliberalism, the pragmatic policy philosophy of Reagan and Thatcher, he would never have gained such popularity as the election revealed. This is because the fundamental logic of neoliberalism clashed with the basic theme behind Japan's economic system, which was built on the denial of class conflicts. For better or for worse, the view had been widely held that Japan was a development-oriented state, as argued by Chalmers Johnson and Yukio Noguchi, so the doctrine of neoliberalism was accepted as supporting an anti-development-oriented policy, with possible favorable effects on the economy in terms of efficiency. Tired of the rent-seeking (such as *amakudari*, the practice of former government officials finding employment in the private sector) practiced by the bureaucrats and the prospect-less social atmosphere under bureaucratic sovereignty and the long-lasting depression, the people's attitude suddenly changed, and the result was the landslide victory of Koizumi. While the economy began to recover mainly because of the export boom, the positive efficiency effect proclaimed by the Johnson-Noguchi theory and the Washington consensus proved by and large erroneous. The equality in income distribution of the high-growth era had vanished, together with the Japanese-style welfare system based on interindustrial protection and sharing. Since the developmental view of Japan lacked solid ground, the neoliberal doctrine proposed as the leading doctrine for Japan was by and large rootless.

The first half of the chapter, comprising sections 8.1 to 8.4, compares the Koizumi reform policy with that of Inoue *zaisei* during 1930–31, which also emphasized market discipline. The second half, comprising sections 8.5 and 8.6, examines the relationship between the concept of neoliberalism and the popular notion of Japan as a developmental state. Section 8.7 sets out some brief concluding remarks.

8.1. Common Features of the Koizumi Reform and Inoue's Fiscal Policy

The policy of lifting the gold embargo implemented by Minister of Finance Junnosuke Inoue under the Hamaguchi administration (July 1929–April 1931) and the second Wakatuki administration (April 1931–December 1931), and the deregulation and structural reform policy carried out by the Koizumi administration (September 2001–April 2006) have many things in common.

First, the two policies were aimed at introducing market discipline as the main theme of economic policy. In the case of Inoue's fiscal policy, the ultimate aim lay in reestablishing the gold standard, but the real aim for Inoue himself seems to have been to enhance market discipline, the so-called *zaikai-seiri*. In the case of Koizumi's reform, he emphasized the necessity of structural reforms and deregulation as well as of challenging bureaucratic dominance.

Second, both policies were introduced as the last resort in tackling the long-lasting stagnation of the economy. The Inoue policy was expected to buoy the stagnant economy, which had been stop-and-go since the end of World War I, and was an attempt to return to the gold standard after the three occasions when chances had been missed. Koizumi's policy also came on stage after the "lost decade," and was intended to be countercyclical , after all the major policy tools had proved to be ineffective in refloating the economy.

Third, both approaches entailed tight fiscal policy in spite of serious deflationary pressure. The Hamaguchi administration revised the already determined national budget for fiscal year 1929, giving rise to a substantial fiscal surplus. The Koizumi administration tried to reduce fiscal deficits by sticking to a self-imposed ceiling on deficit bond issuance.

Fourth, both regimes won landslide victories in the Lower House election during their terms. The Hamaguchi administration obtained a majority in the election of February 1930, and the Koizumi administration won more than two-thirds of the seats in the election of September 2005.

Finally, both Inoue and Koizumi tried to justify their policy by conforming to the global standard of the times. The Hamaguchi administration appointed Kijyuro Shidehara as foreign minister and pursued what came to be known as Shidehara foreign policy, including cooperation with the United States and the United Kingdom, respect for the Washington regime, and a nonintervention policy toward China. Together with the return to the gold standard and open trade, these policies were in accordance with the international order led by the United States and the United Kingdom. The Koizumi administration also supported the international order advocated by the two allied countries. In terms of foreign policy, Koizumi cooperated with US military actions against Afghanistan and Iraq, and at the same time followed and supported the development of the global financial markets.

8.2. Global Standard and Policy Choice in Inoue's Administration

Junnosuke Inoue, minister of finance in the Hamaguchi cabinet, lifted the gold embargo on January 11, 1930, and the exchange rate was set at the same overvalued level as before the suspension of the gold standard. Inoue had carefully prepared for this, with a tight fiscal policy, high Bank of Japan lending rate, and contracts for stand-by credits with the banking groups of London and New York. However, the yen came in for serious speculative attack just after Inoue announced the plan of lifting the gold embargo on November 21, 1929, and the stock of gold reserves decreased substantially. The attack after the suspension of the gold standard by the United Kingdom on September 21, 1931, was even more serious, and Japan's stock of gold was almost exhausted. The Wakatsuki administration was forced to resign, and the gold standard was suspended again by Korenaga Takahashi, the minister of finance in the succeeding administration.

8.2.1. Inoue's Aim in Lifting the Gold Embargo

While the return to the gold standard eventually failed, the Japanese economy was saddled with serious difficulty owing to the tight fiscal and monetary policy as well as the appreciated exchange rate. On top of the shock due to the Great Depression, the Japanese economy fell into its own unprecedented, serious depression, with the so-called Showa Crisis. The successful return to the gold standard was expected to benefit the economy by stabilizing the exchange rate. The enthusiastic support for the policy on the part of raw silk exporters was based on this expectation. For Inoue, however, this did not constitute a major objective for the policy. There is a fair amount of evidence to suggest that his final objective was not exchange rate stability but tight economic policy per se. This was because the Japanese economy had been addicted to overconsumption since the boom during World War I as a result of lax fiscal and monetary policy under the Seiyukai regimes. For one thing, Inoue stuck to tight economic policies after the United Kingdom suspended the gold standard in September 1931, and it became evident to everyone that Japan was unable to continue the policy. For another, the opinion had been growing increasingly strong in financial circles that the purpose of lifting the gold embargo lay in market discipline in the Japanese economy and clearing up inefficient business firms, that is, *zaikai-seiri*. This view became even stronger after the economy had had considerable experience of variation in the exchange rate. When some economists began to argue that the return to the gold standard should be made at a new, depreciated rate, financial circles rose up in arms, claiming that the aim of lifting gold embargo lay in introducing market discipline in the economy by means of the appreciated exchange rate. Their stance originated partly from the notion that the financial side of the economy had already cleared up inefficiency consequent to the financial panic in 1927, and attention was now turning to the real side of the economy. As the leading figure in Japan's financial circles, Inoue, we may suppose, must have shared such views. Furthermore, in Inoue's writings after he became finance minister, priority was always attached to such items as "practicing thrift in public and private life," criticism of "living on borrowing," and the like, and the return to the gold standard was always assigned second or third priority.

Incidentally, *zaikai-seiri* meant weeding out inefficient and weak firms. In prewar Japan, economic policy took the weak to be not workers or poor peasants, but weak producers. Weakness on the part of workers was not admitted in official policy, although the socialists and some enlightened bureaucrats concerned with labor policy were aware of the realities. Poor peasants could be the objects of economic policy only when they were recognized as small and weak producers.

8.2.2. Justification by the Global Standard

It seems that if Inoue were to have claimed explicitly that tight policy per se was the foremost priority, and that the real aim of the return to the gold standard lay in *zaikai-seiri*, the Inoue *zaisei* would have come in for fierce opposition.

Although lifting the gold embargo had long been on the agenda, to be carried out sooner or later, the sharp deflation it entailed would have been sufficient to create doubts about the policy. In order to understand why the Hamaguchi administration's policy was welcomed with such enthusiasm, it is necessary to focus on the whole policy package of the Hamaguchi–Minseito Party regime.

In the policy package of Minseito, the economic aspect—the return to the gold standard and an emphasis on the international division of labor—was complemented by a foreign policy that emphasized cooperation with the United Kingdom and the United States and a flexible policy stance toward China. All this added up to an accommodating stance on the global standards of the times. Although Inoue had been close to Seiyukai before being appointed as the Hamaguchi administration's finance minister, he seems to have become increasingly disappointed with Seyukai's lax approach to spending. At the same time, his conservative stance on the lifting of the gold embargo was well known.

To understand why Inoue decided to lift the gold embargo, we must take into account not only his real aim of implementing *zaikai-seiri* but also his judgment that the policy could meet with public support if presented in a package conforming to global standards. People suffering from long-term economic stagnation and fed up with the policy muddle saw a gleam of hope and relief in the package.

Nevertheless, the policy package was not entirely immune from criticism. For one thing, the view that the international gold standard was not necessarily perfectly congruous with the world economy after World War I was gaining ground; the deflationary bent of the monetary system had already been a serious concern for the policy planners at the Geneva meeting in 1922, and price rigidity owing to oligopoly and the labor unions was recognized as a threat to the price-specie adjustment mechanism. Moreover, fitting in with the international division of labor was not an easy task; the reduction of already weak protection of heavy and chemical industries through such measures as significant tariff reduction was difficult to implement, in view of the increased importance of the industries for the economy. The flexible policy toward China was possible only as long as it did not harm Japanese interests in North-East China, and did not lead to more aggressive moves to boycott Japanese commodities.

8.3. Global Standards and Policy Choice in Koizumi's Policy

Koizumi's approach to deregulation and structural reform comprised three parts: first, the reform of administrative systems such as the postal saving system and various semigovernmental corporations; second, reform in the direction of decentralization or transfer of administrative power to local governments by way of reduction of subsidies, reallocation of local government block grants, and transfer of taxation power to local governments; and third, deregulation in various areas affecting everyday life such as employment, medical care, education, and transportation and communication. Among these, the decentralization policy was scantily implemented; reduction of subsidies was implemented to some extent, but transfer of taxation power was left untouched. With respect to administrative reform, privatization of the postal saving system was the only major accomplishment, although opposition to this policy was still strong, and efforts to reform such semigovernmental organizations as highway public corporations came up against staunch resistance by the bureaucracy. So far, no substantial reform had been undertaken with respect to the public service system.

While reform of areas where the bureaucracy and pork-barrel politicians had vested interests encountered strong opposition and made slow progress, the deregulation of areas touching on everyday life proceeded fairly rapidly. This is reasonable because the major opposition to this policy came only from declining industries, usually composed of weak small and medium-sized firms. According to Eto (2009), 60 percent of the deregulation originally planned by the government had already been accomplished.

8.3.1. The Aim of Deregulation Policy for Koizumi

Most of the prime ministers during the 1980s and the 1990s were reluctant to commit themselves to deregulation. This is partly because of resistance by bureaucrats and politicians concerned with their own electorates, and partly because they feared that deregulation might destroy the delicate mechanisms that protected the weak classes in the economy. The Hashimoto administration (1996–98) took a step forward, and the Koizumi administration embarked on a full-scale deregulation policy. One of the reasons for Koizumi's positive stance on deregulation was that neoliberalism provided a justifying logic, as will be discussed later. Another and probably compelling reason for Koizumi was that, after the long period of stagnation called the "lost decade," the determination grew to utilize deregulation as a measure to set the economy back on its feet. This determination was not based on any rigorous assessment of the policy's effects, but simply derived from the fact that other measures had been tried without significant economic recovery.

Although Koizumi himself claimed that deregulation and structural reform would enhance economic growth, it is not clear how serious he was in this claim. In view of the fact that competition-hampering regulation was strong in declining industries, it was natural to be skeptical about the effects of removing it. Even if regulation caused inefficiencies in those industries, there were many factors responsible for their decline, including the comparative advantage in international trade, and it was by no means certain that simple deregulation could convert them into growing industries. In fact, although the policy provided some segments of business with lucrative opportunities, the macro effect seems to have been negligible. Moreover, because it caused the mass firing of delegated workers and nonregular employees, the subprime crisis triggered criticism of the unfettered deregulation of the labor market brought on by the reform. The Koizumi reform was now facing relentless attacks and charges that it had increased economic inequality.

If Koizumi had showed scant commitment with respect to the growth-enhancing effects of deregulation, what accounted for his extraordinary passion for deregulation and structural reform? In view of the fact that regulations were related to vested interests of bureaucrats and politicians in providing them with *amakudari* opportunities and vote-gathering machinery, it would be natural to consider that Koizumi's real aim was to attack such vested interests. For Koizumi, the privatization of the postal system constituted an attack on the vote-gathering machinery of the LDP, while decentralization aimed at undermining the favor-based politics based on the subsidy flow between the bureaucracy and local communities. The policy of a ceiling on bond financing of the government was also related to this aim, public works projects being its main target.

8.3.2. Justification by the Global Standards

It is to be borne in mind that under the Koizumi regime the unprecedented scandal of missing pension records had yet to be disclosed, so the voters were not entirely disenchanted with the bureaucracy. If Koizumi had paraded anti-bureaucracy slogans in the election campaign, it would not necessarily have brought him victory.

Just as in the case of Inoue, the Koizumi reform or its core part, deregulation and structural reform, was justified by its conformity to global standards. With respect to economic policy, the Koizumi reform was in line with neoliberalism, and as for foreign policy, Koizumi conformed to the Anglo-American line. Emergency legislation as well as the special-measure law aimed at Afghanistan and Iraq effectively strengthened relations with the United States, while Koizumi cared little about the cooling of relations with Korea and China over the Yasukuni and history textbook issue.

8.4. The Difference between Inoue and Koizumi: Strong Counterproposal versus No Counterproposal

In the economic history of Japan, the Inoue and the Koizumi policies are outstanding in that their aim was to introduce market discipline. The two policies have many things in common, as we saw in the first section. In this regard, it is interesting to note that they are distinctively different in having or not having their own counterproposal.

It is well known that, when Inoue's policy of lifting the gold embargo finally failed, Korekiyo Takahashi of the Seiyukai Party took his place and implemented a floating exchange rate, budget deficits, and a low interest rate—exactly the opposite of Inoue's policy. While the Takahasi *zaisei* was a countercyclical macro initiative, it was also a definite counterproposal to Inoue-Hamaguchi in terms of structural policy, which was in fact essentially the traditional stance of Seiyukai. Although in the literature of political history it is often claimed that the policies of the two parties were very similar during the interwar period, the similarity is mostly in areas such as social and rural initiatives, which are directly related to vote mobilization. With respect to the major issues concerning economic and foreign policy, there were salient differences between the two parties. In terms of economic policy, Seiyukai advocated fiscal and import substitution policies favoring heavy and chemical industries, as opposed to the Minseito approach comprising tight fiscal policy and export promotion with a touch of bias against the heavy and chemical industries. In terms of foreign policy, Seiyukai maintained an independent foreign policy with emphasis on national vested interests in China, in diametrical opposition to Minseito's policy, emphasizing cooperation with the United States and the United Kingdom.

Recently, there seems to have developed a marked skepticism about the effectiveness and accomplishment of Koizumi's reform. However, despite the loudness of the criticism, it is surprising that neither the Liberal Democratic Party nor the Democratic Party has been able to come up with an explicit counterproposal to Koizumi's policy. Some Liberal Democratic Party leaders such as Taro Asou criticized Koizumi's effort at market discipline, but he did not propose any theory of economic policy of his own. The Democratic Party, which has recently come into power, emphasizes improvement of living conditions, but it has so far failed to explain why an increase in welfare expenditure is needed within a coherent framework that incorporates both growth and elements of equality in the economy. Why they could not present a counterproposal to the Koizumi model remains an enigma. Let us consider why this enigma emerged.

8.5. Japan as a Hypothetical Development-Oriented State

8.5.1. The Johnson-Noguchi Theory

As far as historical experience up until the high-growth era is concerned, the hypothesis most often considered able to capture the essential characteristic of the Japanese economy is that it is a development-oriented state. This hypothesis was most eloquently spelled out by two authors, Chalmers Johnson and Yukio Noguchi. Johnson (1982) derived this hypothesis by tracing out the historical experience of MITI going back to the Ministry of Agriculture and Commerce in the Meiji period, and Noguchi (1995) by comparing the economic system during the high-growth era with the system that prevailed during World War II. Noguchi is much more cautious than Johnson in the sense that Noguchi is aware that the high-growth system was introduced to address problems of income distribution. However, for the sake of simplicity, we will disregard this difference.

The impact of these two literatures was enormous, partly because the hypothesis was congruent with the Marxian view of the Japanese economy that emphasizes planned and bureaucracy-driven development. This hypothesis, however, is unsupported in two important respects: first, the reasoning on the political decision mechanism determining how an economic system is chosen, and second, the purpose of establishing the system of the high-growth era.

Let me explain the first point. Both Johnson and Noguchi argue that the development-oriented bureaucrats who implemented the wartime planned economy survived through the postwar growth period, and since they had enormous power in the implementation of industrial policy, the Japanese economy became development oriented. Ostensibly, this logic is analogous to the controversy about whether politicians or the bureaucracy wielded greater power in policy implementation. This analogy, however, is wrong because in a democratic society both politicians and bureaucrats are agents for the real principal, the constituents. The decision as to the degree to which the market mechanism is utilized in an economy is determined by the constituents or the median voters of the given society. Both politicians and bureaucrats must respect the decision of the constituents. In other words, unlike political decisions regarding local public goods, such as the tariff rate of a particular product, this falls within the area of general-interest politics. In this sense, the fact that development-oriented bureaucrats had strong power in policy implementation has nothing to do with why Japan has become development oriented. The logic of both Johnson and Noguchi is based on a complete misunderstanding in this regard.

8.5.2. The Purpose of the Economic System during the High-Growth Era

The drawback of the hypothesis that Japan is a development-oriented state is more serious with respect to the second point. The hypothesis implies that the high-growth economic system was established to encourage economic growth thorough growth-oriented industrial policy. Let me explain why this assertion is wrong. First, the regulations mainly targeted declining industries, and second, the system was established so as to avoid the failures of the prewar system based on virtually pure market principles without any formal measures to improve income distribution.

Let us start with the first point. As I have explained elsewhere (Teranishi 2005), the regulation system of the high-growth era economy can be summarized as a system to control the competitive conditions of each industry so as to determine its value added and the division of the value added into profit and wages. In other words, the regulations of competitive conditions of each industrial sector determined the input and output prices, and hence the value added of each sector, and the "spring offensive" system determined the wage rate for each industry, and hence the division of the value added into wages and profits. It is important to note that in this system, competitive conditions were most severely regulated in declining industries. In the case of a growing industry, value added could be high enough without any control of competitive conditions. There is no denying that the bureaucrats in departments such as MITI tried to use this system of controlling income distribution among different industries as a tool of industrial policy. Although they were eager to apply the policy to growing industries, however, such efforts by and large ended in failure, as was seen in the case of the Temporary Measures Law for Special Industries in 1962.

The second reason why the assertion that the high-growth era system was established for the purpose of development is wrong is that the actual process of its establishment did not support this assertion. The postwar economic system was established so as to avoid instability in the socioeconomic system due to aggravation of income distribution and fragility in the banking system. The banking system in the immediate aftermath of the war was on the brink of collapse because of the huge loss caused by the moratorium on wartime loans. In order to save the banks from bankruptcy, control of various interests, including prices of national and corporate bonds, was introduced. Although such controlled interest rates were utilized by bureaucrats for the purpose of credit rationing, the original purpose of control lay in securing the safety of the banking system, not in developmental credit rationing (Teranishi 1993).

With respect to the improvement of income distribution, there were three alternative ways to represent conflicts among the population over the distribution of income. The first alternative was to revive the prewar order based on representation of the interests of regional communities. This system had to be abandoned, however, because postwar reforms such as land reform carried out under pressure by occupation forces deprived local leaders (rich landlords and merchants) of their wealth as well as their ethos as community leaders. The second alternative was a Western-type sociodemocratic mechanism, in which the distributive interests of the population were represented by classes, such as the working class and the capitalist class. In view of the active labor movements and class conflicts that had flared up as the occupation forces encouraged labor movements, this system was considered the most practicable just after the war. However, as the intense labor movements were contained, and class conflicts were accommodated in the cooperative system, the so-called Japanese-style firm system became dominant, and the sociodemocratic system was also abandoned. In this way, the third alternative of representing distributive interests by each industry emerged as the workable distributive mechanism congruent with the Japanese-style firm system. (For detailed examination of the historical process outlined above, refer to Teranishi 2005.)

In sum, the postwar economic system was established with the purpose of realizing an equitable and stable socioeconomic system. Although the competition-hampering mechanism introduced for that purpose was utilized by some development-oriented bureaucrats for the purposes of industrial policy, it was not the original intention of the system.

8.6. Beyond Antidevelopmentalism

8.6.1. Defects of the High-Growth Era System

The competition-hampering system of the high-growth era began to show various defects after the 1980s. First, the coordination of competition-hampering regulations across various industries had come up against international criticism of nontariff trade barriers, dissatisfaction on the part of consumers, and the increase in countercyclical fiscal expenditures channeled, in particular, toward the construction industries. Second, there were growing feelings of hostility against the Japanese firm system, with criticism of the "company man" or "overwork death," leading to deterioration in loyalty to the system on the part of the new middle class. Third, excessive intervention by politicians trying to help their own constituencies and bureaucrats also drew criticism.

Barring a move toward a Western-type sociodemocratic system, the best and the most practical solution was to carry out repairs on the interface between the government and the private sector to correct defects. In view of Japanese experiences during the interwar period and the aftermath of World War II, it seemed best to present a multidimensional system of interest representation and social solidarity. During the interwar period and the immediate postwar period, there were three alternative bases of representation: region (representation of interests through local communities), industry (adjustment of interindustry income difference and solidarity based on industries and firms), and class (representation of interests on the basis of ownership of production factors, labor, and capital). In the future, considerations of historical path dependence would dictate that industry remained an important axis for representation of interests, focusing on the weak side of the industrial structure. In view of the rising criticism against excessive centralization of the economic system, local communities could again be a core to interest representation; competition among regions with respect to living conditions, social welfare, and employment opportunities was expected to activate the economy. Moreover, in view of the increasing conflict of interests among different generations, it would be necessary to incorporate a system of representation of intergenerational interests, accommodating the distributive conflicts regarding public works, the social pension system, and environmental issues.

8.6.2. The Logical Structure of Koizumi Reform

The Koizumi reform, however, was based on entirely different logical grounds. The core reform policy, deregulation and structural reform, was justified using neoliberal arguments and the global standards of the times, coupled with a practically groundless theory of Japan as a developmental state. Let us examine its logical structure in this regard.

As is well known, neoliberalism was then in practice the philosophy of the Reagan administration in the United States and the Thatcher government in the United Kingdom. In the United States, this theory was born in opposition to the populist policy of the Roosevelt administration, which was biased toward labor protection (Shlaez 2007), while in the United Kingdom, neoliberalism emerged from criticism of the corporatist policy pursued by what were essentially social-democratic administrations. The theory gained widespread support as a result of the stagflation of the 1970s, caused by labor union activism and real wage rigidity (Bruno and Sachs 1985). In this sense neoliberalism was a political philosophy in the context of class conflicts and representation of the interests of the various classes. This was perfectly adequate for Western countries with strong tendencies toward social democracy. Japan, however, as mentioned above, had discarded social democracy as a solution for distributive conflicts, and in the case of stagflation triggered by the oil shock, Japan had weathered it by means of real wage flexibility and by applying a distributive mechanism related to interindustry interests.

Let me expand on this point. Neoliberalism maintains that freedom of business activity in competitive markets is the best way to maximize the wealth of each country and indeed the world (Harvey 2005). Free business activity means unfettered pursuit of profits, and this makes it inevitable for labor to be effectively subordinated to capital. The weak side of this model is the working class, which does not have fixed capital (Roemer 1986) and hence is subject to capitalistic exploitation by means of monitoring and coercion of efforts (Bowles and Gintis 1986). Social welfare consists mainly of a social safety net, providing support to individual losers in the competition. On the other hand, in the case of the Japanese model, the weak side of the economy is composed of weak firms in declining industries and small and medium-sized firms. This is completely different from the Western model. In the Inoue *zaisei*, the weak and less-competitive firms were targeted in the weeding-out policy. The high-growth era system protected weak industries, and hence firms within them, as well as small and medium-sized firms. The labor market reform implemented in the context of the Koizumi reform destroyed the employment system in weak industries and small and medium-sized firms, giving rise to massive delegated labor and nonregular employees. This kind of policy is based on a complete misunderstanding of the economic system in Japan.

Moreover, neoliberal doctrine gave rise to the so-called Washington Consensus in its application to developing countries, and in particular the development-oriented states of Latin America. The Washington Consensus implied a highly critical attitude on the part of the International Monetary Fund and World Bank toward development-oriented states. Thanks to the strong influence of the Johnson-Noguchi thesis, the policy prescription of the Washington Consensus found a golden opportunity for application in Japan. However, this application was also based on facile and erroneous reasoning. During the 1960s and 1970s, there occurred rapid expansion of state enterprises in Latin America in order to implement import-substitution policies. It was considered that government involvement was the most effective way to implement these policies, since the government could have at its command the best technology and human resources needed for the policy. The strategy, however, resulted in serious inefficiency and macroeconomic instability. Labor movements, which were particularly radical in the case of state enterprises, brought about serious inflation and appreciation of exchange rates to keep urban prices low. Inflation, together with the inefficiency of state enterprises due to the lack of competition, led to balance-of-payment deficits through overvalued exchange rates, leading to the outbreak of the foreign debt crises in the early 1980s. In Latin America inflation was invariably triggered by labor activism involving state enterprise employees. Their wage demands were quite often met even though this resulted in budget deficits, directly leading to an increase in money supply, fueling inflation. Neoliberal ideas were applied to this situation as a critical response to the overexpansion of government activity in the economy or overpresence of state enterprises that squeezed out private business (Kuczynski 2003; Williamson 1990). This is perfectly appropriate in the case of the Latin American economies, where class conflicts were a major factor behind distributive issues and state enterprise had a huge share in the economy. The situation of Japan, however, was quite different. Here, most of the major economic activities were carried out by the private sector, and interindustry adjustment, not interclass confrontation and labor movements, was the major mechanism in resolving distributive conflicts.

The transplanting of neoliberalism by the Koizumi reform seems to have been carried out on a soil entirely different from that of the Western world or, in particular, from Latin America. One basic reason for this was the widespread acceptance of the Johnson-Noguchi hypothesis of Japan as a developmental state, and the expansion of the neoliberal doctrine as an anti-development-oriented policy. Another was the artful strategy of the Koizumi administration in propagating neoliberalism as the global standard. Finally, Japanese economists shared responsibility on this point, for most major economists seem to have taken an accommodating stance in this regard. The stance of the economists reflects a change in economic theory. As monetarist criticism of Keynesian economics was developed with increasing support from economists, opposition to neoliberalism built on anti-Keynesian theory lost ground.

8.7. Conclusion

The Koizumi reform found justification in neoliberalism, the practical philosophy to activate profit-maximizing behavior by private firms in a context where distributive interests are represented in terms of class conflicts between labor and capital. Although this framework did not fit Japan, where distributive interests were represented by the interindustrial framework, the general acceptance of the hypothesis that Japan was a developmental state presented a convenient ground for the application of neoliberalism. This was because neoliberalism had been extended to the situation of Latin American countries in opposition to developmental states. Since the hypothesis lacked solid ground, there was no logical basis for the Koizumi reform. Even if there were serious criticisms of the Koizumi reform, there does not seem to have been any coherent counterproposal to it. The reason for this lies not in the infallibility of the reform, but in the flaw in the logic used to justify it, failing to take due cognizance of the fallacy of the basic hypothesis of Japan as developmental state.

Some members of the Liberal Democratic Party propose "small government" as a future strategy, and some members of the Democratic Party assert the need for a welfare state. These ideas are futile unless they are elaborated in the context of path dependency in the Japanese economy. If the assertion of "small government" is based on Washington Consensus–type reasoning, and advocates of the welfare state have in mind a class conflict model resembling that of the United States or the United Kingdom, the risk is that these ideas entail the same logical failures as the Koizumi reform.

References

Bowles, Samuel, and Herbert Gintis. 1988. "Contested Exchanges: Political Economy and Modern Economic Theory." *American Economic Review* 72 (2): 145–50.

Bruno, Michael, and Jeffrey Sachs. 1985. *Economics of Worldwide Stagflation*. Cambridge, MA: Harvard University Press.

Eto, Masaru. 2010. "Regulation Reform and Privatization in Structural Reform" (in Japanese). In Juro Teranishi, ed., *Kiseikanwa kouzoukaikaku*. Tokyo: Keioudaigaku shuppannkai.

Harvey, David. 2005. *A Brief History of Neoliberalism*. New York: Oxford University Press.

Johnson, Chalmers. 1982. *MITI and the Japanese Miracle*. Stanford, CA: Stanford University Press.

Kuczynski, Pedro-Pablo. 2003. "Setting the Stage." In John Williamson and Pedro-Pablo Kuczynski, eds., *After the Washington Consensus: Restarting Growth and Reform in Latin America*. Washington, DC: Institute for International Economics.

Noguchi, Yukio. 1995. *1940-System* (in Japanese). Touyoukeizaisinnpousha.

Roemer, John. E. 1986 *Value, Exploitation and Class*. New York: Horwood Academic Press.

Shlaes, Amity. 2007. *The Forgotten Man: A New History of the Great Depression*. New York: HarperCollins.

Teranishi, Juro. 1993. "Emergence and Establishment of the Financial System in Postwar Japan: Government Intervention, Indirect Financing and the Corporate Monitoring System." Paper prepared for the project "Strategies for Rapid Growth: Public Policy and The Asian Miracle," organized by the Country Economics Department, World Bank.

Teranishi, Juro. 2005. *Evolution of the Economic System in Japan*. Northhampton, MA: Edward Elgar.

Williamson, John. 1990. "What Washington Consensus Means by Policy Reform." In John Williamson, ed., *Latin American Adjustment: How Much Has Happened*. Washington, DC: Institute for International Economics. Available at http://www.papelesdesociedad.info/IMG/pdf/john_williamson_what_washington_means_by_policy_reform-2.pdf.

III | Varieties of Neoliberalism

INTERNATIONAL DIMENSIONS

9 | National versus Supranational Collective Goods

THE EVOLUTION OF NEOLIBERAL FEDERALISM

FABIO MASINI

9.1. Introduction

The recent and growing literature concerning the birth and history of neoliberalism (Walpen 2004; Plehwe and Walpen 2006; Plehwe, Walpen, and Neunhöffer 2006; Plickert 2008; Mirowski and Plehwe 2009; Jackson 2010) stresses the importance of supranational economic governance and institutions for the neoliberal project. It is common wisdom that, although mainly pursued at the national level, neoliberal policies require support from a global institutional framework designed to serve the values of neoliberalism, in particular through the provision of two *supranational collective goods*, capital mobility and free trade.

Some authors also underline that the structure of such international governance (at both global and continental levels) is often conceived as a federal model (Prechel and Harms 2007), where supranational institutions are meant to impose "inter-jurisdictional policy competition, which . . . helps to lock-in neoliberal policies at the domestic level" (Harmes 2012, 60), thus reducing the range of actions that national governments can undertake in order to finance the growth and even the preservation of the *national collective goods* that are usually labeled under the category of *welfare state*.

This kind of neoliberal supranational federalism is nevertheless to be better qualified and framed within a specific evolutionary context, requiring some preliminary observations. The first concerns the nature of federalism advocated by neoliberals. As Harmes (2012, 67) suggests: "Rather than advocating federalism in general, neoliberal theory argues for a specific type of federalism that is explicitly designed to limit social democratic forms of government intervention." It is therefore necessary to understand the specific features of the federal idea advocated by neoliberal intellectuals. The second point is that the antiwelfarist bias in neoliberal federalism, trading-off supranational and national collective goods, only applies to the last decades, in particular since what may be called the Hayek-Friedman-Buchanan approach to neoliberalism has grown more and more powerful worldwide, both intellectually and politically (Graefe 2006).

The aim of this chapter is to enquire into the origins of this approach and to show that the situation was very different and more pluralistic at the beginning of the intellectual effort that characterized the "neoliberal thought collective" (Mirowski and Plehwe 2009): only after World War II was there a radicalization of the trade-offs between the two levels (national and supranational) of collective goods in the neoliberal agenda. Building on a previous paper (Masini 2012a), I argue that the way federalism was conceived in different neoliberal approaches to the international order can help understand us one of the most subtle ways in which neoliberalism increasingly supported an antiwelfarist policymaking.

In order to illustrate this, it is crucial to show briefly the emergence of heterogeneous responses to the crisis of civilization after World War I and underline the existence of two very different approaches to federalism within neoliberal thought: one instrumental to defend the market from any collective decision-making process and prevent discretionality in public policies, therefore negatively impacting the provision of national collective goods (section 9.2); the other one aiming at a constitutional decision-making process where both—national and supranational—levels of government are given the legitimate power to decide and enforce the provision of collective goods in a genuine multilevel governing system (section 9.3). As I shall illustrate, this debate evolved into a more specific attack against the welfare state in the fifties, through a competitive model of fiscal federalism (section 9.4).

9.2. Freedom from Wants or Freedom from the State?

After World War I—for more than two decades—the values of classical liberalism were patently in danger. The two pillars upon which the first globalization era was founded, *capital mobility* and *free trade*, were destroyed. Wilson's international liberalism soon proved to be utopian and naive. A new creative effort of social design and imagination was needed to guarantee the provision of these two supranational public goods, crucial to the liberal tradition.

At the same time, especially after 1929, new social needs were to be satisfied in order to avoid massive poverty and unemployment. After what was seen as a manifest failure of free markets, socialist and corporatist national economic planning seemed to gain credibility as the only viable alternative approaches to the satisfaction of human needs.

The liberal intellectuals during the interwar period developed divergent ideas on these issues. On the one side, some dwelled on the need to found *new liberal* values based on the desire to free human beings from wants, therefore accepting some forms of social welfare in order to alleviate the economic, social, and political marginalization resulting from unemployment. Keynes and Beveridge but also Schumpeter were among the leading exponents of this particular way to revive liberalism. The market is a fundamental social and economic institution, but it can fail. In such cases, a credible and strong intervention by public authorities is necessary to help the market regain its positive social function.

On the other side, although less monolithic than usually argued (Denord 2009, 48ff.), the *neoliberal* thought collective, which started to be gathered around the Institut des Hautes Études Internationales of Geneva in the early thirties and would later become a mature intellectual (with the 1938 Lippman's Colloquium of Paris) and political (with the foundation of the Mont Pelerin Society in 1947) project, shared some common attitudes about these problems.

In its most radical view, the major challenge to civilization was found to be state intervention in the free play of economic forces. What had failed was not the free market but the attempt to influence and distort it by means of political regulations. The illegitimate pre-eminence of collective political authorities over the free choices of individuals on the satisfaction of human needs called for a strong claim against any form of state interference, in particular in the realm of arbitrary wealth redistribution: "In neoliberal theory, therefore, government is a monopolistic rent seeker whose intervention in the economy is unlikely to be either benevolent or effective" (Harmes 2012, 64).

It is precisely from these arguments that an important reflection starts among some neoliberal intellectuals on the question of the decentralization of power and on federalism. As Buchanan (1995, 259) would later suggest, "A coherent classical liberal must generally be supportive of federal political structures, because any division of authority must, necessarily, tend to limit the potential range of political coercion." Or as Mantzavinos (2010, 102) has recently synthetized: "Federalism as a constitutional structure provides a system of 'checks and balances' which in the long run promotes the liberty of individuals of the respective polity. Federalism is a constitutionally anchored constraint onto political power and onto the possibility of curtailing individual liberty."

Nevertheless, as I shall illustrate, two different paths can be taken form this shared belief in the positive effect of federalism on liberty. Basically, one is related to the preservation of individuals' *economic* freedom thanks to a federal authority called to limit the interference of national states—something similar to what has been labeled "market-preserving federalism" (Weingast 1995) the other to the guarantee of individuals' *political* freedom of choice at all levels of government where collective goods are required, from the local to the global dimension.

As concerns the first, which will be dealt in the remaining part of this section, we should dwell on Mises's and Hayek's contributions. They shared important social, political, and philosophical views, also as concerns the role of international institutions and the global public goods they are supposed to provide. In *Liberalismus*, Mises (1927, 111) tackles the crucial question of "how to create the social conditions that will eliminate the causes of war." In *Nation, Staat und Wirtshaft* he had already given an answer to that: "The first requirement in this regard is private property. When private property must be respected even in time of war . . . an important motive for waging war has already been excluded." According to him, "Liberalism . . . is indifferent towards the State itself" (Mises 1919, 66) unless it proves detrimental to the establishment of a free-market international framework. In that case, the problem becomes "limiting State power to a minimum" (Mises 1919, 126).

In *Nation, Staat, und Wirtschaft*, Mises had indeed underlined the political aspect of economic freedom but also the economic goal behind political action: "Liberalism, which assumes full economic freedom, tries to solve the difficulties which the different political institutions pose to the development of the market, detaching economics from the State" (Mises 1919, 35). Liberalism implies, under this point of view, a political struggle designed to free economics from the influence of politics. Peaceful international relations are, therefore, as in Bentham and Mill, the byproduct of economic freedom: "The starting-point of [the] entire [liberal] political philosophy is the conviction that the division of labor is international and not merely national" (Mises 1927, 148). Indeed, when criticizing the Covenant of the League of Nations, Mises (1927, 149–50) argues against it because it does not adequately guarantee private property and economic freedom from political power, not because the League is ineffective in making, passing, and enforcing international law.

The solution lies in the general acceptance (to be pursued in each country) of *liberal principles*: "This frame of mind can be nothing less than the unqualified, unconditional acceptance of liberalism. Liberal thinking must permeate all nations, liberal principles must pervade all political institutions, if the prerequisites of peace are to be created and the causes of war eliminated. As long as nations cling to protective tariffs, immigration barriers, compulsory education, interventionism, and etatism new conflicts capable of breaking out at any time into open warfare will continually arise to plague mankind" (Mises 1927, 150–51). Mises's strategy is what Sally (1998a, 1998b) defines as *liberalism from below*, according to which the goal of international peace can be served through a liberal agenda to be pursued at the level of single national countries, eventually supported by international economic institutions to guarantee the best operation of the market.

Building on these concepts of the nature and scope of international institutions, Hayek started to reflect in the early thirties on these topics, later claiming to be in favor of federal supranational institutions. The reasons why Hayek started to think about federalism are two. On the one side, he was looking for institutional tools that could reduce the room for public intervention in the economy. The degeneration of the political debate in fascism, Nazism, and corporatism during the thirties made it more and more urgent to raise obstacles to the arrogant distortions of politics in economic matters. The defense of the free interplay of the market was a way to defend individual freedom from the state. But in Hayek's view, even more detrimental was the alternative, within liberals themselves, defended by economists like Harrod and Keynes who argued in favor of monetary (and economic) nationalism. Not yet radically critical about rationalist constructivism, Hayek thought that advocating a European federation might be a good opportunity to limit the power of nation-states over the economy.

The second reason why Hayek turned to the federal model is that, after he moved to London in 1931, he had the chance to listen to Lionel Robbins's strong claims in favor of a European federation. Hayek, nevertheless, held different views from Robbins concerning the reasons why civilization was in danger, which in turn would determine a profound difference in the way they approached the idea of supranational federal institutions, as I shall illustrate. Although rooted in previous works (Hayek 1931, 1933a, 1933b), his first book on these questions is *Monetary Nationalism and International Stability*, published in 1937. He would later come back to these matters in 1939 with *Economic Conditions of Inter-state Federalism* and in 1944 with the world-renowned *Road to Serfdom*, where he deals extensively with federalism in chapter 15, "The Prospects of International Order."

Hayek's reference to the international institutional framework based on a federal political structure in his writings of 1937 and 1939 is clearly aimed at reducing the intervention of (national) public authorities in the realm of economic relationships (Hayek 1937, 77). The transfer of monetary sovereignty from nation-states to a supranational authority is merely a means to minimize public interventions in the working of the global market, not a matter of conflict resolution (as it was for Robbins, as we shall see in the next section). Under the intellectual influence of Mises, international institutions are for Hayek the best substitute for the complete negation of any public (national) intervention in the economy.

For this reason only, that is, in order to promote this kind of market-oriented federalism, in 1939 Hayek joined the Federal Union, founded in London to promote some sort of political, military, and economic federation between Britain and France, as his contributions to the debate within the association demonstrate (Ransome 1991). Along the same lines he published an article in *New Commonwealth Quarterly*, also in 1939, titled "Economic Conditions of Inter-state Federalism," where he argues in favor of federal supranational institutions to support the principles of economic freedom. But, again, it is clearly a negative-sum game as concerns public interventions in the economy: "The conclusion that, in a federation, certain economic powers, which are now generally wielded by the national states, could be exercised neither by the federation nor by the individual states, implies, that there would have to be less government all around if federation is to be practicable" (Hayek 1939, 266).

His concept can be better grasped by these lines: "The need is for an international authority which, without power to direct the different people what they must do, must be able to restrain them from action which will damage others. The powers which must be devolved on an international authority are not the new powers assumed by the states in recent times, but that minimum of powers of the ultra-liberal 'laissez-faire' state. . . . The form of international government under which certain strictly defined powers are transferred to an international authority, while in all other respects the individual countries remain responsible for their internal affairs, is, of course, that of federation" (Hayek 1944, 172–73). It is quite clear why this approach would later evolve in a more radical concept of federalism where the federal authority is thought of as a sort of functional, technical organism constraining national policymaking into narrow paths of public spending, as in Friedman (1962) and Buchanan.

The federal authority is not designed to provide international public goods that the inherent clash of national interests makes it impossible to provide in the necessary amount, and not even to defend states from each other, but to defend individuals from states. In Hayek's opinion: "An international authority which effectively limits the powers of the state over the individual will be one of the best safeguards of peace. The international Rule of Law must become a safeguard as much against the tyranny of the state over the individual as against the tyranny of the new super-state over the national communities. Neither an omnipotent super-state, nor a loose association of 'free nations,' but a community of nations of free men must be our goal" (Hayek 1944, 175). Although this last sentence much resembles one of Robbins's (1937a, 245) most renowned claims, the role of the supranational level is here meant only to defend individuals from undue interferences of nation-states in their free choices, not to create a new place where collective supranational decisions may be taken democratically.

In the following years, the disillusion with the institutional choices of the international organizations of the postwar era, an increasing detachment from Robbins and London, and a very different intellectual climate and agenda in the United States when he moved there, marked a new phase: Hayek completely abandoned any reference to federalism à la Robbins and went on pursuing a neoliberal agenda (à la Mises) where economic freedom is not the byproduct of a worldwide constitutional arrangement based on the federal principles but is a goal in itself, to be pursued in each national political arena and coordinated worldwide. In synthesis, apart from a very short period in his life, not only could Hayek's political liberalism be labeled "instrumental" (Kley 1994), but also his claim for political federalism can be said to be *instrumental* to an economic and social Weltanschauung aimed at preserving the spontaneous social order expressed by the market from the interference of any collective political body. This is the attitude that would exert a major influence on the neoliberal thought in the following decades and which would also exert some influence in the integration process of the European Union in the last 30 years (for different interpretations on this, see Streeck 2014; Masini 2015).

9.3. Sovereignty, Liberal Planning, and Constitutional Federalism

The main feature of Mises's *liberalism from below* and Hayek's *instrumental federalism* is that any effort to design some international institution is devoted only to elicit national state sovereignties from interfering with the operation of the free market. This is a different question from the one addressed by two other major exponents of the early neoliberal thought collective, Lionel Robbins and Luigi Einaudi. Their approach to the crisis of civilization after World War I was quite different from the approach of Mises and Hayek. They both found it to be attributable to the existence of absolute and exclusive national sovereignties, which make it intrinsically impossible to rely on diplomatic arrangements for international conflict resolution and therefore to find solutions to the problems of collective action that are necessary to provide international public goods, first of all *peace*.

Einaudi had dealt extensively with this problem soon after World War I, although his first contribution on this point dates back to 1897 (Einaudi 1897). Anticipating Sen (1970) on the "impossibility of a Paretian liberal," and building on his intellectual background deeply rooted in the British liberals (Cressati 1992, 31; Giordano 2006, 65ff.), Einaudi claims that freedom, at the international level, does not depend on the possibility of acting according only to national sovereign choices but on a set of rules where international decisions are taken by majority principle and where, therefore, "state sovereignty has to be limited" (Morelli 1990, 21). His crucial point is that the absolute and exclusive sovereignty of each national state, embodied in the veto rule at the international diplomatic level, makes it impossible to pursue any collective action and hence to provide a collective public good such as international peace, which is in turn fundamental to provide other liberal values such as the effective operation of the markets.

If this is the analysis, the way out is a system where supranational choices are the result of a democratic decision-making process: "From this imperfect phase when any one of the six powers, through its opposition, could make any plan accepted by all the others inapplicable, we will slowly come to a point where the majority will be able to impose decisions on the minority without having recourse to the *ultima ratio* of war" (Einaudi 1897, 37–38). Such concepts would be further restated at the end of World War I. In two newspaper articles that appeared in *Corriere della Sera* in January and December 1918, Einaudi underlined that the major weakness of the Wilsonian project lay in its confederative architecture, which did not question the absolute sovereignty of nation-states: "Everybody implicitly admits that the allied—or confederated—states should remain completely sovereign and independent" (Einaudi 1918a, 82). Thinking of US experience, he contrasted "a society of nations in terms of a confederation of sovereign states, with the magnificent success of another kind of society of nations, which eventually transforms the previously sovereign states into provinces of a whole and wider sovereign state" (83).

In the second article, Einaudi makes a step further. He argues that "the dogma of sovereignty, *absolute* and *perfect in itself,* is mostly maleficent" (1918b, 147) and that "the self-sufficient, isolated and sovereign state is a fiction of imagination" (151). Therefore, "It is necessary to destroy and ban forever the dogma of perfect sovereignty, if we want the society of nations to be born vital" (151). And some lines further: "Only integrated nations can reciprocally constrain themselves to secure themselves, as parts of a superior state organism, against the attempts of hegemony toward which, in the present anarchical situation, the strongest state is unavoidably attracted by the deadly dogma of absolute sovereignty" (156).

Even more interesting is an article published in 1919 in *Corriere della Sera*, where Einaudi tackled the proposal by Wilson to take the territory of Fiume (now in Croatia) away from Italy and give it to the Austro-Hungarian regime. Einaudi recognizes the importance of "nationalistic" feelings that, if denied, might become a source of political uncertainty in international relations and of military conflict. But he asserts that constitutional economic arrangements and institutions could be designed to ensure a collective, transnational use of such territories. Einaudi aims to challenge the identification of *nationality* with *state sovereignty*, and he is convinced that the only juridical system that could achieve this goal is a federal constitutional arrangement along the lines subscribed at the second Philadelphia convention of 1787, where sovereignty is *shared* by different levels of government and citizens are loyal to both national and supranational bodies.

In the following decades, freedom, in all its forms, was shrinking under Italian fascism. In 1931 university professors were obliged to sign an oath of allegiance to the regime; some months later Mussolini (1933, 264) declared, "Today we bury economic liberalism" and most (nonfascist) scientific and academic journals were closed. In this very unsympathetic context, Einaudi tried to defend the economics profession from the interference of the ideologies of the political regime and developed a peculiar approach to economic epistemology, based on a positivistic approach to Robbins's *Essay on the Nature and Significance of Economic Science*, but also a militant role for the economist in society. Economics is detached from politics, and so should it remain; but economists are supposed to testify the *truth* of economic laws against the pretensions of political ideologies.

It is in the very heart of this cultural atmosphere that, in the second half of the thirties, Einaudi came back to questions concerning the institutional architecture of international liberalism. Einaudi had traveled extensively in the previous years and met representatives of that thought collective, which would later become the Mont Pelerin Society (Rappard, Mises, Hayek, Robbins, etc.). During these years, one of the most influential books for him was Robbins's (1937a) *Economic Planning and International Order.* After reading it, Einaudi immediately sent it to his friend and colleague Ernesto Rossi, imprisoned for antifascism on the Island of Ventotene, where the book became the reference volume for the elaboration of the federalist *Manifesto for a United Europe* (written with Altiero Spinelli) and for the foundation of the European Federalist Movement, in 1943, to which Einaudi immediately adhered.

Einaudi and Robbins shared many common values and a very similar cultural background, well rooted in the classical British economic and political heritage. But the main character of their common view concerned the international order and is to be found in the British federalist tradition: a source of cultural and later political inspiration for Einaudi; a cultural heritage of which Robbins became the most important follower and protagonist in the thirties. According to O'Brien (1988, 136ff.) Robbins's interest in the international aspects of economics is attributable to Mill, Hamilton, Senior, Torrens, Cannan, and Bentham. Nevertheless, in his *Autobiography* Robbins, explaining the birth of his 1937 book—the first one on the constitutional architecture of an international liberal project—based on the lectures he was invited to give in the summer of 1935 at the Institut des Hautes Études Internationales in Geneva, only cited Hamilton's *The Federalist* as intellectual a source.

What were the main contents of that book, and why can we claim that, when it was published, it was the last product of the British liberal federalist tradition (Pinder 1990; Masini 1994; Burgess 1995)? His master at the London School of Economics, Edwin Cannan, had explicitly taken a position in favor of an international economic and monetary architecture designed along the lines of constitutional federalism, with the speech he gave at the LSE on "International Anarchy from the Economic Point of View" and the article "A Plea for Large Political Units," both written in 1916 but published only in 1927, within the book *An Economist's Protest.* Cannan, in turn, was particularly influenced by Henry Sidgwick, who deals extensively with federal governments in chapter 26 of his *Elements of Politics* of 1891.

Furthermore, Robbins lived in the very active and vivid cultural and intellectual London of Philipp Kerr (later Marquis of Lothian), Lionel Curtis, and

Arnold Toynbee. All of them in the twenties and thirties had pamphleted in favor of a European federation to promote an international political architecture founded on liberal principles and actively participated in the federalist struggle launched in 1938 with the foundation of the association Federal Union (which would later create the Federal Trust). It is interesting here to recall that the Federal Union was a very peculiar intellectual and political experience. Although it lasted a very few years, it gathered such culturally different economists as Friedrich Hayek, James Meade, Markus Fleming, William Beveridge, Barbara Wootton, and of course Robbins. The composition of the Economists' Committee shows that the federalist approach was indeed a struggle at a constitutional level, which most of them considered a prerequisite for a peaceful political debate, to which each could bring his ideological heritage.

Robbins's key point was that peace is not a mere and temporary absence of conflicts but a permanent condition that requires a specific economic, political, and institutional structure. The causes of war are therefore to be found both in inefficient institutions and in market failures depending on a perverse concept of *sovereignty*, which is exclusively attributed to nation-states: "The ultimate condition giving rise to those clashes of national economic interest which lead to international war is the existence of independent national sovereignties" (Robbins 1939b, 99). In this respect, Robbins maintained that classical liberalism was "anarchic," as international relations are only tackled through national diplomatic efforts, without any superior coercive institution. But the existence of systems of power with an exclusive and absolute sovereignty is not coherent with the necessity to safeguard peaceful international relations, nor with economic efficiency. The economy is in fact founded on the production and consumption of private and public goods. As concerns the former, they need to be produced and exchanged in a plurality of territorially concentric markets because each good and service is provided to satisfy the needs of more or less wide groups of individuals. Each market for each good needs to be backed and guaranteed by specific rules and juridical systems. Similarly, there are collective and shared needs that require the production of public goods that are not to be provided necessarily at the national level. In both cases, the economy needs an institutional, political, and juridical system that has to be structured from the local to the global dimension, following a principle that we would now call "subsidiarity."

According to Robbins (1937a, 1937b, 1939a, 1939b, 1940), the most adequate constitutional framework coherent with these urges is the federal one. Federalism provides an optimal constitutional equilibrium between decentralization and centralization, between local and global. "Independent Sovereignty must be limited" (Robbins 1939b, 104) and "the national States must learn to regard themselves as the functions of international local government" (Robbins 1939a, 105). A mere confederative agreement among national states, like those characterized at several international conferences in the thirties, would be unable to provide the collective public goods that are necessary to achieve a truly peaceful international framework and the constructive operation of global market forces. What is required is a constitutional architecture based on a multilevel federal system that allows decentralized choices and, at the same time, central strategic unity. In Robbins's own words, "There must be neither alliance nor complete unification, but Federation; neither *Staatenbund*, nor *Einheitsstaat*, but *Bundesstaat*" (1937a, 245).

For Robbins, the federal structure did not necessarily imply less government in a negative-sum game, as for Hayek. Federal authorities might decide whether or not to intervene in economics and to what extent (Robbins 1940, 240–41). Of course, I am not suggesting that Robbins would have argued in favor of socialist policies, but simply that this kind of political struggle (for example, between liberal and socialist policies) was to be framed within an appropriate constitutional set of rules and institutions where supranational decisions were also taken in a democratic way and not left to the law of the strongest, which usually governs diplomatic conferences. A federal structure is a constitutional architecture where different ideological approaches can politically confront each other, not necessarily a means to reduce public intervention in the economy.

Robbins's *constitutional federalism*, was therefore the opposite of Hayek's *instrumental federalism*, presenting the provision of concentric collective goods not as a trade-off but as a constitutional question to be faced ex ante according to the assessment of their spillover effects. In this respect, Robbins's open and multilayer approach to liberalism could interpret the heterogeneous approaches and ideologies that met at the founding meeting of the Mont Pelerin Society much better than could Hayek's. It is not by chance that if one compares the two versions of the final statement of the meeting, differences appear to be relevant: Robbins was indeed asked to redraft it in a way that made a compromise possible (Mirowski and Plehwe 2009, 22–25; Hartwell 1995, 41).

9.4 Collective Goods and Action: Polycentrism versus Federalism

In the interwar period, the pathological intrusion of politics into public institutions (Soviet central planning, corporatism, fascism, Nazism) ignited the debate against economic planning. After World War II, there was a widespread feeling that new models of institutional design were necessary. On one side, there was the Keynesian optimism that states could manage economic policy to maximize social welfare. On the other side, it became manifest that policymaking was strongly influenced by powerful lobbies and interest groups, which oriented policymaking strategies irrespective of the general welfare. The idea of the government as a welfare-maximizing collective agent acting in the interest of the majority of the constituency was dramatically challenged.

This also led to a reconsideration of the role and extent of public intervention in the economy, eventually culminating in the radical critique by the public choice school.

In between these two extreme diagnoses on the role of public institutions, a new approach to their role came through the recognition of the importance of collective preferences and action. As J. R. Commons had already noted as early as the 1930s: "This is an age of collective action . . . collective action is the general and dominating fact of social life. Human beings are born into this process of collective action and become individualized by the rules of collective action. Thus an institution is collective action in control, liberation, and expansion of individual action" (1950, 23). "Groups" came to be considered a third subject between (and beyond) the market and the state, judged as exerting a positive influence on social welfare. The problem was no longer how to defend the public sphere by sectional interests expressed by influential groups, as it was in the thirties, but how groups (any kind: local administrations, informal associations, international organizations) could help solve government failures. This paved the way to studying the relationship between public goods and public authority more generally.

As concerns the theoretical apparatus conceptualizing public (national) goods and public (national) action, the Samuelson (1954) and Musgrave (1939, 1959) solution to the optimal provision of public goods, implying externalities that are assumed to concern the whole (nation) state, is the need for a (national) governmental provision, in order to avoid free-riding problems. In the Pigouvian tradition, Musgrave and Samuelson were trying to understand how to make the state efficiently solve market failures. After World War II, *public goods* were increasingly and more widely accepted as a multifaceted system of *collective goods* assigned to concentric levels of government (Commons 1950; Tiebout 1956; Musgrave 1959), with different degrees of rivalry in consumption: from local to national and supranational layers. At the same time, it was recognized that certain goods are not easily assigned to—or efficiently provided by—administrative jurisdictions, and a different direction of research is taken (eventually leading to Ostrom 1990) concerning informal grouping.

Tiebout (1956), in particular, challenged the idea of a monodimensional nature of (federal/supranational) "public" goods, also identifying local/national public goods whose consumption (and supply) patterns are at subfederal or subnational level. Actually, although his writings are very differently interpreted, Tiebout's concern was to allow for government competition, making local governments mere producers of goods that can be priced and chosen on the market. Certainly, it is a very special market, requiring consumers, who "vote with their feet," to make a choice of mobility. If the individual does not agree with collective choices, he can exit the community in search of a different group where his preferences are better matched. A look at the assumptions of Tiebout's models may be interesting. First, the collective good the individual is seeking to consume has externalities that must coincide exactly with local constituencies (Tiebout 1956, 419), which is very unlikely. The second assumption is that an alternative provider of local/national public goods may always exist (at small transaction costs). But this is not always the case: I may be attracted by a lower income tax jurisdiction, where some collective goods provided by the outgoing jurisdiction are not provided by the new one. The third assumption is that any individual can change (local or national) constituency but is not allowed to form a transjurisdictional group: no civil society association is envisaged as a possible provider of collective goods. Only administrative jurisdictions, competing with one another, are allowed to provide collective goods. This implies that competitiveness is the only mechanism required to provide incentives for public policies. Local (or national) jurisdictions will compete to match best the preferences of the individuals they want to have. No coercion is necessary, but a *rush to the bottom* in the provision of collective goods and an uneven distribution of wealth between localities is the most probable outcome. Competitive, decentralized provision of public goods in a multilayer (federal) system may result in the underprovision of them in some places, leading to further reduction of the budget assigned to them.

The problem raised by Tiebout was later developed in an article titled "An Economic Theory of Fiscal Decentralization," allegedly influencing the *Economic Theory of Clubs* by Buchanan (1965) (see Fischel 2000, 8), since the model of local government by Tiebout seems a basic example of Buchanan's theory (even though there is no mention of the article in the work), and the work of Vincent and Elinor Ostrom. Tiebout and Vincent Ostrom met at the University of California, Los Angeles, where Tiebout had moved in the 1950s and Ostrom had received his Ph.D. in political science. There they also met Robert Warren, who was assistant professor of political science at the University of Washington. Tiebout's analysis provided the theoretical background for the study they made together in 1961 (Ostrom, Tiebout, and Warren 1961) on *polycentric governance*. In that work, they argue that it is possible to bring the principle of excludability (typical of private goods in Samuelson's analytical framework) into public goods, thus generating *club goods*, whose provision and consumption should be considered confined to (geographical or membership) parameters of access within a local community: "A public good on a neighbourhood or community scale can be viewed as 'packaged' within appropriate boundaries so that others outside the boundaries may be excluded from its use" (Ostrom, Tiebout, and Warren 1961, 834).

The central government works on such a large scale that it risks not matching people's preferences, while many of the interests of smaller groups of individuals might be suitably arranged within a smaller political community: "Interests of smaller publics might be properly negotiated within the confines of a smaller political community without requiring the attention of centralized decision-makers concerned with the big system. This task of recognizing the smaller publics is a problem of 'field' or 'area' organization" (Ostrom, Tiebout, and Warren 1961, 838). In order to better design the appropriate boundaries of government in dealing with the problem of scale connected to the provision of public goods, the authors draw political frames as structures to deal with the problem, and define criteria of control, efficiency, political representation, and local self-determination, assuming that public goods can be internalized. Their first suggestion is to build a *polycentric political system* within the public dimension, through a model of multiple jurisdictions reflecting a multiplicity of interests in various public goods demanded by the inhabitants of a metropolitan region. Second, the polycentric system is based on the satisfaction of the needs of a broader community—beyond the geographical or functional limits of each of the formal entities within the metropolitan region. The authors argue that polycentric governance is also supposed to provide a variety of public goods with many scales of organization and in supplying optimal arrangements for the production and consumption of public goods: "With the development of quasi-market conditions in production, much of the flexibility and responsiveness of market organization can be realized in the public service economy" (Ostrom, Tiebout, and Warren 1961, 839).

The concept of polycentrism, which applies to subnational, national, and supranational layers of jurisdiction, is rooted in a vision of society as constituted by individual agents organized in a spontaneous order, and *polycentrism*, described by Michael Polanyi (1951), later developed by Hayek in *The Constitution of Liberty* in 1964, is a way to organize such society. Polycentrism and polycentric governance were fundamental issues of Michael Polanyi's *The Logic of Liberty* (1951), and both Buchanan and Polanyi were members of the Mont Pelerin Society. It is worth noting also that Ostrom was a representative of the Bloomington school, one of the three leading centers of public choice theory, together with Buchanan's and Tullock's Virginia school of political economy and Riker's Rochester University (Boettke and Coyne 2005, 147).

Tiebout's model (but and also Polanyi's, Ostrom's, and Warren's) pointed to a market provision and competition in the provision of public goods that made such provision uncertain and unequal. A different approach is in Musgrave (1957, 1959). Also talking about the United States, his first claim concerns the existence of some collective goods that should be provided by the federal government not because they are difficult to price or to exclude, but because they satisfy basic needs that should not be dealt with by market mechanisms. They are *merit goods*. They should be provided by the government irrespective of consumers' explicit demand and of private supply (education is a typical example). This rests on the assumption of self-interested, utility-maximizing agents who are nevertheless unable to fully understand all the social and intertemporal consequences of their choices. The government can provide these kinds of public goods (which would not be provided by firms) because it can force people to pay through general taxation: if it were not for taxation, there would be no public goods and vice versa.

A second point is fiscal federalism. Fiscal federalism fully recognizes that the provision of public goods is dependent on different constituencies, as in Tiebout. But contrary to Tiebout's model, Musgrave recognizes the existence of externalities among political constituencies and designs fiscal federalism to solve problems of incoherence between the extent of externalities and the extent of the governing body legitimated to choose on them. As was the case for Robbins, Musgrave's fiscal federalism assumes that every collective good can be provided by a specific level of government: no overlapping situations can exist because when externalities arise from the consumption or production of a particular good, the provision of that very good is assigned to a greater constituency (from *local* to, virtually, *global*). Public authorities, through their concentric and articulated structure, match all the requirements of the society. This approach to fiscal federalism has been criticized as tending to centralize too many functions (and it is precisely in this critique that Elinor Ostrom's analyses find a favorable ground for growth).

It might be interesting to recall at least another perspective in line with Musgrave, illustrated by Olson (1965). He underlines that "unless there is coercion or some other special device to make individuals act in their common interest, rational, self-interested individuals will not act to achieve their common or group interest" (1965, 2). Incentives can play a role, but the problem with them is that it is difficult to find a mechanism that provides incentives *to all* the members of the community. One therefore needs either an individually based weighting system or a Pareto suboptimal solution. This is not necessarily a problem, but it is not clear why the market should be more legitimate than a democratic council in deciding who should bear the onus of financing the collective good. Olson's (1965) idea was that when the decision-making mechanism is not framed within a juridical context where democratic legitimacy (and certainty of a final decision) is constitutionally enforceable, the most plausible result of collective choice is the status quo, where no choice at all is taken. If this can be socially optimal from a Pareto point of view, it usually implies the underprovision of essential collective goods whose lack may undermine the very existence of a community. A solution may be to build a constitutional rule obliging stakeholders to take a decision; and to make this decision work without any veto rule. This means having a governmental body to which competence over the production of that good is assigned, as is the case with Robbins and Musgrave.

Although the debate in the fifties and sixties hardly dwelt on the role of international institutions, the main arguments fit perfectly the more or less explicit trade-off between supranational order and the welfare state. After World War II the range of public goods whose provision was under careful scrutiny included not only peace, but the whole range of public (collective) goods, at each layer of government. And the market-based, competitive solution provided by Tiebout, Ostrom, and others exerted a major academic influence, especially in the last few decades, when the public choice school became with Buchanan and Tullock a leading approach to public intervention in the economy.

9.5. Conclusion

The outbreak of World War I, the Russian Revolution, and later the Great Depression challenged liberal values and ideology. The mere restoration of monetary cooperation was insufficient to provide the stable economic framework required to help a balanced recovery and to secure against the rise of etatism and totalitarian regimes. A new, creative effort to relaunch the values of international liberalism was needed. Hence the intellectual fervor that would bring about the foundation of several new approaches to liberalism. One of them was neoliberalism.

Since the mid-1930s, the neoliberal thought collective contained very different concepts of supranational institutions. In particular, although several neoliberal intellectuals supported a federal supranational system of power, a latent dispute emerged between two radically different concepts of federalism. On the one side, the delegation of the provision of two crucial global public goods, capital mobility and a free market, to a supranational authority would imply less room for political interference in economics and, later on, greater jurisdictional competition, in turn implying less opportunity to finance welfare policies at the national level. On the other side, federalism was meant as a metaeconomic, constitutional system aiming to avoid the inherent clash between absolute and exclusive national sovereignties and at creating a shared system of concentric sovereign institutions designed to provide, at subnational, national, and supranational levels, some specific collective goods. While in the former case, peace is implied as the byproduct of the defense of market structures, in the latter it is the other way around: peace is the supranational collective good to be provided through effective and legitimate collective action before any effective political struggle for the achievement of liberal values will be possible. This dichotomy would still persist in the fifties and sixties, in the debate over the relationship among different layers of government and the optimal provision of collective goods.

This picture suggests several remarks. The first is that any distinction between right-wing and left-wing federalism—which is often used in the literature—is not able to capture the key point of the story told here. Neither Robbins nor Einaudi during the thirties and forties, nor Tiebout or even Musgrave in the fifties, can be described as a left-wing intellectual. The crucial distinction is the one I have been trying to describe, opposing market-oriented instrumental federalism to constitutional federalism. This also means that it is not federalism per se that can be deemed responsible for the trade-off between national and supranational public goods, but a very special approach to it. Only instrumental federalism, based merely on a defense of the market, where jurisdictional subnational competition provides a macroeconomic framework imposing a decreasing trend in national public expenses, makes this trade-off emerge.

The second point concerns the question of enforcement. The reason why Hayek gave great attention to a federal supranational model is that all confederative, cooperative solutions suggested in the interwar period neglected the question of how the provision of supranational public goods, such as free trade and capital mobility, should be made enforceable. Instrumental federalism favors a supranational federation with a very limited but at the same time overwhelmingly strong power so that it can better avoid underprovision of these public goods at the global level due to clash of national interests. This testifies to Hayek's faith in the capacity of a federal supranational authority to fulfill its tasks, although they are very limited in scope, suggesting that Hayek's critique of rational constructivism was not yet fully in force, at least until the end of World War II.

A third point concerns the decreasing strength with which neoliberalism has challenged the legitimacy of nation-states' engaging in welfarist policies, indeed tolerating, even encouraging this behavior to the point that neoliberalism is sometimes associated with favoring a strong state (Gamble 1979; Mirowski and Plehwe 2010; Harmes 2012, 64). This is no contradiction: in order to hinder national social policies, it is necessary that the decision-making process linked to their provision be on a (subfederal) level different from the one where the (federal, regulating) monetary authority is. It is therefore not necessary to advocate ex ante a weak welfare state at the national level because it will be constrained ex post by the supranational guarantee of free trade and capital movements.

The last point is that the existence of two very different approaches to federalism and its role in designing an international order testifies to a great pluralism that accompanied the birth and early growth of the neoliberal thought collective. We might wonder why such pluralism faded and disappeared during the last 50 years. In this respect I can only suggest a couple of tentative explanations. One is theoretical: the pathbreaking *Tiebout model*, following his 1956 article, favored the development of an approach to (fiscal) federalism where the "exit" (market) strategy prevails over the "voice" strategy to be pursued through a democratic political decision-making process. Competitive federalism came therefore to be studied and advocated more than constitutional federalism, which was almost forgotten. The other reason is that this kind of neoliberal, competitive federalism seems to imply a minor loss of national sovereignty and is more acceptable to public opinion and politicians. In fact, instrumental federalism brings about a greater loss of national sovereignty—for example, the ability to finance national public goods—imposing supranational, nondemocratic constraints over national democratic choices, than does constitutional federalism, where sovereignty is rescued on a multilevel system of collective democratic choices. But an apparently loose supranational institution with very limited scope seems to better guarantee the survival of national sovereignties.

We should recognize that this recent neoliberal strategy has been very effective, at least in Europe, if even left-wing movements and parties have fallen into this trap, arguing in favor of a return to ineffective and dangerous national expansionary policies without calling for a transfer of competences over the welfare state from nation-states to a supranational federation, which would be the only way to ensure its effective provision of welfare in the present macroeconomic framework of high economic interdependence worldwide.

Acknowledgments

This chapter is the result of several discussions in very different international meetings, in particular Tokyo 2010 and 2011, and Florence, Padova, and Copenhagen 2012; and it shares some sections with Masini 2012a, 2012b, 2015. I thank Dieter Plehwe and all the participants in those meetings for invaluable comments.

References

Boettke, P. J., and C. J. Coyne. 2005. "Methodological Individualism, Spontaneous Order and the Research Program of the Workshop in Political Theory and Policy Analysis." *Journal of Economic Behavior and Organization* 57:145–58.

Buchanan, J. M. 1965. "An Economic Theory of Clubs." *Economica*, n.s. 32 (125): 1–14.

Buchanan J. M. 1995. "Federalism and Individual Sovereignty." *Cato Journal* 15:259–68.

Burgess, M. 1995. *The British Tradition of Federalism*. London: Leicester University Press.

Commons, J. R. 1950. *The Economics of Collective Action*. London: Macmillan.

Cressati, C. 1992. *L'Europa necessaria: Il federalismo liberale di Luigi Einaudi* (*The Necessity of Europe: The Liberal Federalism of Luigi Einaudi*). Turin: Giappichelli.

Denord, F. 2009. "French Neoliberalism and 1st Divisions: From the Colloque Walter Lippmann to the Fifth Republic." In P. Mirowski and D. Plehwe, eds., *The Road from Mont Pèlerin: The Making of the Neoliberal Thought Collective*, 45–67. Cambridge, MA: Harvard University Press.

Einaudi, L. 1897. "Un sacerdote della stampa e gli Stati Uniti europei" ("A Priest of the Press and the United States of Europe"). *La Stampa*, August 20, 1–2.

[Einaudi, L.] Junius. 1918a. "La Società delle Nazioni è un ideale possibile?" ("Is the Society of Nations Still a Viable Goal?"). *Corriere della Sera*, January 5. In [Einaudi, L.] Junius (1920). *Lettere politiche di Junius (Junius's political letters)*, 79–94. Bari: Laterza.

[Einaudi, L.] Junius. 1918b. "Il dogma della sovranità e l'idea della Società delle Nazioni" ("The Dogma of Sovereignty and the Idea of the Society of Nations"). *Corriere della Sera*, December 28. In [Einaudi, L.] Junius (1920). *Lettere politiche di Junius (Junius's political letters)*, 143–56. Bari: Laterza.

[Einaudi, L.] Junius. 1919. "Fiume, la società delle nazioni ed il dogma della sovranità" ("Fiume, the Society of Nations and the Dogma of sovereignty"). *Corriere della Sera*, May 6. In [Einaudi, L.] Junius (1920). *Lettere politiche di Junius (Junius's political letters)*, 157–168. Bari: Laterza.

Fischel, W. A. 2000. "Municipal Corporations, Homeowners, and the Benefit View of the Property Tax." In Wallace E. Oates, ed., *Property Taxation and Local Public Finance*. Cambridge, MA: Lincoln Institute for Land.

Friedman, M. 1962. *Capitalism and Freedom*. Chicago: University of Chicago Press.

Giordano, A. 2006. *Il pensiero politico di Luigi Einaudi* (*The Political Thought of Luigi Einaudi*). Genoa: Name Edizioni.

Graefe, P. 2006. "Neoliberal Federalism and Social Democratic Approaches to Social Assistance in the Canadian Provinces in the 1990s." Paper presented at the Canadian Political Science Association, York University, June 3.

Harmes, A. 2012. "The Rise of Neoliberal Nationalism." *Review of International Political Economy* 19 (1): 59–86.

Hartwell, R. M. 1995. *A History of the Mont Pèlerin Society*. Indianapolis: Liberty Fund.

Hayek, F. A. von. 1931. *Prices and Production*. London: Routledge and Kegan Paul.

Hayek, F. A. von. 1933a. *Monetary Theory and Trade Cycle*. London: Jonathan Cape.

Hayek, F. A. von. 1933b. "Über 'neutrales Geld.'" *Zeitschrift für Nationalökonomie* 4: 659–61. Translated as "On 'Neutral Money'" in Hayek 1984. *Money, Capital and Fluctuations. Early Essays*. Edited by Roy McCloughry, 159–62. London: Routledge and Kegan.

Hayek, F. A. von. 1937. *Monetary Nationalism and International Stability*. London: Longmans Green.

Hayek, F. A. von. 1939. "Economic Conditions of Inter-state Federalism." *New Commonwealth Quarterly* 5 (2): 131–49. Reprinted in *Individualism and Economic Order* (Chicago: University of Chicago Press, 1948), 255–72.

Hayek, F. A. von. 1944. *The Road to Serfdom*. London: Routledge and Kegan.

Jackson, B. 2010. "At the Origins of Neo-liberalism: The Free Economy and the Strong State, 1930–1947." *Historical Journal* 53 (1): 129–51.

Kley, R. 1994. *Hayek's Social and Political Thought*. Oxford: Clarendon Press.

Mantzavinos, C. 2010. "Federalism and Individual Liberty." *Constitutional Political Economy* 21:101–18.

Masini, F. 1994. "Lionel Robbins e la svolta federalista nella tradizione liberale inglese" ("Lionel Robbins and the Federalist Turn in the British Liberal Tradition"). *Storia del pensiero economico* 28:69–92.

Masini, F. 2012a. "Designing the Institutions of International Liberalism: Some Contributions from the Interwar Period." *Constitutional Political Economy* 23 (1): 45–65.

Masini, F. 2012b. "Luigi Einaudi and the Making of the Neoliberal Thought." *History of Economic Thought and Policy* 1 (1): 39–59.

Masini, F. 2015. "European Integration: Contrasting Models and Perspectives." In R. Fiorentini and G. Montani, eds., *The European Union and Supranational Political Economy*, 44–64. London: Routledge.

Mirowski, P., and D. Plehwe, eds. 2009. *The Road from Mont Pèlerin: The Making of the Neoliberal Thought Collective*. Cambridge, MA: Harvard University Press.

Mises, L. von. 1919. *Nation, Staat, und Wirtschaft*. Translated by Leland B. Yeager as *Nation, State and Economy* (New York: New York University Press, 1983).

Mises, L. von. 1927. *Liberalismus*. Jena: Gustav Fischer Verlag. Translated as *Liberalism in The Classical Tradition* (New York: Foundation for Economic Education, 1996).

Morelli, U. 1990. *Contro il mito dello stato sovrano: Luigi Einaudi e l'unità europea (Against the Myth of the sovereign State: Luigi Einaudi and the European Union)*. Milan: Franco Angeli.

Musgrave, R. A. 1939. "The Voluntary Exchange Theory of Public Economy." *Quarterly Journal of Economics* 52 (February): 213–17.

Musgrave, R. A. 1957. "A Multiple Theory of the Budget." *FinanzArchiv*, n.s. 25 (1): 33–43.

Musgrave, R. A. 1959. *The Theory of Public Finance*. New York: McGraw Hill.

Mussolini, B. 1933. "Discorso all'Assemblea del Consiglio Nazionale delle Corporazioni" (Speech before the Assembly of the National Council of Corporations), Rome, November 14. In A. Montemaggiori, ed., *Dizionario della dottrina fascista* (Turin: Paravia, 1934), 264.

O'Brien, D. P. 1988. *Lionel Robbins*. London: Macmillan.

Olson, M. 1965. *The Logic of Collective Action*. Cambridge, MA: Harvard University Press.

Ostrom, E. 1990. *Governing the Commons: The Evolution of Institutions for Collective Action*. Cambridge: Cambridge University Press.

Ostrom, V., M. Tiebout, and R. Warren. 1961. «The Organization of Government in Metropolitan Areas: A Theoretical Inquiry." *American Political Science Review* 55 (4): 831–42.

Pinder, J. 1990. "The Federal Idea and the British Liberal Tradition." *Federalist* 32 (1): 9–32.

Plehwe, D., and B. Walpen. 2006. "Between Network and Complex Organization: The Making of Neoliberal Knowledge and Hegemony." In D. Plehwe, B. Walpen, and G. Neunhöffer, eds., *Neoliberal Hegemony: A Global Critique*, 27–50. London: Routledge.

Plehwe, D., B. Walpen, and G. Neunhöffer, eds. 2006. *Neoliberal Hegemony: A Global Critique*. London: Routledge.

Plickert, P. 2008. *Wandlungen des Neoliberalismus: Eine Studie zu Entwicklung und Ausstrahlung der "Mont Pèlerin Society"*. Stuttgart: Lucius.

Polanyi, M. 1951. *The Logic of Liberty*. Chicago: University of Chicago Press.

Prechel, H., ed. 2007. *Politics and Neoliberalism: Structure, Process and Outcome*. Amsterdam: Elsevier.

Prechel, H., and J. B. Harms. 2007. "Politics and Neoliberalism: Theory and Ideology." In H. Prechel, ed., *Politics and Neoliberalism: Structure, Process and Outcome*, 3–17. Amsterdam: Elsevier.

Ransome, P., ed. 1991. *Towards the United States of Europe: Studies in the Making of the European Constitution*. London: Lothian Foundation Press.

Robbins, L. C. 1937a. *Economic Planning and International Order*. London: Macmillan.

Robbins, L. C. 1937b. "The Economics of Territorial Sovereignty." In C. A. Woodward Manning, ed., *Peaceful Change*, 41–60. London: Macmillan.

Robbins, L. C. 1939a. *The Economic Basis of Class Conflicts*. London: Macmillan.

Robbins, L. C. 1939b. *The Economic Causes of War*. London: Jonathan Cape.

Robbins, L. C. 1940. "Economic Aspects of Federation." In M. Chaning-Pearce, ed., *Federal Union: A Symposium*, 167–86. London: Jonathan Cape.

Sally, R. 1998a. "Classical Liberalism and International Economic Order: An Advance Sketch." *Constitutional Political Economy* 9 (1): 19–44.

Sally, R. 1998b. *Classical Liberalism and International Economic Order: Studies in Theory and Intellectual History*. London: Routledge.

Streeck, W. 2014b. *Buying Time*. London: Verso.

Tiebout, C. M. 1956. "A Pure Theory of Local Expenditures." *Journal of Political Economy* 64 (October): 416–24.

Walpen, B. 2004. *Die offenen Feinde und ihre Gesellschaft: Eine hegemonietheoretische Studie zur Mont Pèlerin Society*. Hamburg: VSA.

Weingast, B. 1995. "The Economic Role of Political Institutions: Market Preserving Federalism and Economic Development." *Journal of Law, Economics, and Organization* 11:1–31.

10 | Neoliberal Think Tanks and the Crisis

DIETER PLEHWE

10.1. In the Absence of Paradigm Shift: Observation of Maintenance Efforts

In the early stages of the global financial crisis the public debate focused on the collapse of a highly speculative system of financialized capitalism. The irresponsible behavior of corporate and public management of banks, and the failure of public supervisory bodies were at the center of public attention. The crisis was regarded as a market failure of giant proportions. A few years onward observers express distress about the return to business as usual and what is widely regarded a failure to promote substantial reregulation of the financial sector. Critical voices both in Europe and in the United States have seen approaches to reform being narrowed down in international (G8, G20, EU, etc.) negotiations. There have been and continue to be adjustments to the previous regulatory arrangements (Helleiner and Pagliari 2009), but by and large it remains surprising how much tolerance seems to exist with regard to the continuities of the regulatory status quo before the crisis. Possibly worse, the crisis has been used to firmly entrench and constitutionalize austerity regimes in Europe, which arguably push neoliberal ordering of social affairs to new extremes (see Blyth 2013; compare Mirowski 2013).

Why has there been a great gulf between popular sentiments and intellectual perceptions of the need to more profoundly change the regulatory system, and a fairly narrow range of options pursued? Structural transformations of the globalized economy can be considered an important part of the answer to this puzzle (Zimmermann 2009). The world has been changed after decades of transformations inspired by neoliberal perspectives. At the same time it remains a puzzle to be explained exactly why neoliberal interpretations of the causes of the crisis and neoliberal proposals for remedy still command a considerable amount of authority in spite of the fundamental contradictions evident in what has evidently been a huge market failure demanding bold public action. Both in Europe and in the United States governments seem to (have to) rely on the same community of (business oriented) experts who were part of the progressive move toward deregulation, financial integration, and financialization. But industry experts and lobbyists also had to face the crisis and the reactions of the public, including the wide range of critical experts from organizations like ATTAC (Association for the Taxation of financial Transactions and Aid to Citizens) and trade unions. It is interesting, therefore, to ask how elites and experts themselves react to the crisis. Do they learn from critiques, possibly absorb some of the counterwisdom, or do they develop other strategies to cope with the at times strong and radical criticism of the establishment? Has there been a shift in the composition of groups that are influential in public discussions? Since certain proposals advocated by non-governmental organizations like ATTAC—most prominently the Tobin tax—have been picked up by conservative politicians and parties (like Christian Democracy in Germany), one might be inclined to concede a certain shift in public debates after all.

Yet in spite of a certain amount of regulatory overhaul and critical reflections with regard to the merit of self-regulation, scholars have curiously noted the absence of a paradigm shift following the second large-scale crisis of capitalism after the Great Depression. The Great Depression ushered in the era of social liberalism and Keynesian economic planning. The crisis of Fordism in the 1970s ushered in the era of neoliberalism. The global financial crisis of 2008 following in turn does not appear to be leading to paradigm shift of similar importance (Zimmermann 2009). In lieu of a paradigm shift attention has to turn to reasons for and the forces behind paradigm maintenance (including minor adjustment). Why does it still seem to be convincing to argue in favor of privatization of banks saved from bankruptcy by alleging the inferiority of public management?[1] Why do austerity measures, which lead to a continuing retrenchment of welfare regimes, belong to the key policies pursued despite the abysmal record of austerity projects?

In order to better explain neoliberal paradigm maintenance, I conceive of the need to re-examine more closely those who were behind the neoliberal reforms of the past. How did the scholars and policy advisers who were key to intellectual, political, and institutional entrepreneurship of the great neoliberal reform era following the crisis of the 1970s react to the crisis? Several scholars have written about the surprising resilience of neoliberalism in light of the massive critique during the first years of the global financial crisis of 2008 by way of emphasizing structural and institutional configurations, sometimes in combination with economic and political power elites (compare Crouch 2011; Schmidt and Thatcher 2013; Cahill 2014). Only Mirowski (2013) has, so far, examined closely the neoliberal thought collectives of and around the Mont Pelerin Society (compare Mirowski and Plehwe 2009; Plehwe, Walpen, and Neunhöffer 2006), though he concentrates on status quo maintenance in the economic profession. A closer look at the interdisciplinary and transprofessional circles of the Mont Pelerin Society and related think tank networks reveals a powerful nexus of neoliberal authority, intellectual power, and political influence. The neoliberal groups that pushed for, legitimized, and defended the globalization and deregulation of financial markets are still in place and need closer attention in order to better comprehend the structure and direction of ongoing debates and negotiations with regard to the reregulation of globalized capitalism in general, and austerity-driven reforms of the welfare state in particular. Unlike the examination of business experts involved in positions of government decision-making, the role of the wider field of policy-oriented research and consulting has not received much attention so far, and the transnational network of neoliberal intellectuals and think tanks continue to mostly operate under the radar.[2]

In order to more fully comprehend the evolution of public and expert debates, we need to consider the workings of a new class of professionals who are operating within and behind the think tank, research, media, and PR efforts capable of attacking—or maintaining—policy paradigms with regard to policy-related research in general, and in the relevant fields of financial regulation, public finance, and welfare reforms in particular. In order to assess the expert debate it is not only technical expertise that matters, but normative framing and the ways in which frames and expertise are embedded in agents and agency. Discourse coalition theory enables us to link structural, material, and ideational aspects of public debates (Hajer 1994; Plehwe 2009). Discourse coalitions link current struggles to the bedrock of intellectual and conceptual ingredients, and thereby help to go beyond a short-term and narrow empiricist focus of mainstream political science (on advocacy coalitions, for example, compare Fischer 2003, 73f.).

In the case of Great Britain, right-wing think tanks have been credited for successfully changing the terms and frames of debating the global financial crisis. The crisis-of-capitalism debate in the United Kingdom has once again been successfully turned into a discourse on a crisis of the public sector (Carrigan 2010).[3] The capacity to change the terms of debates had already been identified by John Saloma III (1984) as the key to understanding the role (and power) of think tanks of the New Right in the United States. Saloma's case study focused on affirmative action, which had been reinterpreted as a practice of (reverse) discrimination. Tom Medvetz (2013) has demonstrated the think tank capacity of the New Right once more in the field of welfare research, which was reframed in the United States during the 1980s to address problems of dependency instead of problems of inequality.

Such an ability to reconceptualize political issues transcends traditional models of politics, according to Saloma (1984), who thereby anticipated contemporary postdemocracy arguments. Although this great reinterpretation effort may have been more important during the early years of the rise of neoliberal hegemonic constellations, the capacity to organize, restructure, and maintain public discourses certainly requires particular attention to the specialized agencies that have been developed to accomplish such goals rather than limit attention to the academic experts of a particular policy field or issue area.

In order to assess the claims made with regard to the ability of think tanks to recontextualize the debate over the global financial crisis, we need to look at what neoliberal intellectuals and the think tank networks developed to back their activities have been doing in the most recent years. Before taking on this task, section 10.2 will introduce the most important intellectual networks sustaining neoliberalism. I will trace the origins of the progressive move toward global financial integration after World War II to a key group of members of the Mont Pelerin Society in order to identify clearly what can and indeed must still be regarded a core group of neoliberal intellectual leadership, *comprehensive* transnational discourse community (Plehwe 2010).[4] Section 10.3 will examine the papers given at a special conference organized by the Mont Pelerin Society in New York in 2009 on the subject of the crisis and explore some of the global think tank network activities developed in the aftermath of the meeting. Section 10.4 will present the results of a scan of the Stockholm network, the major neoliberal think tank network in Europe. Here we will observe and systematize the spread of positions and opinions voiced on the issue of the financial crisis. The conclusion will use the major findings to reconsider arguments on the issue of paradigm shift and the future varieties of neoliberalism.

10.2. Mont Pelerin Society: Intellectual Origins of Speculative Globalization

The Mont Pelerin Society (MPS) of neoliberal intellectuals founded by Friedrich August von Hayek, Wilhelm Röpke, Albert Hunold, and others in 1947 in Switzerland has been a key subject of research efforts dedicated to better understanding the organizational and intellectual underpinnings of the rise of neoliberalism (Walpen 2004; Plehwe, Walpen, and Neunhöffer 2006; Plickert 2008; Mirowski and Plehwe 2009; Burgin 2012). The association is probably still unknown to most scholars and experts, who certainly will have heard about many of the individual scholars who are members of the MPS including eight winners of the economics Nobel Prize: Hayek, Friedman, Stigler, Buchanan, Becker, Allais, Coase, and most recently experimental economist Vernon Smith (compare Offer and Söderberg 2016).

Problems and issues of monetary policy and international finance are central to the academic and political agenda of both the Mont Pelerin Society at large and many individual members. Apart from some of the leading economics professors in this field who are members of the MPS, a large number of central bankers, private bankers, and employees of the international financial institutions from across the world complete the neoliberal finance community (compare Schmelzer 2010). In addition to advocating free trade, privatization, and deregulation, the progressive liberalization of capital and financial markets has figured prominently in the programs advanced by neoliberal economists in particular. Eric Helleiner (1994) alerted readers in his seminal work on the re-emergence of global finance to the prominence of certain MPS members in key debates. Helleiner's explanation for the US policy shift toward abandoning the gold exchange standard of the early 1970s emphasizes the leadership of (MPS) neoliberal intellectuals, and the emergence of a coalition of private bankers, industrialists, and public officials in support of neoliberal ideas in the early 1970s (Helleiner 1994, 122). Gottfried Haberler's role in particular as adviser to President Nixon on international financial questions, Milton Friedman's close relationship with Treasury secretary George Shultz (who held an industrial relations professorship at Chicago in the late 1950s and early 1960s), and "Austrian economics" influencing key officials like Thomas Willett[5] (Council of Economic Advisors) and Paul Volcker are mentioned: "Drawing on Hayek, Röpke and other European neoliberals, these officials rejected the embedded liberal approach to capital movements that had inspired the restrictive Bretton Woods financial order" (Helleiner 1990, 115). Digging deeper into the matter, Matthias Schmelzer (2010) has examined in detail the debates between gold standard advocates and flexible exchange rate advocates in the MPS during the 1950s and 1960s, and the ultimately successful attempt to subsequently organize an international consensus among central bankers and private bankers.

While gold standard and flexible exchange rate advocates were united in their desire to subject states to the rigid discipline of the market, they differed with regard to the method considered adequate to this task. A return to the gold standard would have directly removed the discretion of governments and central banks with regard to monetary policy and exchange rates, while flexible exchange rates would accomplish this task only in a roundabout way. The reason for Haberler, Friedman, and Machlup to diverge from the position of the old generation and Machlup's teacher Ludwig von Mises in particular was twofold. A return to the gold standard would theoretically come at the price of restrictions on capital movements and would not be feasible in any case. The Haberler faction argued that a gold standard solution would have forced many countries to maintain restrictions on capital mobility in line with the so-called Triffin or policy trilemma: According to this view, only two of the following three policy goals can be combined: (1) stable exchange rates, (2) monetary autonomy, (3) unrestricted capital mobility. Because of expanded state functions in the economy, states would not give up monetary autonomy and therefore most likely would have to give up on the freedom of capital given a regime of fixed exchange rates. Furthermore, the group was certain that a return to the gold standard was a political project doomed to fail, almost completely lacking support (except for some forces in France). Ultimately, the superior aim was a continuing drive to liberalize capital markets, and flexible exchange rates were regarded adequate to indirectly (in the long term) enforce fiscal discipline.

Advocacy in favor of flexible exchange rates at the time ran into huge problems. Flexible exchange rates were associated with economic nationalism, speculation, turbulence, and chaos, reminding some of the disintegration of the world market during the time after the gold standard had been abandoned in the early 1930s. The move toward flexible exchange rates could certainly be interpreted as a move toward economic nationalism. Certainly not all economists who started to oppose the Bretton Woods international monetary order did so to embrace economic globalization. But the major obstacle was memories of economic disorder and flexible exchange rates (Schmelzer 2010).

To quell such fears the neoliberal economists relied on a case study of more recent Canadian experiences with flexible exchange (Friedman and Roosa 1967), and launched a massive cycle of conferences and papers to convince experts and bankers of the merit of flexible exchange rates, not least if not primarily in order not to give up on capital market liberalization. It thus can be clearly stated that financial market liberalization belongs to the key elements of the neoliberal transformation of state regulation of the economy, and thus to the drivers of the recent decades of corporate and financial globalization (compare Mirowski and Plehwe 2009; Kogut and Macpherson 2008).

If the Mont Pelerin scholars were instrumental promoters of the original policy shift in the United States, and the ultimate paradigm shift in favor financial liberalization and the consequential expansion of highly speculative markets, the global financial crisis certainly can also be seen as a crisis of the wisdom and advisory position of the neoliberal intellectuals.

10.3. Debating the Crisis at Headquarters: The Mont Pelerin Society Goes Wall Street

The global financial crisis has indeed been perceived as a strong challenge by the members of the Mont Pelerin Society. In 2009, the current president of the Mont Pelerin Society, UCLA professor of development economics Deepak Lal, together with the longtime MPS secretary treasurer, Ed Feulner (former MPS president and head of the Heritage Foundation), organized an MPS special meeting on the financial crisis in New York City. Special meetings complement regular biannual global and regional MPS conferences, which have been the alternating opportunity of members of the transnational community to meet face to face since the early 1970s. Additional special meetings have been organized occasionally to address specific concerns.

The title of the conference spelled out the major fears of neoliberals. Under the headline "The End of Globalizing Capitalism? Classical Liberal Responses to the Global Financial Crisis" more than 100 members and about 100 guests debated a total of 18 lectures, the speech of the president, and four keynote presentations (Harvard historian Niall Ferguson, media tycoon Steve Forbes, Dutch critic of Islam Ayaan Hirsi Ali, and Gary Becker). Milton Friedman's longtime collaborator Anna Schwartz also belonged to the distinguished roster of speakers. Both the written and oral material on record[6] allows discerning some of the key patterns of neoliberal argumentation with regard to the crisis. Most of the presentations display the shared core positions of the transnational community, though we can find diverse and even contradictory positions, as we shall see.

The basic pattern can be interpreted as a counterattack against popular critiques of the market and capitalism. The state and political choices rather than the market and economic behavior are emphasized in the neoliberal analysis of the origins of the crisis. But in spite of the unsurprising reiteration of the neoliberal party line in general, individual examinations of the causes of the crisis reveal a more profound level of reflection. We can also observe important dimensions of neoliberal reform reasoning in response to the crisis and most notably the revival of (German-Swiss) ordoliberal lines of neoliberal thought (compare Ptak 2009). I will attempt to highlight key positions of select contributions that are representative of the whole range of authors presenting in New York City. Since I discuss individual presentations at some length, the rather short contributions of the authors will be referenced as such to make for an easier reading of our cursory discussion.

The first speaker, MPS president Deepak Lal, can be considered one of the most influential development economists of the Washington Consensus era. Among economists, he certainly must be considered a highly creative and innovative thinker because of his efforts to integrate cultural dimensions in the analysis of market behavior (Lal 1998). Unlike his otherwise admired predecessor in neoliberal development economics, Hungarian-born Peter Bauer, the Indian native Lal promoted a truly universal rather than a restricted Western understanding of neoliberalism (Plehwe 2009). Lal (2009) startled his audience in New York by reminding listeners first of the approximation of key neoliberals like Hayek and Lionel Robbins to positions of John Maynard Keynes with regard to the crisis of the 1930s. If cyclical downturns turn into depression, state interventions to change the course of economic processes are deemed necessary. Lal also stipulated a common Wicksellian heritage shared by Hayek and Keynes in an apparent effort to claim space for neoliberal economists in the economic Premier League. Lal refrained from discussing the impact of the coordinated stimulus efforts of governments in 2008/9 to avoid sliding into depression. But since the first part of the MPS meeting was dedicated to distinguishing the present crisis from the Great Depression, the hint about

Keynesianism as *ultima ratio* of neoliberal interventionism mainly served to draw a line between the 1930s and the present. Lal also invoked Keynes as a critic of infrastructure investments to revive the economy because of their longer-term impact, and referred to him as a witness in support of demanding tax relief, which has a short-term impact and is in principle more compatible with the neoliberal agenda. Without discussing issues of redistribution that are central to Keynes, the arguably most important economist of the age of social liberalism thus was introduced by Lal to cast doubt on current Keynesian policies and as a supporter of neoliberal reasoning.

But Lal also cast doubt on his own camp in direct and indirect ways, discussing the politics of easy money, global imbalances, and avarice. He asked why the crisis came at a time with many good friends at the helm (of the US Federal Reserve, for example). Low-interest policies were pursued under Alan Greenspan and his advisers, who included key MPS members like Milton Friedman. The possibly most interesting audio material from Anna Schwartz's presentation is damaged, unfortunately. But a "sound money campaign" has been launched in the aftermath of the New York meeting by MPS related think tank networks.[7] We can safely take Lal's reflections as an indicator of the priority given to monetary politics once again, and as a genuine sphere of neoliberal self-criticism requiring a return to the roots rather than a reformulation of original neoliberal agendas.

Although Lal had no doubt with regard to the key role of the state and of regulatory politics as ultimate causes of the crisis, and while he clearly spoke out against the revival of theories of market failure, he did address global economic imbalances (discussed at length in a series of articles written for the Indian business daily *Business Standard*). Global economic imbalances were held to be the cause of speculation. Lal compared the present export surplus of countries like Germany and Japan with the case of the oil-exporting countries in the 1970s leading up to the world debt crisis of the 1980s. Although he refrained from deducing political measures from this analysis, he appeared to perceive a need to remedy what can be regarded as unsustainable macroeconomic imbalances. *Financial Times* reporter Martin Wolf seconded Lal on this topic in his own presentation in greater detail.

Last but not least Lal subjected the predominance of avarice to severe criticism in the Scottish tradition of the Enlightenment. He found virtuous and chivalrous values—most notably sympathy, going along with business acumen—to be more prevalent in India and other Asian countries than among British noblemen, picking out the bankers of the City of London.

Yet regardless of moments of critical self-reflection, Lal turned primarily against competing schools of thought. He identified potential protectionism as a result of the crisis as a grave Keynesian mistake because Keynes had provided legitimacy for protectionist policies under specific circumstances. The MPS president urgently warned against a revival of mercantilist perspectives.

Extending the agenda of globalization unsurprisingly constituted another sphere for strategic action promoted via MPS-related think tanks (to be further discussed below).

The presentation of the MPS president skillfully combined an attack against the key opposition, Keynesianism, arguably perceived to grow stronger in the face of the crisis, with elements of self-critique. Yet even though his speech was delivered in a tone of modesty peppered with tributes to intellectual foes, Lal unmistakably held on to the core of neoliberal convictions. He distinctly did not demand, let alone promote, a search for a new synthesis of Keynesianism and neoliberalism, of welfare theories of market failure and neoliberal theories of state failure. He rather called for a return to neoliberalism's own values and insights to "renew the neoliberal mandate" (his title). If the conference title has been chosen in a defensive manner surreptitiously speaking about classical liberalism, Lal himself proudly held up the banner of neoliberalism. His call to renew the mandate included the inscription of a neoliberal school of thought held in lower esteem during the heyday of aggressive globalization: ordoliberalism.

Harvard historian Niall Ferguson first reminded his audience of the role of the historians in the early history of the Mont Pelerin Society in order to claim attention for history rather than mathematics (Ferguson 2009). His rigid anti-Keynesian and antiplanning attitude was declared immediately after the friendly scolding of economists. Ferguson spoke out vigorously against a revival of Keynesian planning efforts financed by the accumulation of public debt, and against the nationalization of private corporations. According to him there is an ill-conceived lack of patience. Monetary stimulus did not fail to provide results, according to Ferguson, but fiscal stimulus had been rushed. The financial crisis was considered a crisis of globalization. Much like Lal, he perceived the rise of protectionism to be the most important coincidence with the Great Depression. Instead of avoiding a depression, the repression of the banking crisis was held to potentially cause it because the provision of liquidity precluded the clearing process in the market.

Yet technical questions paled in the face of what Ferguson regarded as the gravest danger: the possibility that the free-market economy might be considered a failure. His own warning against an imminent crisis back in 2006 instead rested on historical insights in the evolution of the financial sector. His major finding: regulation caused the crisis, not the market. But the following summary of his book contradicted this simplified message. Ferguson blamed the lack of liquidity and high debt ratio of banks on the regulatory framework reached in the Basle I and II agreements. Lowering the equity requirements proved to be inadequate, European banks in particular being held to maintain high debt levels as a consequence. Because of the lack of fences between banks and hedge funds, the former had basically transformed themselves into the latter. Ferguson observed a conflict of interest in the rating agencies because they were financed by the corporations they regulate. Even if Ferguson absolved the market and blamed regulation, his analysis evidently suggested that he supported better and different regulation rather than deregulation.

Ferguson relied on Frank Knight to distinguish between risk and uncertainty. Based on this difference, he suggested that the development of markets of derivatives constituted a nonsensical experiment. While the state is unlikely to play a strong role in derivatives, Ferguson was quite right to insist on the role of the state in the real estate market. Subsidies in form of tax breaks for housing property were instrumental to maintaining the American dream, which had been extended to less fortunate parts of the population by way of cheap credits from semi-public housing societies. The model pursued constituted a neoliberal alternative to the welfare state, a sort of discounter Fordism (Walmartism). Lower classes managed to maintain consumption standards by way of incurring debts on their property. As long as the value of the property kept rising, the mechanism worked just fine. Ferguson settled the score with what he calls "Chinmerica," an imaginary wonderland combining the partners of China and America in a way that allows one partner to spend money while the other has to save. China was held to still be a planned economy because of capital market controls and currency manipulation. Because China did not rely on free markets, according to Ferguson, the evolution cannot be blamed on market failure.

Even though Ferguson elaborated on concrete deficits in government regulations, he refrained from discussing regulatory reforms, ending on a note of both fatalism and optimism. He held financial crises to constitute an intrinsic feature of capitalism unlikely to be prevented by any regulatory framework. Because the stronger regulations back in the 1970s had not succeeded in preventing financial crisis, there was no good reason to return to the old regulatory framework. The fundamental cause is uncertainty, and thus rooted in psychology. Experimental economists in the meantime have established the irrationality of the individual.[8] Ferguson's optimism on the other hand was related to an evolutionary argument. Functioning natural selection involves periodic mass mortality. Alluding to Schumpeter, Ferguson declared creative destruction to be essential to capitalist development. The principle of too big to fail should accordingly not exist. He considered the crisis itself to constitute the "natural" selection and reform process.

In his conclusion Ferguson reminded his audience of the founding meeting of 1947 to ask why the ordoliberal school (of Walter Eucken and others) had been marginalized. His rhetorical question: Do we care for free entrepreneurship or for a competitive order? He presented the order principle as fit to overcome this apparent choice, charging his listeners to rediscover the ideas for an effective order of competition before Keynesian economists succeeded in turning the wheel of history backward. Ferguson maintained it to be the key task of neoliberals to develop a credible framework for the resurrection of free markets. In order to make this more than a moral goal, the political and regulatory foundations of the free market have to be reconsidered.

If Ferguson and most of the other academics considered many dimensions of the global crisis sometimes at odds with their conclusions, the media tycoon Forbes had nothing to deliver but platitudes. The global financial crisis became in his hands a monumental crisis of government without any reflection on contributions of private forces, including the media, speaking out in favor of the free market (controlled by people like him). Not even at the level of individual values was he ready to support Lal's attack on avarice, though he probably had a point suggesting that it was unlikely that Wall Street after 200 years of existence would have suddenly been overwhelmed by greed. The response to the crisis by President Obama was declared to be full of horrible mistakes. There was no reason for pessimism, however. Forbes noted that students of Ronald Reagan would remember that even the Iron Curtain could be opened. The multimillionaire predicted natural frictions in society, which would find expression in protests against state policies like health reform. Forbes demanded that the participants develop a plan to be ready for coming opportunities to provide political direction again.

Gary Becker assisted Forbes by way of suggesting that the most important principle in economics is the same as in medicine: Do no harm. He rejected the common notion that it is better to do something than nothing. Random action was worse than abstinence, according to Becker. While he did not suggest a return to the self-restraint of the 1930s—because government does have a role to play—Becker found the policies pursued by Presidents Bush and Obama to be of dubious effectiveness. He considered Obama's measures to be inconsistent and unorganized. He singled out the rescue of the car industry, suggesting it provided excessive wages and contributed to an artificially high degree of organization of trade unions.

Many presentations gave an impression of a deep crisis of neoliberalism, at least in particular locations at least. Hannes Gissurarson, the key policy adviser to the Oddsen government in charge of the Icelandic road to radical neoliberalism in the 1990s and 2000s, delivered a speech on the "strange death of a liberal island." Gissurarson blamed the British government for treating Iceland like a terrorist organization by way of suspending monetary transactions. But Gissurarson did admit the lack of an institution that could have acted as lender of last resort because Iceland did not join the European Union. Gissurarson de facto blamed himself: His group of Icelandic neoliberals, who had invited Hayek, Friedman, Buchanan, and other leading MPS members as young politicians in Iceland during the 1980s,[9] resented the regulatory requirements demanded from full members of the EU.

What are the conclusions to be drawn from the presentations at the MPS special meeting? Reconsidering Deepak Lal's general message delivered under the headline of his presidential address, "A Mandate Renewed," it seems to be clear that present-day neoliberals, unlike the original founders of MPS neoliberalism back in 1930s (Walpen 2004; Denord 2009), do not see any need for basic revisions of their thinking. They propagate a return to their own strongholds and talents in addition to minor technical reforms that remain controversial. At least two strategic initiatives were decided: A sound money project and a new multilingual free trade project targeting peripheral countries apparently considered easy prey for the advocacy of protectionism.

The sound money project was first reported in *Highlight*, an online newspaper published by the Atlas Economic Research Foundation:

> Following a recent Mont Pelerin Society meeting in New York City, the Atlas Sound Money Project held its inaugural high level strategy session with monetary scholars including: Lawrence H. White (F.A. Hayek Professor of Economic History, University of Missouri–St. Louis), Deepak Lal (President of the Mont Pelerin Society), Peter J. Boettke (Professor of Economics, George Mason University), and Gerald P. O'Driscoll (former vice president of the Federal Reserve Bank of Dallas and Senior Fellow, Cato Institute). (*Highlight*, Spring 2009)

The report explains the background of the new initiative. It mentions the easy money politics during the long boom from 1983 until 2000 and the loss of monetary policy competence in the think tank community. Interestingly, it was suggested that think tank professionals had neglected research in favor of lobbying. *Highlight* announced a survey to establish the current level of competence on monetary issues within the think tank community, essay competitions, and the development of online resources and conferences. New social media like Facebook would be relied on to promote a sound money perspective.

The new free trade initiative was reported first in the autumn issue of *Highlight*. Headed by Tom G. Palmer, the multilingual project was taken over by Atlas from the Cato Institute. The aim of the project is to expand the support for free trade in countries considered difficult from a neoliberal perspective. After September 11 attention was directed to the Middle East. "Lamp of Liberty" projects were considered to be of particular importance in such "border regions." Palmer's political PR strategy of aggressive marketing was inspired by an unnamed Norwegian businessman who explained to him the relevance of brands, and by the Internet retailer Amazon (Highlights Winter 2009, 3). A global project team was reported to have developed 13 Internet platforms in different languages including Farsi, Hindi, Swahili, Russian, Vietnamese, and Arabic, but also in English, French, and Portuguese.[10]

> The Initiative coordinates a network of ten major programs and many subsidiary projects working together across linguistic, cultural, and regional contexts to bring the ideas and policies of individual liberty, toleration, free markets, the

rule of law, and peace to populations around the world. The various teams publish books, maintain websites that offer a wealth of texts and audio and video presentations, syndicate articles to the print media, and organize seminars for students, conferences for policy makers, and much more.[11]

The project, still ongoing, employs many different media tools. AfricanLiberty.org, for example, features more than 20 videos on topics ranging from mistakes of Keynesianism to African history and freedom to the reasons for tax heavens. Books are featured as well, including classics from Hayek and Bastiat, but also Johan Norberg's statistical compendium "In Defence of Global Capitalism" (published by the Swedish think tank Timbro). Apart from online resources, conferences and seminars are organized for students and scholars.

While such projects are centralized, top-down efforts, regional think tank networks can also be examined in order to observe bottom-up efforts advanced by a variety of neoliberal think tanks at the local level. The following section will turn to the European Stockholm network in order to observe the range of positions and activities developed among more than 120 organizations on the issue of the global financial crisis.

10.4. The Global Financial Crisis in the Eyes of Members of the Stockholm Network

In the course of the 1990s many neoliberal think tanks were founded, especially in Central and Eastern Europe (Horn 2005). At the same time the networking and coordination among neoliberal think tanks was intensified. In 1997, the Stockholm network of neoliberal think tanks in Europe was founded by the British journalist Helen Disney. More than 120 members are currently listed on the website.[12] Members cannot be said to form a unified and homogeneous group. They represent a wide spectrum of neoliberal forces. Given the close links to US-based think tanks and think tank networks, the Stockholm network unsurprisingly copied some of the methods developed across the Atlantic to assist in capacity building. Regular resource bank meetings bring together think tank professionals from across Europe, and offer help and support with regard to funding and other issues.[13] Because Helen Disney has also founded a PR firm to run the network (Market House International), the purpose of the umbrella organization is not fully transparent. Most member organizations are charities, but the close relation to multinational corporations like Pfizer and Exxon Mobile indicates an overlap toward the more arcane parts of lobbying efforts. Unlike the United States, however, Europe still lacks transparency requirements that would enable researchers to more fully account for their corporate relationships. While the nexus between corporations and think tanks is clearly of importance, the following analysis is directed toward a better understanding of decentralized efforts of the members of the Stockholm network that probably do not need direction from corporations.

Unsurprisingly the financial crisis figured prominently both in the umbrella organization Stockholm network and in the member organizations. At least 47 of the 128 think tanks displayed documents on the topic (published 2007–2010). The material of 34 additional think tanks could not be assessed because of language constraints. The Stockholm network magazine *Eyes on Europe* (2009) featured the headline "Why Do the Markets Still Have a Role"? Criticism of the market is rejected in general, though several questions with regard to the crisis and consequences are raised including issues of transparency, reforms of equity requirements, and supervision. Only after clearly coming out in favor of reforms requiring increasing control and oversight does Helen Disney warn us not to place too much trust in the holy grail of regulation. Life and arguments clearly have become more complicated for neoliberal public intellectuals.

The member organizations feature both practical reform contributions and arguments pertaining to the crisis discourse itself. Some institutes are exclusively involved in the interpretation of the crisis from a neoliberal perspective, including several that are highly vested in the excessively utopian attitude of the Austrian school of economics following Mises and Hayek (advocating the need for a neutral monetary policy best accomplished by abolishing political discretion with regard to monetary matters). Other institutes feature more pragmatic arguments frequently grounded in ordoliberal traditions. I identified the two (certainly overgeneralized) positions by the following criterion: If public financial market regulation, whether by way of monetary policy or even fiscal policy instruments, is considered wrong in principle, the perspective is considered Austro-radical. If such instruments are considered acceptable only in specific ways, the perspective is described as pragmatic/ordoliberal. A number of think tanks do not waste much time on abstract theory. They are committed to technocratic advice in straightforward ways. The distribution and combination of positions presented in table 10.1 represent published material on record in the Internet only.

Crisis discourse-oriented think tanks and thinks tanks that also feature contributions to the reform debate roughly balance each other out. Austrian radical contributions dominate pragmatic publications on the whole. Two causes of the crisis are singled out: the intervention of the state in monetary policy in principle (the Austrian line) and the misleading of private behavior due to specific regulations. The latter most frequently emphasizes the inflation of credit by semi-public building societies like Fannie Mae and Freddie Mac in the United States. While the first line argues in a rigorous manner mostly at a highly abstract and general level, the second line typically features historical and empirical arguments, and occasionally offers complex and differentiated analysis. In such contributions we can find arguments

TABLE 10.1 Perspectives of Members of the Stockholm Network on the Global Financial Crisis

COUNTRY	PAPERS		TYPE OF CRISIS DISCOURSE		REFORM ARGUMENTS	TOTAL
	YES	NO	AUSTRO-RADICAL	PRAGMATIC		
UK	6	9		2(1)	5	15
Germany	7	5	3	4	5	12
Belgium	4	7	2(1)	1	4	11
France	6	2	1	2	2	8
Poland	3	5	1	2	3	8
Slovakia	1	7	1			8
Italy	4	3			1	7
Spain	2	3	(1)			5
Bulgaria	2	3	1	(1)	2	5
Czech Republic	1	4	(1)		1	5
Rumania	1	3	1			4
Sweden	1	2				3
Switzerland	3	0	1(1)	1	1	3
Denmark	1	1				2
Israel	1	1	(1)			2
Lithuania	1	0	1		1	1
Norway	1	0	(1)			1
The Netherlands	1	0	1			1
Total	**46**	**55**	**13(6)**	**12(1)**	**25**	**101**

SOURCE: www.stockholm-network.org and Internet pages of network members (2007–10).
I gratefully acknowledge research assistance by Werner Krämer. In brackets: identification unsure.

about the regulatory deficits of globalization and crisis management inspired by ordoliberal theory.

Radical positions are strongly voiced by German and Swiss think tanks like the Institute für unternehmerische Freiheit, the Hayek Society, and Liberales Institut. A small group of authors, including Torsten Polleit, Michael von Prollius, Frank Schäffler, and Norbert Tofall, produce the majority of publications. A small group of radical "Austrians" is capable of producing a disproportional share of contributions to the think tank literature on the topic.

How do the largest and probably best-financed subgroups of think tanks in the four larger countries (United Kingdom, Germany, France, and Italy) compare? British think tanks among the Stockholm network members seem to rely less on ideological justifications. They are mostly involved in discussions of regulatory change from a neoliberal perspective and can therefore be regarded to constitute a sort of neoliberal technocracy. Two British think tanks

(Policy Exchange and Reform) emphasize structural imbalances in international financial and production streams as central causes of the crisis (like Martin Wolf of the *Financial Times* at the MPS meeting discussed before).

In Germany, think tanks present much more material featuring worldview-dominated discussions on the topic. This is true both for publications from German "Austrians" and for German "Germans" (ordoliberals). It will be particularly important to watch out for the ways in which German ordoliberal perspectives are fed into international circuits, for example, through the Freiburg-based Center for European Policy dedicated to assessing European policymaking from an ordo perspective. Probably not by coincidence, one can observe ordoliberal perspectives featured particularly by Belgian (Brussels) think tanks as well. Italian and French think tanks (notably featuring frequent writers like MPS member Pascal Salin) are predominantly involved in fundamental debates on the crisis, and neglect more detailed discussions on regulatory reforms by and large.

With due recognition of all kinds of differences and contradictions between Stockholm network members, a common trait can be discerned with regard to blaming public authorities for the financial crisis and defending private market actors. Many authors representing the Austrian radical wing can be regarded to even fall back behind positions taken by Lal, who recognized the approximation of Hayek and Robbins to a Keynesian perspective on the Great Depression. Michael Prollius, of the Institut für unternehmerische Freiheit and founder of the Forum Ordnungspolitik, thinks it is possibly the gravest mistake to believe that the New Deal contributed anything toward overcoming the Great Depression. To the contrary, he claimed that the policies pursued by Presidents Hoover and Roosevelt were the reason behind the extraordinary length and depth of the economic crisis (Prollius 2009). Prollius carefully explored the neoliberal bookshelf to correct the alleged misinterpretations of the New Deal in line with the writings of Murray Rothbard and other followers of Ludwig von Mises, who held the New Deal primarily responsible for the development of the postwar elements of planning and welfare state capitalism. If Ferguson reminded neoliberal audiences of the ordoliberal reservoir to be tapped in order to preempt reform proposals from Keynesian competitors, tapping the Austrian heritage had the primary purpose of nurturing doubts with regard to the character of state regulation in principle. A principled distance from state regulation in the belief of superiority of unregulated market activities should not be equated to neoclassical models of full competition and equilibrium since the Austrian understanding conceives of dynamic processes of "creative destruction" (Schumpeter) rather than describing markets that are both complete and static.

If the presentation so far has made some effort to juxtapose the two major lines of neoliberal thought in reaction to the global financial crisis, this has been done for analytical reasons rather than to represent two clearly distinct camps within the Stockholm network. Individual contributions on the crisis by leading neoliberal economists in Germany can be pointed out that combine Austrian and ordoliberal lines of analysis. Straubhaar, Wohlgemut, and Zweynert (2009), for example, present a sophisticated argument against what they hold to constitute vulgar Keynesian responses to the crisis by way of drawing on ordoliberal principles of regulation and an Austrian understanding of the business cycle. Much like Lal, the authors make an effort to enlist what they hold to be the valuable Keynes—the understanding of the problems of uncertainty and limited recourse to state intervention to overcome liquidity traps—to combat a return to "big government" in the name of Keynes.

A careful analysis of the different schools of thought united under the umbrella of neoliberalism has to recognize the common elements of understanding and joint efforts of Austrian and ordoliberal varieties of neoliberalism, including convictions about the neutrality of economic policy, the primacy of monetary stability, the need to oppose discretionary intervention in the economic process, and the minimization of state ownership and participation in capital accumulation. Notably with regard to monetary policy the different wings also feature occasionally sharp disagreement with regard to the methods enlisted to secure these premises. In reaction to the global financial crisis, one can observe a division of labor within the neoliberal networks. To break the momentum of reformist action Austrian positions are most valuable because they are highly effective in casting doubt on the effectiveness of reregulation, and thereby can be effectively used to undermine support for reform or to slow reform processes down. Ordoliberal positions are valuable because they are better prepared to enter the competition for the scope and instruments of reregulation, usually in an effort to prevent far-reaching reregulation and to limit the impact on private ownership and market activities regardless of rhetoric that can sometimes sound quite radical (against monopoly, etc.). The highest value linked to the Austrian perspective is individual freedom, whereas ordoliberals emphasize competition and effectiveness. In combination, the joint project can develop formidable strength in support of paradigm maintenance even in times of enduring crisis of globalized capitalism.

10.5. Conclusion: What's Left for Neoliberal Private Authorities?

Based on the survey of MPS deliberations on the question of the financial crisis and the scan of the Stockholm network contributions, it is safe to suggest that neoliberal discourse coalitions can rely on a well-organized hinterland of think tank networks engaged in a wide range of intellectual productions. The positions developed and conveyed by leading intellectuals and think tank professionals through think tank channels are ready made for public opinion struggles carried out in the media beyond expert communities, and in civil society at large. In addition to the closed circuits of technical experts that have been described elsewhere (including Plehwe 2009), we can point to the larger phenomenon of a neoliberal discourse coalition that is ready to defend the major neoliberal storylines and the status quo ante crisis in the wider spheres of public and media discourse. It is not possible based on the research conducted so far to provide an impact assessment of the productions discussed in this chapter. If Carrigan (2010) is right to credit the British think tanks he scrutinized for changing the terms of the debate on the financial crisis, it might be an adequate hypothesis to be advanced for the neoliberal think tank networks at large, although the impact may differ to a certain extent from country to country, and from time to time. Think tank productions alone clearly are not enough to explain such a capacity, though. The paradigm shift in monetary policy during the late 1960s and early 1970s—the shift toward flexible exchange rates—has been accomplished by a core group of neoliberal intellectuals with the assistance of a small group of think tanks compared to the neoliberal networks that exist today. While the media, public, and expert discussions arguably were more restricted 40 years ago, the capacities of the neoliberal networks may be considered much larger and yet more restricted nowadays, on the topic of global finance at least. It appears likely, however, that the troops Lal and others can enlist in support of neoliberal storylines are strong enough to defend key elements of the hegemonic discourse of the heyday of neoliberal globalization. Bernhard Walpen (2009) is probably right to suggest that neoliberals currently are ruling rather than leading—too many remain unconvinced of the present state of regulatory reform, but without being able to move debates in a new direction. Modification of neoliberal paradigms is more likely than replacement under these conditions.

References

Becker, Gary. 2008. Keynote lecture, MPS Special Meeting, New York. www.montpelerin.org/nyc2k9.cfm.

Blanchard, Olivier, Giovanni Dell'Ariccia, and Paolo Mauro. 2010. "Rethinking Macroeconomic Policy." IMF Staff Position Note, February 12.

Burgin, Angus. 2012. *The Great Persuasion: Reinventing Free Markets since the Depression*. Cambridge, MA: Harvard University Press.

Carrigan, Mark. 2010. "How Right-Wing Think-Tanks Laid the Foundation for the Coalition's Agenda." Liberal Conspiracy, August 9. http://liberalconspiracy.org/2010/08/09/how-right-wing-think-tanks-laid-the-foundation-for-the-coalitions-agenda/.

Ferguson, Niall. 2008. Keynote lecture, MPS Special Meeting, New York. www.montpelerin.org/nyc2k9.cfm.

Fischer, Frank. 2003. *Reframing Public Policy: Discursive Politics and Deliberative Practices*. New York: Oxford University Press.

Forbes, Steve. 2008. Keynote lecture, MPS Special Meeting, New York. www.montpelerin.org/nyc2k9.cfm.

Frank, Thomas. 2004. *What's the Matter with Kansas?* New York: Metropolitan Books.

Friedman, Milton, and Robert Roosa. 1967. *The Balance of Payments: Free versus Fixed Exchange Rates*. Washington, DC: American Enterprise Institute.

Gissurarson, Hannes H., 2008. "The Strange Death of Liberal Iceland." www.montpelerin.org/nyc2k9.cfm.

Hajer, Maarten A. 1993. "Discourse Coalitions and the Institutionalization of Practice: The Case of Acid Rain in Britain." In Fischer, Frank and John Forrester, eds., *The Argumentative Turn in Policy Analysis and Planning*, 43–76. Durham, NC: Duke University Press.

Helleiner, Eric. 1994. *States and the Reemergence of Global Finance: From Bretton Woods to the 1990s*. Ithaca, NY: Cornell University Press.

Helleiner, Eric, and Stefano Pagliari. 2009. "Crisis and the Reform of International Financial Regulation". In Helleiner Eric, Pagliari Stefano, and Zimmermann Hubert, eds., *Global Finance in Crisis. The Politics of International Regulatory Change*, 1–17. London: Routledge.

Horn, Karen. 2005. "Die wirtschaftlichen Freigeister stellen sich auf die Hinterbeine: Selbst in wirtschaftlich schwierigen Zeiten entstehen auf der Welt immer mehr 'Think Tanks.'" *Frankfurter Allgemeine Zeitung*, August 11, 11.

Kogut, Bruce, and J. Muir Macpherson. 2008. "The Decision to Privatize: Economists and the Construction of Ideas and Policies." In Beth A. Simmons, Frank Dobbin, and Geoffrey Garrett, eds., *The Global Diffusion of Markets and Democracy*, 104–40. Cambridge: Cambridge University Press.

Lal, Deepak. 2008. "The Mont Pelerin Society: A Mandate Renewed." Presidential address. www.montpelerin.org/nyc2k9.cfm.

Mirowski, Phil, and Dieter Plehwe, eds. 2009. *The Road from Mont Pèlerin: The Making of the Neoliberal Thought Collective*. Cambridge, MA: Harvard University Press.

Offer, Avner, and Gabriel Söderberg. 2016. The Nobel Factor. The Prize in Economics, Social Democracy, And The Market Turn. Princeton, NJ: Princeton University Press.

Plehwe, Dieter. 2009. "Schützt die Krise vor der Beratung?" *Gegenblende*, August 20. http://dgbdebatte.blogspot.com/search/label/Politikberatung.

Plehwe, Dieter. 2010. "The Making of a Comprehensive Transnational Discourse Community." Marie-Laure Djelic and Sigrid Quack, eds., *Transnational Communities: Shaping Global Economic Governance*, 305–26. Cambridge: Cambridge University Press.

Plehwe, Dieter, Bernhard Walpen, and Gisela Neunhöffer, eds. 2006. *Neoliberal Hegemony: A Global Critique*. London: Routledge.

Plickert, Philip. 2008. *Wandlungen des Neoliberalismus*. Marktwirtschaftliche Reformpolitik, Schriftenreie der Aktionsgemeinschaft Soziale Marktwirtschaft. Stuttgart: Lucius & Lucius.

Prollius, Michael von. 2009. "Kann die Regierung die Rezession bekämpfen?" Commentary for the Institut für unternehmerische Freiheit. http://iuf-berlin.org/kommentare/2359.php.

Ptak, Ralf. 2009. "Neoliberalism in Germany: Revisiting the Ordoliberal Foundations of the Social Market Economy." In Philip Mirowski and Dieter Plehwe, eds., *The Road from Mont Pèlerin: The Making of the Neoliberal Thought Collective*, 89–138. Cambridge, MA: Harvard University Press.

Saloma, John S., III. 1984. *Ominous Politics: The New Conservative Labyrinth.* New York: Hill and Wang.

Schmelzer, Matthias. 2010. *Freiheit für Wechselkurse und Kapital! Die Ursprünge neoliberaler Währungspolitik und die Mont Pelerin Society.* Marburg: Metropolis Verlag.

Straubhaar, Thomas, Michael Wohlgemuth, and Joachim Zweynert. 2009. "Rückkehr des Keynesianismus: Anmerkungen aus ordnungspolitischer Sicht. In "Aus Politik und Zeitgeschichte," supplement to *Das Parlament* 20 (May 11). www.bundestag.de/das-parlament/2009/20/Beilage/index.html.

Thum, Marcel and Harald Hau. 2009. "Subprime Crisis and Board (In-)Competence: Private vs. Public Banks in Germany." *Economic Policy* 60:701–52.

Walpen, Bernhard. 2004. *Die offenen Feinde und ihre Gesellschaft.* Hamburg: VSA.

Wolf, Martin. 2008. "Global Imbalances." www.montpelerin.org/nyc2k9.cfm.

Zimmermann, Hubert. 2009. "Conclusion: Whither Global Financial Regulation?." In Eric Helleiner, Stefano Pagliari, and Hubert Zimmermann, eds., *Global Finance in Crisis*, 170–75. Routledge: London.

| Conclusion

THIS VOLUME REVEALS THE complexity of the positions toward the welfare state taken by economists, most of whom could be counted as liberal in one way or another. Liberal economists were both at the heart of the original development of the welfare state and at the center of the countermovement against the welfare state. The nature of the interaction between liberalism and the welfare state, and the role of economists, varied greatly between countries. In some countries the merger of liberal economic concerns and solidarity norms of Christian or socialist provenance eventually paved the way to the universalization of welfare provisions, whereas in others, liberal and conservative philosophy limited welfare provisions. However, in the age of welfare state retrenchment, cost-cutting, and reorganization, the norm on which most countries seem to have converged includes a package of means-tested programs, minimized universal programs combined with private insurance and temporary relief in times of crisis, no matter which variety of welfare regime had been developed during the heyday of social liberalism. The major force behind the countermovement against the welfare state has been a coalition of economic interests and market ideology, the latter increasingly becoming a transnational movement. For a long time, this countermovement was restricted by the institutional configuration of the welfare state, which was not easily dissolved (Hall and Lamont 2013).

However, transformations of welfare regimes can be better explained if closer attention is paid to the mobilization of specific economic ideas in the reform of the welfare state. While many liberal economists were involved in working out ways to take welfare provision out of the market in the early days of the welfare state—advancing concepts of social citizenship—the dominant strand in the neoliberal economic thinking that offered ongoing criticism of welfare states across the world advanced notions of more or less social-market citizenship. Even where there is agreement on the need for minimum standards and social protection, the welfare state is no longer a project designed to decrease inequality. In other words, the history of liberalism and welfare have gone through a cycle: from laissez-faire and private charity to social citizenship and public welfare; and then from there to market citizenship relying on a mixture of private and modified public welfare.

In contemporary discourse, liberalism has become associated with opposition to the welfare state. Over the past 30 to 40 years, explicit economic arguments against the welfare state have been developing much faster than those in its support. Demographic challenges and problems of public debt have increasingly replaced moral hazard as the driving force of welfare state retrenchment, with the result that the main argument has shifted from the merits of the welfare state itself to the necessity to solve macroeconomic imbalances. Defenses of the welfare state, such the argument that welfare transfers can act as a major stabilizer (made by Paul Krugman) and arguments about how inequality holds back growth (made by the OECD: Cingano 2014), echo this view and are therefore limited.[1] They turn social welfare provision from being a pragmatic device for minimum protection into a technocratic institution of macroeconomic coordination and labor market control.

However, despite the widespread failure of economists sympathetic toward the welfare state to produce economic arguments in its favor that were sufficiently powerful to counter arguments against it, there is, as the chapters in this volume show, no inherent conflict between liberalism and the welfare state. Prior to the rise of modern neoliberalism, which has succeeded in making arguments about the welfare state much more uniform across countries, economists did not see any conflict between liberalism and the welfare state. Even the early neoliberals were less opposed to more comprehensive welfare provision than is the case today. The nowadays dominant narratives of redistribution versus efficiency and of practical constraints (due to competition, globalization, etc.) requiring retrenchment of the welfare state fail to capture the diverse and changing contributions even of liberal economists to the welfare debate across countries and time. Take, for example, the "New Liberal" supporters of the welfare state such as Keynes and Beveridge, and the early "Neoliberals," such as Hayek, Robbins, and Müller-Armack. Their views diverged on account of their broader perspective on economics, economic policymaking, and social development, yet they were united in their opposition to collectivism, and they converged on the innovative idea of a minimum standard of welfare in the course of the 1930s. Economists may have held to the dominant liberal, conservative, and social democratic worldviews, but there was no simple connection between such worldviews and economic ideas. If we acknowledge this variety we can make much more sense of the distance of the real types from the ideal types (e.g., the social democratic dimension of NHS in the United Kingdom, the neoliberal dimension of limited public welfare in Japan, the mix of public and commercial welfare in Germany) than if we talk simply in terms of different welfare regimes as a whole.

In both Japan and in Germany, the private sector and employment politics played a stronger role with regard to early postwar welfare state thinking than was the case in Britain. The liberal market economy and allegedly liberal welfare state United Kingdom developed into a more universal welfare state regime during a time in which state spending on social policy was quite restricted in the coordinated market economies of Japan and Germany. In an odd mixture, Japan combined the most minimalist of all (OECD) public welfare regimes with a Keynesian growth model that advanced company-based welfare benefits way beyond what was offered in restrictive liberal regimes like the United States. Germany evolved from a rather restrictive neoliberal regime into a more universal regime, because Christian Democrat and Social Democratic perspectives prevailed over neoliberal perspectives, which had informed the postwar regime of the social-market economy. Ludwig Erhard had opposed the public pension system and industrial democracy, but he had to compromise with regard to cornerstones of the intergenerational contract and codetermination system. While the German variety of neoliberalism, ordoliberalism, nevertheless secured a strong emphasis on the private sector and competitiveness, a comprehensive expansion of the German welfare state resulted from an attempted merger of ordoliberal and Keynesian perspectives. While German economists perceived a strong need for enhanced macroeconomic management in the course of the 1960s, the inventors of the new bag of economic ideas predicated Keynesian style macroengineering on ordoliberal principles. When they failed to restrict the Social Democratic coalition government and the German *Länder* in the upswing of the early 1970s, the leading ordo-Keynesians left the government and the party—both Karl Schiller and Herbert Giersch turned into vocal critiques of the economic policy regime they had helped to create in the first place, as Hagemann explains in this volume. Germany's de facto transformation of the originally neoliberal social-market economy into a Social Democratic version faced stubborn opposition from an increasingly supply-side-oriented cohort of neoliberal economists. Over time this opposition helped to restrict Germany's welfare regime and eventually helped to commercialize and reduce the system following unification, as Kinderman observes in his chapter.

In Japan in turn, the ingenious division of welfare-related labor between the state and the corporate sector remained relatively stable until the 1990s as well. It is intriguing to observe the close link of the business world and certain camps of (neo)liberal ideas in Japan dating back to the immediate postwar era, which was, however, more strongly influenced by a range of new and social liberals influenced from British sources, as pointed out by Nishizawa and Ikeda. But in all three countries, a strong link was constructed between business interests and neoliberal critiques of the welfare state. The chapters by Rollings, Nishizawa, and Kinderman in particular explain the common influence, which was also characterized by international ties. Japan was less insulated from the varieties of Western liberalism than many might think, with both German ordoliberals and Austrian school economics playing a considerable role, if on the margins of the ruling Liberal Party system. While neoliberals informed the rollback of the welfare state in Britain under Thatcher beginning in the early 1980s, the axis of corporate interests and neoliberal intellectuals and the coproduction of economic thought in these circles came to bear more strongly on Japanese and German developments in the 1990s and 2000s—paradoxically most strongly under a Social Democratic government in Germany. In any case, we learn much more about the drivers of changes within and across welfare regimes when recognizing economists, alliances of political economists (frequently supported by think tanks and networks), and economic thought tailored to the specific needs of a social economic context: targeting employment politics in Japan, unemployment insurance in Germany, and the institutional configuration of trade union strength in the United Kingdom. We can also learn about struggles and surprising failures. The National Health System was subject to attacks, but could not be dismantled due to strong resistance against health austerity measures, while the mixed private-public health system in Germany was already closer to ideas of commercialization neoliberals successfully pushed in reforms of the German health and care services.

A focus on varieties of liberalism and neoliberalism in the realm of economic ideas takes the welfare state debate beyond the prevailing focus on major ideologies (of liberalism, conservatism, and socialism) and institutional configurations. This focus takes the debate also beyond the superficial equation of economic and neoliberal ideas. Economic ideas are seen in the different light of a battleground between different wings of liberalism and neoliberalism and other worldviews. For those who are concerned about both the history and the field of economics, it is most important not to equate economics with liberalism or neoliberalism *tout court*, and hence to avoid the essentialism implied in talking of the power of economic ideas without specifying what kind of economic ideas these are. This is why, when talking about debates over the welfare state, it is useful to talk in terms of the political and economic power of ideas of liberal social citizenship at the origin of the modern welfare state, and of the political and economic power of ideas of neoliberal market citizenship when we turn to contemporary arguments for retrenchment, cost-cutting, and market-oriented reforms of the welfare state.

One of the reasons why there has not been more recognition of the varieties of liberalism and neoliberalism in discussions so far is that there has been a desire to advance hegemonic claims in favor of one or the other version of liberalism. Both social (progressive, left leaning if you wish) liberals and neoliberals (or conservative, leaning toward the right side of the political spectrum) can be found to deny the right to the liberal title to the other side. Modern social liberals, still seeking comprehensive welfare provision as the foundation of a free society, and emphasizing the way political liberalism has evolved over the centuries, treat Hayek and the neoliberals as "pretenders" or old-fashioned liberals.[2] Conversely, modern neoliberals claim continuity with classical liberalism, emphasizing the importance of property rights, individualism, and freedom of contract. For them, social liberals are no longer liberals, and rather have to be considered socialists or social democrats. Rather than side with one of these contradictory claims, it makes sense to recognize the enormous variety of positions found within liberalism.

There is not even homogeneity within these two positions: neither social/progressive liberalism nor anticollectivist neoliberalism/classical liberalism can be considered a homogeneous body of thought existing in isolation from other strands of thought. Complicating his own efforts to exclude Hayek from the liberal family, Michael Freeden writes convincingly about "the elusiveness of European (anti-)liberalism" (Freeden 2015, 33). How otherwise to make sense of the flirting with dictatorship (in Latin America of the 1970s, for example) by many neoliberals hostile to advances of socialist government? Twenty years earlier the circumstances of the time required ordoliberals (in Germany in the 1950s) to consider issues of social integration much more strongly than neoliberals usually did during the later period of established welfare state capitalism, which had generated a whole range of critiques of social citizenship and generous welfare regimes. If varieties of welfare are considered from the vantage point of egalitarian notions of social citizenship all the way down to notions of social minimum standards not inimical to the market (one of the Mont Pelerin founding conference principles formulated by Lionel Robbins), we can observe the whole range of liberal and neoliberal positions. While the equality principle pushed back ideas of natural inequality and modified capitalist class society by way of reducing if not compensating labor market-related and social risks, the inequality principle inherent to capitalist class society has been advancing again by way of welfare state retrenchment. Alfred Marshall observed this fundamental conflict between equality and inequality principles. He concluded by way of suggesting a possible mediation between the hostile siblings through the welfare state. It is possible that he would be more skeptical nowadays, but this we do not know, of course. The task would seem quite different now than it was back in Marshall's days: How to reconcile the normative ideal of the equality principle requiring social citizenship beyond national borders with the dynamic forces of inequality driven by globalized capitalism? Can there be social citizenship in a postnational world? Or is some sort of social-market citizenship the only viable option left for cosmopolitan capitalism (Herbert Giersch 1989)? Which of course translates into cosmopolitan inequality! The answer is surely not expected from economists only, but we are confident that economists will have to contribute significantly to an answer.

The chapters in this volume, in showing that the history of the welfare state is bound up with the history of liberalism and that, for most of the twentieth century, liberal economists were strongly in favor of the welfare state for ethical and instrumental reasons, bring out a dimension of the history of liberalism that is often overlooked. They also serve as a reminder that liberal economists were more ambitious in what they believed a state conforming to fundamental liberal values might be able to achieve.

References

Cingano, Federico. 2014. "Trends in Income Inequality and Its Impact on Economic Growth." OECD Social, Employment and Migration Working Papers No. 163. www.oecd.org/els/soc/trends-in-income-inequality-and-its-impact-on-economic-growth-SEM-WP163.pdf.

Freeden, Michael. 1996. *Ideologies and Political Theory: A Conceptual Approach*. Oxford: Oxford University Press.

Freeden, Michael. 2015. "The Elusiveness of European (Anti-)liberalism." In Gosewinkel, Dieter, ed., *Anti-liberal Europe: A Neglected Story of Europeanization*, 33–46. New York: Berghahn.

Giersch, Herbert. 1989. "Anmerkungen zum weltwirtschaftlichen Denkansatz." *Weltwirtschaftliches Archiv* 125(1): 1–16.

Hall, Peter, and Michele Lamont. 2013. *Social Resilience in the Neo-Liberal Era*. Cambridge: Cambridge University Press.

NOTES

Introduction

1. Data on inequality developments in different countries can be found here: http://inequalitywatch.eu. The stunning success of Thomas Piketty's book *Capital in the Twenty-First Century* (2013) can hardly be explained without the growing concern about rising inequality since the global financial crisis. On the link between inequality and the financial crisis see Atkinson and Morelli 2011. Both OECD and the World Bank featured focus areas on rising inequality after the crisis; compare http://www.oecd.org/els/soc/dividedwestandwhyinequalitykeepsrising.htm, http://www.worldbank.org/en/topic/isp.

2. *The Guardian*, January 8, 2013. http://www.theguardian.com/commentisfree/2013/jan/08/welfare-state-1942-2013-obituary. King Willem-Alexander from the Netherlands likewise declared the end of the welfare state in 2013: http://www.independent.co.uk/news/world/europe/dutch-king-willemalexander-declares-the-end-of-the-welfare-state-8822421.html. Compare also Svalvors and Taylor-Gooby 1999; Wacquant 2010.

3. "Towards Common Principles of Flexicurity: More and Better Jobs through Flexibility and Security" was published in June 2007.

4. The term was first introduced by the Social Democratic prime minister of Denmark, Poul Nyrup Rasmussen.

5. Folster and Sanandiji's (2014) book on the renaissance of reforms, which was initiated by Swedish employer organizations, is widely cited in recently founded Austrian think tanks like Agenda Austria ("learning from others"). Compare also the role of the OECD in supporting welfare state reforms discussed in Armingeon and Beyeler 2004.

6. *Neoliberalism* is a highly contested term. The term was used as a label for an attempt to rethink liberalism that began in the late 1930s, when a group of liberal thinkers became pessimistic about the growth of collectivism. These thinkers are discussed in more detail below. The view taken here is that while the term is abused, and while the boundaries of what and who count as neoliberal are far from clear-cut, the term is serviceable.

7. This alludes to the arguments of Pickett and Wilkinson (2009).

8. Liberal welfare regimes are considered limited in terms of scope and depth, accordingly. Yet the very existence of public liberal welfare regimes attests to the departure from the era of private charity.

Chapter 1

1. This is discussed below.

2. "Am I a Liberal," in Keynes 1972–89, 9:297.

3. Keynes 1972–89, 10, chap. 39. The purpose of Keynes's essay was ostensibly to engage another essay read a few months earlier by David Garnett on the response (not favorable) of the novelist D. H. Lawrence to Bloomsbury. This discussion of Keynes's ethics and its subsequent fate includes some material from Backhouse and Bateman 2012.

4. See Bateman 1988 for a full discussion of Keynes's early work on probability in his Apostles papers.

5. This was the perception. Whether this was the reality is a different matter that we do not need to pursue here. Bart Schultz (2004) has argued that the Apostles had more in common with Sidgwick than they acknowledged.

6. This paragraph summarizes part of an argument developed at much greater length in Backhouse 2010.

7. This second point is a central argument of Backhouse and Bateman (2010), who describe several cases in which Keynes encouraged the people who were reshaping (or rebuilding) his theory on a new foundation.

Chapter 2

1. In the event, the Labour government paid pensions in full when the National Insurance Act was implemented in 1948.

Chapter 3

1. The successful currency reform that took place on June 20, 1948, in the three Western zones was mainly based on the 1946 American Colm-Dodge-Goldsmith (1955) plan for the liquidation of war financing and the financial rehabilitation of Germany, with Gerhard Colm as the main architect.

2. Some parts of the paper are based on Hagemann 2013.

3. For greater details on Miksch see Goldschmidt and Berndt 2005.

4. See Goldschmidt 2002 for a detailed analysis of Eucken's life and work.

5. See Rieter and Schmolz 1993, 96–103, for a more detailed discussion of these debates.

6. There is a clear link in conceptualizing a division of labor between the market and the government and a liberal economic policy between the Freiburg school and the old Chicago school, as later consistently pointed out by James Buchanan. In specifying the constituent principles of a market economy, Eucken (1952, 255) explicitly refers to *Economic Policy for a Free Society* by Henry C. Simons (1948) who throughout advocated the use of government power to eliminate private monopoly in all its forms and to allow the benefits of free competition to be enjoyed by all, as well as the need of stricter rules in monetary policy.

7. See Eucken 1952, book 4.

8. Röpke had been a "pre-Keynesian" advocating a credit-financed investment program as an initial ignition to overcome the Great Depression but later became a staunch anti-Keynesian, attacking the inflationary bias of permanent Keynesian demand management policies.

9. See Deutsche Bundesbank 1998, particularly the contributions by Neumann, Holtfrerich, von Hagen, Baltensperger, and Richter.

10. For a comprehensive survey of the decisive figures and their main contributions see the excellent compilation edited by Goldschmidt and Wohlgemuth (2008a). See also the contributions in Peacock and Willgerodt 1989. For more critical views see Haselbach (1991), Ptak (2004) and Plehwe (2006).

11. When Erhard became German chancellor in 1963, Müller-Armack resigned from his position in the Ministry of Economics.

12. A key role was played by the managing editor, Erich Welter (1900–1982), who had studied economics with Oppenheimer and Eucken's teacher Hermann Schumacher at Berlin, where he also came into closer contact with Eucken. Welter made a dual career as a journalist (he was the last editor-in-chief of the liberal *Vossische Zeitung* in Berlin 1932–34 and cofounder of the FAZ in 1949) and in academics. From 1948–1965 he was full professor of Economics at the University of Mainz.

13. Volumes 2 and 3 were also translated into English as, respectively, *Prices and Equilibrium: An Introduction to Static and Dynamic Analysis* and *Money, Income, and Employment* (London: George Allen & Unwin, 1962; still available as Routledge Reprints and ebooks today), and characterized by Kurt Rothschild in the *American Economic Review* as "one of the best introductions to modern economic analysis available" (1964, 4). The last German edition of volume 3, which was published posthumously (1973), contains a brilliant attack against the monetarist counterrevolution initiated by Milton Friedman, which was now gaining ground also in Germany.

14. On Schneider's life and work see the excellent article by Häuser (2010).

15. For a detailed analysis of the activities of the committee in the period of catching-up to the Anglo-Saxon developments of the first two decades, in which Keynesianism was rather dominant, see Schefold 2004b.

16. For a concise discussion of this decisive turning point in the economic program and the development of the SPD "from Marx to Market," see Nützenadel 2005, 234–44.

17. The SVR in the annual reports to the government has to assess overall economic developments in the past year and to outline economic prospects for the coming year. It is explicitly forbidden to make policy "recommendations," which has always been a controversial issue. Thus in its 2013–14 report the majority explicitly opposed the introduction of minimum wages in Germany, which had been agreed by the partners in the third Grand Coalition.

Chapter 4

1. Since then interrupted twice, first by the Murayama (Socialist Party) coalition government in 1994–98, then by the new Democratic Party in 2009–12.

2. Ouchi 1970, 410–12. Shakaihoshoseido Shingikai Jimukyoku ed. 1971, 3. In fact, immediately after the war in 1946, a Social Security Study Group was set up by several academics and drew up the "Plan for Social Security," strongly influenced by the Beveridge report. An Enquiry into Social Insurance was also set up in the Welfare Ministry in 1946, whose subcommittee consisted of the same four academics as the above Social Security Study Group. Enquiry drew up "Outline of Social Security System," following the basic ideas of the Beveridge report (for these see Tamai 1992, 300–306).

3. Around 1974, the year Hayek received the Nobel Prize, he began a series of occasional visits to Japan. He drafted the Nobel Prize memorial lecture in Izu (a resort not far from Tokyo) in the autumn of 1974. Nakayama Ichiro was instrumental in bringing out a book based on Nishiyama's interviews with Hayek in 1976 (see below in this chapter).

4. See Backhouse and Nishizawa 2010, part 2.

5. The origins of the Japanese Ruskin Society date back to these days; it was probably Kawakami Hajime and Fukuda Tokuzo who provided the inspiration to read Ruskin. See Daniels and Tsuzuki 2002, chaps. 2, 11, 12.

6. For the 150th anniversary of Adam Smith's birth Ueda Teijiro wrote "The Economic Policy of Adam Smith": he argued in support of Smith's criticism of mercantilism, a system that had defended the merchants' and manufactures' monopoly on trade and industry. Around the same time, Ueda wrote in support of Muto Sanji (Kanebo Cotton Spinning Co.) and his "Commercial and Industrial Party"—a political party that opposed monopolistic and privileged classes that colluded with politicians; and called for a rallying of the middle business classes (Ueda 1976a, 442–43).

7. The Maintenance of Public Order Act passed in 1925 in Japan.

8. Nishizawa 2010. Fukuda praised Britain's Liberal reform of the old-age pensions act of 1908 and highly commended the foundation of the first Labour government in 1924. He also applauded Keynes's *Economic Consequences of Peace* in the highest terms. Fukuda 1926b, 1465–69.

9. See Nishizawa 2014. Fukuda attended Webb's lecture "Policy of National Minimum" at Keio Gijuku in October 1911.

10. Presumably the idea of "doubling wages" came from Fukuda, or Brentano and Fukuda's *Labour Economics* (*Rodokeizai-ron*, 1899), which argued for efficient wages. Nakayama highly praised this work in his paper "Welfare Economics and Fukuda Tokuzo" ("Koseikeizaigaku to Fukuda Tokuzo," 1974), in Minoguchi and Hayasaka 1978.

11. See Nishizawa 2002.

12. The first Japanese translation was by the economic section of the Treasury in 1948. The Beveridge report was introduced in the prewar years in articles published in the *Social Policy Bulletin* (*Shakai-seisaku-jiho*) by the Conciliation Society (Kyochokai) in 1943 and 1944 (see Tamai 1992, 298–99).

13. Tsuru 1971. The paper titled "In Place of GNP" was first presented at the Symposium on Political Economy of Environment, Paris, 1971.

14. See Miyamoto 1986.

15. Fukuda also referred to Hobhouse's *Metaphysical Theory of the State* (1918), following an eminent liberalist, Hasegawa Nyozekan. Hasegawa introduced Hobhouse's criticism of Hegelian and German philosophical statism, and Fukuda used Hobhouse in his arguments on "discovery of society" for social policy. Fukuda 1926a.

16. Kishi was a very able bureaucrat of the prewar Ministry of Trade and Industry and deeply involved in the planned and controlled economy of Manchuria and Japan. He then became the permanent secretary of the Ministry but clashed with the liberalist minister Kobayashi Ichizo, a liberal-minded man of the business world who founded the Hankyu Railway Company; he was also the director of Tokyo Electricity Company, for which Kikawada worked. Kobayashi in his role as minister asked Yamamoto Katsuichi to produce a critique of the controlled economy.

17. In fact, Ikeda was finance minister in the Ishibashi government; Ishibashi had picked out Ikeda for the role of permanent secretary of the Finance ministry when he was its minister. Ishibashi later referred to "My disciple Mr. Ikeda"([Watashino Deshi, Ikeda-kun]) in the *Memorial Essays for Teacher Ikeda Hayato* (*Ikeda Hayato Sensei wo Shinobu)* (as quoted in Tsutsui 1986, 414). Ikeda Hayato was PM from 1960 to 1964 after Kishi Nobusuke.

18. See Nishizawa 2001. See also Nishizawa 2007, chap. 5, sec. 6. Section 4.3 of the present chapter is largely based on these texts.

19. The second volume of Ueda's *Collected Works* (1975) was entitled *Economic Discourse of Joint Stock Companies* (*Kabushikigaisha Keizairon*). Ueda's disciple Aoba Fumio, who was active in the postwar business community, as I discuss below, wrote the "Commentary" for this volume.

20. Ueda 1942, 32.

21. For Keizai-doyukai's proposal and Nakayama, Sakurada, and Kikawada, see Nishizawa 2002, 13–14; Okazaki 1996, 107–11, 193–99.

22. Ueda's disciple Aoba, as general secretary of the JERI (Japan Economic Research Institute), said about JERI research topics, like the forward march of liberalism and the role of business enterprise, and roles of government business and private business, that he owed much to his teacher Ueda's *Enterprise and Society*. Aoba 1989, 23.

23. Fukuda (sometime finance minister who met Hayek in 1965 in Japan) and Aoba were acquainted through the private advisory group (called Niki-kai) to the PM, formed and started when Sato Eisaku was PM in 1964; the original members of Niki-kai included Kiuchi Nobutane.

24. Okazaki 1996, 90.

25. Takamiya 1978. It is said that Kikawada kept the *Ordo* in his study.

26. When Hayek was awarded the Nobel Prize, the media came up with many comments. An editor of the newspaper *Mainichi* (Tamaoki Kazuhiro), who had worked for EPA (Economic Planning Agency), experienced some difficulty in tracking down a good commentator for Hayek; he asked Kikawada about Hayek. Kikawada's comment appeared in *Mainichi*, October 10, 1974.

27. Okazaki 1996, 229. Keizai-doyukai set up the Committee for Promoting New Liberalism in 1973. One of main issues was to investigate the theory and practice of "ordered liberalism." Against the background of the strains of high-speed economic growth, environmental disruption, and oil shocks, the committee considered business from the social viewpoint, and approached the issue of the market principle with order; its intermediate report stated that an issue of increasing importance was "how to institute order and the principle of regulation by the public in order to maintain the positive aspects of the market principle, i.e., to develop and maximize individuals' faculties" (Okazaki 1996, 227).

28. Aoba 1985, 1.

29. Kaji 1994, 88. For a road from Mont Pelerin in Japan, cf. Nishizawa's presentation to the conference "More Roads from Mont Pelerin: Neoliberalism Studies" in Berlin March 20–22. 2016.

Sekai Keizai Chosakai (World Economic Research Society) was originally founded in 1941 with the main purpose of analyzing foreign economic affairs.

30. Yamamoto sent a galley proof of the book to Kiuchi Nobutane, who was greatly impressed and excited by Yamamoto's ideas. See, Yamamoto 1980, 155–56.

31. This leaflet was published by the Tokyo Yamamoto-kai; it was reproduced as a chapter in Yamamoto, *Welfare State Decays the Nation*, 1975, having replaced the subtitle as title (1961b, 99–124).

32. Parts of Röpke's lectures and questions were published in the journal *Keizai-ourai*, May 1961. A questioner at the first lecture on inflation was Nakayama Ichiro; the second lecture was on the "economic order in a free society," and the questioners were Kikawada Kazutaka and Minato Moriatsu of Keizai-doyukai (28–39, 40–51).

Yamada Yuzo, who met Röpke in Geneva in 1953, had written "Professor Röpke and Neoliberalism" in the previous issue of same journal, April 1961.

33. Röpke's *Civitas Humana* (1944) was translated into Japanese by Kitamura Hiroshi in 1952. Kitamura also translated Röpke's *Die Krise des Kollektivismus und Das Kulturideal des Liberalismus* (1947) in 1949.

34. See Yamada 1954. Some translations and books on Eucken by Oizumi Yukio (a former student of Ueda Teijiro, taught at Takamatsu Higher Commercial School—currently Kagawa University) were published in the 1940s and 1950s.

35. For Yamamoto, see Okon 1977; and Doi 2001.

36. Yamamoto took a political stance alongside Ishibashi Tanzan during the conflicts between Yoshida and Hatoyama, and collaborated in drawing up the liberal policy draft (simplification of the administration, tax reduction, abolition of controls, privatization). Yamamoto became vice minister of industry and trade in 1954–55 under Ishibashi. Yamamoto had drawn up the "General Principles of Liberal Economic Policy" in 1947 at the request of Ishibashi as finance minister (Makino 2010, 102–3; Yamamoto 1980: 385).

37. Yamada 1954, 44–62.

38. For Naniwada, see Tezuka 2015.

39. Here the scope of my analysis is fairly limited. I refrain from going into the details of the role of monetarism in the Bank of Japan, itself an interesting topic to be investigated.

40. For details, see the following comments by Hayek:

> Simons I should have had a great hope for, and his death was a catastrophe. The others are in a methodological line; they are in effect macroeconomists and not microeconomists. . . . Milton and I agree on almost everything except monetary policy. In this sense, the old group who saw this ethic derive from Wesley Clair Mitchell's creation of the Institute of National Economic Research (National Bureau of Economic Research), led by Arthur Burns—another personal friend of mine with whom I do not agree on economics—and they are in effect logical positivists, methodologically. They believe economic phenomena can be explained from aggregates and averages. (Kresge and Wenar 1994, 144)

41. The following information is mainly based on an interview in August 26, 2014, in Koga's office at Waseda University. We are obliged to Koga Katsujiro, who kindly gave us permission to reproduce the essential part of it.

Chapter 5

1. On Hayek's thinking on the welfare state see Peden in this volume.

2. Harvey 2005, 19–23. See also Stedman Jones 2012. See Beech in this volume for consideration of the political dimensions of these developments.

3. Turner 2008, 4–10; Plehwe 2009, 4–5, 14–15. As an attempt to define neoliberalism in terms of key elements see Mirowski 2009.

4. The CBI's organizational structure followed that of the FBI fairly closely. There was a president, a businessman elected for a two-year term, the FBI Grand Council (later CBI Council) on which a large number of businessmen sat and which was the peak decision-making body. Below that were a series of ad hoc and standing committees. In addition, there was a staff, headed by the director-general.

5. Sir Campbell Adamson, http://www.oxforddnb.com/view/article/74490.

6. http://www.gazettes-online.co.uk/issues/33300/pages/5102/page.pdf.

7. Cockett 1994, 119; Tribe 2009, 87; and www.liberaalarchief.be/MPS2005.pdf, inventory of MPS General Meetings.

8. www.liberaalarchief.be/MPS2005.pdf, inventory of MPS General Meetings; and Hartwell 1995.

9. FBI 1957, 7 and 14. This was produced prior to the *Report* of the Radcliffe Committee on the Working of the Monetary System (1959) and the right-wing critique of the report published by the IEA, Seldon 1960.

10. Modern Records Centre, University of Warwick (hereafter MRC) MSS200/C/3/DG1/2123ii, "Shenfield, 'Industrial Policy Group: A Programme," September 5, 1967.

11. MRC MSS200/C/3/DG1/2701/ii, Shenfield. "The Regulation of the Economy: Part II," May 19, 1961.

12. MRC MSS200/C/3/DG1/2099iii, Shenfield, "The Rehabilitation of the Economy," January 17, 1968.

13. MRC MSS200/C/1/4/2, Economic Committee meeting, January 3, 1967.

14. MRC MSS200/C/3/DG1/42, "Industrial Policy Group Memorandum No. 2: Government Expenditure," April 1968, 9.

15. MRC MSS200/C/3/DG1/42, "Industrial Policy Group Memorandum No. 2: Government Expenditure," April 1968, 9.

16. MRC MSS 200/C/3/DG1/42, 'Shenfield, "Occupational Pension Schemes," June 24, 1968.

17. Some of his works from this period have been collected in Barry 1998.

18. Jewkes, John, *Oxford Dictionary of National Biography*, http://www.oxforddnb.com/view/article/39975.

19. Jewkes and Jewkes 1961, vii. See also the contribution by Peden in this volume.

20. John Jewkes, "Entrepreneurs on the Defensive: The Industrial Policy Group: The Failure of an Experiment" in Jewkes 1978, 174.

21. MRC MSS200/C/3/DG2/68, Bracewell-Milnes, "IPG Chairman's paper No. 2—'Topics for Future Study by the Group,' " February 25, 1970. Unfortunately there appear to be no papers on the IPG in the CBI archives after 1970.

22. Among his publications are Bracewell-Milnes 1974, 1976a, 1976b; Bracewell Milnes and Huiskamp 1977; Bracewell-Milnes 1979, 1980, 1982; Bracewell-Milnes and Teja 1991.

23. *The Mont Pelèrin Society Winter Newsletter* 64 (2012): 15. https://www.montpelerin.org/montpelerin/documents/MPS_December_2012_newsletter.pdf.

24. UK National Archives (hereafter TNA) T277/2064, BR (68)1, January 31, 1968.

25. MRC MSS200/C/1/1/E.300.69-E.350.69, E.338.69, "CBI Budget Representations 1970."

26. MRC MSS 200/C/1/4/3, E.497.70, Economic Committee meeting, November 30, 1970.

27. MRC MSS 200/C/1/4/3, E.23.71, Economic Committee meeting, January 4, 1971.

28. MRC MSS 200/C/1/4/3, E.33.71, Special Joint Meeting of the Taxation Panel and the Economic Committee, January 11, 1971.

29. "Business Diary: An Unexpected Swansong," *The Times*, February 6, 1973, 19; and "Director Quits in CBI Tax Clash," *Financial Times*, February 7, 1973.

30. "Business Diary: An Unexpected Swansong," *The Times*, February 6, 1973, 19; "Director Quits in CBI Tax Clash," *Financial Times*, February 7, 1973.

31. MRC MSS 200/C/1/1/E/72, E.489.72, Taxation Panel meeting, December 23, 1972. The Taxation Panel consisted of members of the full Taxation Committee that met more regularly.

32. MRC MSS 200/C/1/1/C/73, C11(1)73, minutes of CBI Council, January 17, 1973. Estate duty was the tax paid on the estates of dead people. The duty was very high but largely avoidable, as there was no gifts tax.

33. Ibid.

34. Ibid.

35. MRC MSS 200/C/1/1/C/73, C21(3)73, "Director-General's Report to the Council," March 1973.

36. "No Gratitude in the CBI," *The Times*, March 16, 1973, 16.

37. "A Split at the CBI," *Financial Times*, January 23, 1973.

38. MRC MSS200/C/3/DG1/46-7, Bracewell-Milnes, "Third Draft of IPG Paper on Taxation," October 26, 1968.

39. MRC MSS200/C/3/DG2/68, N. Tate, "Industrial Policy Group Meeting (16/4/70)," April 15, 1970.

40. Stedman Jones 2012 and Cockett 1994 are typical here.

41. For an exploration of these issues see Brittan 1973.

Chapter 7

1. Gesamtmetall represents Germany's metal and electrical industry, the country's largest industrial sector, which includes the automobile industry and encompasses almost 7,000 companies and well over 2 million employees.

2. 10 million euros per year from 2000 to 2009, 8.8 million euros per year from 2009 to 2014.

3. www.insm.de.

4. Barry and Wilkinson (2011) see employers' associations' tendency to project their interests beyond the collective bargaining arena as a broader trend connected with the decline of institutional industrial relations.

5. The chemical industry's employers' association, VCI, almost joined the INSM, but the former feared that the latter would endanger its cooperative relations with unions.

6. The "old" social-market economy was supposed to have existed before it was "hijacked" by special interest groups and distorted by excessive welfare-state interventionism. As early as 1958, when German social policy was in its infancy, the ordoliberal theorist Wilhelm Röpke thought that West German economic policy had taken a turn toward excessive interventionism. He declared that the state should place itself as a "guardian of the market" above societal interest groups (Haselbach 1991, 172).

7. Tasso Enzweiler was one of the INSM's managing directors between 2002 and 2006. Although no longer affiliated with the INSM (he has gone into the consulting business), Enzweiler's doctoral dissertation was supervised by Ulrich van Suntum, an academic economist who has been associated with the INSM since its beginnings. Entitled "Ways out of the Reform Log Jam" (Enzweiler 2013), his dissertation is built on public choice foundations: labor market regulations, employment protection, and CME institutions are not instruments for comparative institutional advantage. Instead, they provide insiders with rents and impede market functioning.

8. If the INSM had been based on a different concept—for example, ordoliberal Walter Eucken's idea of a *Wettbewerbsordnung*, or "competitive order"—its popular legitimacy would be harder to defend.

9. See Kinderman 2014 for more detailed and comprehensive explanation.

10. Wolfgang Streeck's important work on the *commonalities* of capitalism is obviously relevant here.

Chapter 10

1. For Germany, two economists found losses of public banks to be greater than losses of private banks, and offer additional arguments for economic superiority of private banking (Thum and Hau 2009).

2. The great documentary by Helgi Felixson on the collapse of Iceland (*God Bless Iceland*) emphasized the responsibility of government leaders and private bankers in particular. Iceland's key neoliberal policy adviser, Prof. Hannes Gissuarson, escaped the attention. Charles H. Ferguson's great documentary *Inside Job* does throw light on the role of economic professors who were advising governments and banks involved in the crisis. Because *Inside Job* focuses on US academics only, the transnational networks of policy-related neoliberal pundits remain in the dark in this film as well, unfortunately.

3. Carrigan (2010) surveyed 73 reports produced by five right-wing think tanks.

4. Comprehensiveness refers to both a general transdisciplinary and transprofessional character driven by a common Weltanschauung, and the (think tank) capacity to produce knowledge at various upstream and downstream levels of expert and public discourses.

5. Willett was educated at the University of Virginia during the Buchanan/Nutter era and together with Gottfried Haberler published "U.S. Balance-of-Payments Policies and International Monetary Reform" (American Enterprise Institute for Public Policy Research, 1968).

6. Online at www.montpelerin.org/nyc2k9.dfm.

7. Www.soundmoneyproject.org.

8. The latest economics Nobel in the ranks of the MPS, Vernon Smith, has been awarded the prize precisely for his work to promote experimental economics (compare Frank 2004, 80f. on the role of the Koch Foundation with regard to the career of Vernon Smith). Rather than assuming rationality, researchers look for institutional designs to support individuals making choices in line with rational expectations.

9. When the MPS met in Iceland in 2005, the group celebrated the great success of the Icelandic model. On display at the MPS homepage are historical photographs documenting the early meetings of Icelandic politicians with famous MPS leaders during the 1980s (www.mps-iceland.org/?gluggi=iceland&nafn=iceland/impact).

10. Compare atlasnetwork.org/globalinitiative/websites/.

11. Http://atlasnetwork.org/globalinitiative/websites/.

12. Www.stockholm-network.org.

13. Compare www.rbeurope.org.

Conclusion

1. It is worth noting that Krugman has also pointed out the difference between maintaining macroeconomic stability and maintaining social stability (http://krugman.blogs.nytimes.com/2009/03/27/european-stability/comment-page-1/).

2. For an extensive discussion of the variety of liberalism, see Freeden 1996.

INDEX